C-1606 CAREER EXAMINATION SERIES

This is your
PASSBOOK for...

Maintenance Mechanic (Automated Mail Processing Equipment) (USPS)

Test Preparation Study Guide
Questions & Answers

COPYRIGHT NOTICE

This book is SOLELY intended for, is sold ONLY to, and its use is RESTRICTED to individual, bona fide applicants or candidates who qualify by virtue of having seriously filed applications for appropriate license, certificate, professional and/or promotional advancement, higher school matriculation, scholarship, or other legitimate requirements of education and/or governmental authorities.

This book is NOT intended for use, class instruction, tutoring, training, duplication, copying, reprinting, excerption, or adaptation, etc., by:

1) Other publishers
2) Proprietors and/or Instructors of "Coaching" and/or Preparatory Courses
3) Personnel and/or Training Divisions of commercial, industrial, and governmental organizations
4) Schools, colleges, or universities and/or their departments and staffs, including teachers and other personnel
5) Testing Agencies or Bureaus
6) Study groups which seek by the purchase of a single volume to copy and/or duplicate and/or adapt this material for use by the group as a whole without having purchased individual volumes for each of the members of the group
7) Et al.

Such persons would be in violation of appropriate Federal and State statutes.

PROVISION OF LICENSING AGREEMENTS – Recognized educational, commercial, industrial, and governmental institutions and organizations, and others legitimately engaged in educational pursuits, including training, testing, and measurement activities, may address request for a licensing agreement to the copyright owners, who will determine whether, and under what conditions, including fees and charges, the materials in this book may be used them. In other words, a licensing facility exists for the legitimate use of the material in this book on other than an individual basis. However, it is asseverated and affirmed here that the material in this book CANNOT be used without the receipt of the express permission of such a licensing agreement from the Publishers. Inquiries re licensing should be addressed to the company, attention rights and permissions department.

All rights reserved, including the right of reproduction in whole or in part, in any form or by any means, electronic or mechanical, including photocopying, recording, or by any information storage and retrieval system, without permission in writing from the Publisher.

Copyright © 2024 by
National Learning Corporation

212 Michael Drive, Syosset, NY 11791
(516) 921-8888 • www.passbooks.com
E-mail: info@passbooks.com

PUBLISHED IN THE UNITED STATES OF AMERICA

PASSBOOK® SERIES

THE *PASSBOOK® SERIES* has been created to prepare applicants and candidates for the ultimate academic battlefield – the examination room.

At some time in our lives, each and every one of us may be required to take an examination – for validation, matriculation, admission, qualification, registration, certification, or licensure.

Based on the assumption that every applicant or candidate has met the basic formal educational standards, has taken the required number of courses, and read the necessary texts, the *PASSBOOK® SERIES* furnishes the one special preparation which may assure passing with confidence, instead of failing with insecurity. Examination questions – together with answers – are furnished as the basic vehicle for study so that the mysteries of the examination and its compounding difficulties may be eliminated or diminished by a sure method.

This book is meant to help you pass your examination provided that you qualify and are serious in your objective.

The entire field is reviewed through the huge store of content information which is succinctly presented through a provocative and challenging approach – the question-and-answer method.

A climate of success is established by furnishing the correct answers at the end of each test.

You soon learn to recognize types of questions, forms of questions, and patterns of questioning. You may even begin to anticipate expected outcomes.

You perceive that many questions are repeated or adapted so that you can gain acute insights, which may enable you to score many sure points.

You learn how to confront new questions, or types of questions, and to attack them confidently and work out the correct answers.

You note objectives and emphases, and recognize pitfalls and dangers, so that you may make positive educational adjustments.

Moreover, you are kept fully informed in relation to new concepts, methods, practices, and directions in the field.

You discover that you are actually taking the examination all the time: you are preparing for the examination by "taking" an examination, not by reading extraneous and/or supererogatory textbooks.

In short, this PASSBOOK®, used directedly, should be an important factor in helping you to pass your test.

MAINTENANCE MECHANIC AUTOMATED MAIL PROCESSING EQUIPMENT

SAMPLE QUESTIONS

EXAMINATION

933

UNITED STATES POSTAL SERVICE

SAMPLE QUESTIONS - TEST M/N 933

The purpose of this booklet is to illustrate the types of questions that will be used in Test M/M 933. The samples will also show how the questions in the test are to be answered.

Test M/N 933 measures 16 Knowledge, Skills, and Abilities (KSAs) used by a variety of maintenance positions. Exhibit A lists the actual KSAs that are measured, and Exhibit B lists the positions that use this examination. However, not all KSAs that are measured in this test are scored for every position listed. The qualification standard for each position lists the KSAs required for the position. Only those questions that measure KSAs required for the position(s) for which you are applying will be scored for the position(s).

The suggested answers to each question are lettered A, B, C, etc. Select the BEST answer and make a heavy pencil mark in the corresponding space on the Sample Answer Sheet. Each mark must be dense black. Each mark must cover more than half the space and must not extend into neighboring spaces. If the answer to Sample 1 is B, you would mark the Sample Answer Sheet like this:

After recording your answers, compare them with those in the Correct Answers to Sample Questions. If they do not agree, carefully re-read the questions that were missed to get a clear understanding of what each question is asking.

During the test, directions for answering questions in Part I will be given orally, either by a cassette tape or by the examiner. You are to listen closely to the directions and follow them. To practice for this part of the test you might have a friend read the direction to you while you mark your answers on the Sample Answer Sheet. Directions for answering questions in Part II will be completely described in the test booklet.

STUDY CAREFULLY BEFORE YOU GO TO THE EXAMINATION ROOM

PART I

In Part I of the test, you will be told to follow directions by writing in a test booklet and then on an answer sheet. The test booklet will have lines of material like the following five samples:

SAMPLE QUESTIONS

SAMPLE 1.   5 _____

SAMPLE 2.   1 6 4 3 7

SAMPLE 3.   D B A E C

SAMPLE 4.   (8__) (5__) (2__) (9__) (10__)

SAMPLE 5.   (7__) [6__] (1__) [12__]

To practice this test, have someone read the instructions on the next page to you and you follow the instructions. When they tell you to darken the space on the Sample Answer Sheet, use the one on this page.

```
               SAMPLE ANSWER SHEET
 1 Ⓐ Ⓑ Ⓒ Ⓓ Ⓔ      5 Ⓐ Ⓑ Ⓒ Ⓓ Ⓔ      9 Ⓐ Ⓑ Ⓒ Ⓓ Ⓔ
 2 Ⓐ Ⓑ Ⓒ Ⓓ Ⓔ      6 Ⓐ Ⓑ Ⓒ Ⓓ Ⓔ     10 Ⓐ Ⓑ Ⓒ Ⓓ Ⓔ
 3 Ⓐ Ⓑ Ⓒ Ⓓ Ⓔ      7 Ⓐ Ⓑ Ⓒ Ⓓ Ⓔ     11 Ⓐ Ⓑ Ⓒ Ⓓ Ⓔ
 4 Ⓐ Ⓑ Ⓒ Ⓓ Ⓔ      8 Ⓐ Ⓑ Ⓒ Ⓓ Ⓔ     12 Ⓐ Ⓑ Ⓒ Ⓓ Ⓔ
```

Instructions to be read (the words in parentheses should not be read aloud).

You are to follow the instructions that I shall read to you. I cannot repeat them.

Look at the samples. Sample 1 has a number and a line beside it. On the line write an A. (Pause 2 seconds.) Now on the Sample Answer Sheet, find number 5 (pause 2 seconds) and darken the space for the letter you just wrote on the line. (Pause 2 seconds.)

Look at Sample 2. (Pause slightly.) Draw a line under the third number. (Pause 2 seconds.) Now look on the Sample Answer Sheet, find the number under which you just drew a line and darken space B as in baker for that number. (Pause 5 seconds.)

Look at Sample 3. (Pause slightly.) Draw a line under the third letter in the line. (Pause 2 seconds.) Now on your Sample Answer Sheet, find number 9 (pause 2 seconds) and darken the space for the letter under which you drew a line. (Pause 5 seconds.)

Look at the five circles in Sample 4. (Pause slightly.) Each circle has a number and a line in it. Write D as in dog on the blank in the last circle. (Pause 2 seconds.) Now on the Sample Answer Sheet, darken the space for the number-letter combination that is in the circle you just wrote in. (Pause 5 seconds.)

Look at Sample 5. (Pause slightly.) There are two circles and two boxes of different sizes with numbers in them. (Pause slightly.) If 4 is more than 2 and if 5 is less than 3, write A in the smaller circle. (Pause slightly.) Otherwise write C in the larger box. (Pause 2 seconds.) Now on the Sample Answer Sheet, darken the space for the number-letter combination in the circle or box in which you just wrote. (Pause 5 seconds.)

Now look at the Sample Answer Sheet. (Pause slightly.) You should have darkened spaces 4B, 5A, 9A, 10D, and 12C on the Sample Answer Sheet. (If the person preparing to take the examination made any mistakes, try to help him or her understand why the mistakes are wrong.)

SAMPLE ANSWER QUESTIONS

1 Ⓐ Ⓑ Ⓒ Ⓓ Ⓔ
2 Ⓐ Ⓑ Ⓒ Ⓓ Ⓔ
3 Ⓐ Ⓑ Ⓒ Ⓓ Ⓔ
4 Ⓐ Ⓑ Ⓒ Ⓓ Ⓔ
5 Ⓐ Ⓑ Ⓒ Ⓓ Ⓔ
6 Ⓐ Ⓑ Ⓒ Ⓓ Ⓔ
7 Ⓐ Ⓑ Ⓒ Ⓓ Ⓔ
8 Ⓐ Ⓑ Ⓒ Ⓓ Ⓔ
9 Ⓐ Ⓑ Ⓒ Ⓓ Ⓔ
10 Ⓐ Ⓑ Ⓒ Ⓓ Ⓔ
11 Ⓐ Ⓑ Ⓒ Ⓓ Ⓔ
12 Ⓐ Ⓑ Ⓒ Ⓓ Ⓔ
13 Ⓐ Ⓑ Ⓒ Ⓓ Ⓔ
14 Ⓐ Ⓑ Ⓒ Ⓓ Ⓔ
15 Ⓐ Ⓑ Ⓒ Ⓓ Ⓔ
16 Ⓐ Ⓑ Ⓒ Ⓓ Ⓔ
17 Ⓐ Ⓑ Ⓒ Ⓓ Ⓔ

18 Ⓐ Ⓑ Ⓒ Ⓓ Ⓔ
19 Ⓐ Ⓑ Ⓒ Ⓓ Ⓔ
20 Ⓐ Ⓑ Ⓒ Ⓓ Ⓔ
21 Ⓐ Ⓑ Ⓒ Ⓓ Ⓔ
22 Ⓐ Ⓑ Ⓒ Ⓓ Ⓔ
23 Ⓐ Ⓑ Ⓒ Ⓓ Ⓔ
24 Ⓐ Ⓑ Ⓒ Ⓓ Ⓔ
25 Ⓐ Ⓑ Ⓒ Ⓓ Ⓔ
26 Ⓐ Ⓑ Ⓒ Ⓓ Ⓔ
27 Ⓐ Ⓑ Ⓒ Ⓓ Ⓔ
28 Ⓐ Ⓑ Ⓒ Ⓓ Ⓔ
29 Ⓐ Ⓑ Ⓒ Ⓓ Ⓔ
30 Ⓐ Ⓑ Ⓒ Ⓓ Ⓔ
31 Ⓐ Ⓑ Ⓒ Ⓓ Ⓔ
32 Ⓐ Ⓑ Ⓒ Ⓓ Ⓔ
33 Ⓐ Ⓑ Ⓒ Ⓓ Ⓔ
34 Ⓐ Ⓑ Ⓒ Ⓓ Ⓔ

PART II

1. The primary function of a take-up pulley in a belt conveyor is to

   A) carry the belt on the return trip.
   B) track the belt.
   C) maintain proper belt tension.
   D) change the direction of the belt.
   E) regulate the speed of the belt.

2. Which device is used to transfer power and rotary mechanical motion from one shaft to another?

   A) Bearing
   B) Lever
   C) Idler roller
   D) Gear
   E) Bushing

3. What special care is required in the storage of hard steel roller bearings? They should be

   A) cleaned and spun dry with compressed air.
   B) oiled once a month.
   C) stored in a humid place.
   D) wrapped in oiled paper.
   E) stored at temperatures below 90 degrees Fahrenheit.

4. Which is the correct method to lubricate a roller chain?

   A) Use brush to apply lubricant while chain is in motion
   B) Use squirt can to apply lubricant while chain is in motion
   C) Use brush to apply lubricant while chain is not in motion
   D) Soak chain in pan of lubricant and hang to allow excess to drain
   E) Chains do not need lubrication

5. A circuit has two resistors of equal value in series. The voltage and current in the circuit are 20 volts and 2 amp respectively. What is the value of EACH resistor?

   A) 5 ohms
   B) 10 ohms
   C) 15 ohms
   D) 20 ohms
   E) Not enough information given

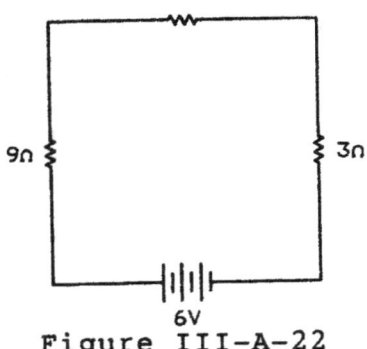

Figure III-A-22

6. Which of the following circuit is shown in Figure III-A-22?

   A) Series circuit
   B) Parallel circuit
   C) Series, parallel circuit
   D) Solid state circuit
   E) None of the above

7. What is the total net capacitance of two 60 farad capacitors connected in series?

   A) 30 F
   B) 60 F
   C) 90 F
   D) 120 F
   E) 360 F

8. If two 30 mH inductors are connected in series, what is the total net inductance of the combination?

   A) 15 mH
   B) 20 mH
   C) 30 mH
   D) 45 mH
   E) 60 mH

Figure 75-25-1

9. Crowbars, light bulbs and vacuum bags are to be stored in the cabinet shown in Figure 75-25-1. Considering the balance of weight, what would be the safest arrangement?

A) Top drawer - Crowbars
   Middle drawer - Light bulbs
   Bottom drawer - Vacuum bags
B) Top drawer - Crowbars
   Middle drawer - Vacuum bags
   Bottom drawer - Light bulbs
C) Top drawer - Vacuum bags
   Middle drawer - Crowbars
   Bottom drawer - Light bulbs
D) Top drawer - Vacuum bags
   Middle drawer - Light bulbs
   Bottom drawer - Crowbars
E) Top drawer - Light bulbs
   Middle drawer - Vacuum bags
   Bottom drawer - Crowbars

10. Contaminants have caused bearings to fail prematurely. Which pair of the items listed below should be kept away from bearings?

A) Dirt and oil
B) Grease and water
C) Oil and grease
D) Dirt and moisture
E) Water and oil

11. The electrical circuit term "open circuit" refers to a closed loop being opened. When an ohmmeter is connected into this type of circuit, one can expect the meter to

A) read infinity.
B) read infinity and slowly return to ZERO.
C) read ZERO.
D) read ZERO and slowly return to infinity.
E) None of the above

12. Which is most appropriate for pulling a heavy load?

A) Electric lift
B) Fork lift
C) Tow conveyor
D) Dolly
E) Pallet truck

13. In order to operate a breast drill, which direction should you turn it?

A) Clockwise
B) Counterclockwise
C) Up and down
D) Back and forth
E) Right, then left

14. Which is the correct tool for tightening or loosening a water pipe?

A) Slip joint pliers
B) Household pliers
C) Monkey wrench
D) Water pump pliers
E) Pipe wrench

15. What is one purpose of a chuck key?

    A) Open doors
    B) Remove drill bits
    C) Remove screws
    D) Remove set screws
    E) Unlock chucks

16. When smoke is generated as a result of using a portable electric drill for cutting holes into a piece of angle iron, one should

    A) use a fire watch.
    B) cease the drilling operation.
    C) use an exhaust fan to remove smoke.
    D) use a prescribed coolant solution to reduce friction.
    E) call the Fire Department.

17. The primary purpose of soldering is to

    A) melt solder to a molten state.
    B) heat metal parts to the right temperature be be joined.
    C) join metal parts by melting the parts.
    D) harden metal.
    E) join metal parts.

18. Which of the following statements is correct concerning a soldering gun?

    A) Tip is not replaceable
    B) Cannot be used in cramped places
    C) heats only when trigger is pressed
    D) Not rated by the number of watts it uses
    E) Has no light

19. What unit of measurement is read on a dial torque wrench?

    A) Pounds
    B) Inches
    C) Centimeters
    D) Foot-pounds
    E) Degrees

20. Which instrument is used to test insulation breakdown of a conductor?

    A) Ohmmeter
    B) Ammeter
    C) Megger
    D) Wheatstone bridge
    E) Voltmeter

21. 1/2 of 1/4 =

    A) 1/12
    B) 1/8
    C) 1/4
    D) 1/2
    E) 8

22. 2.6 - .5 =

    A) 2.0
    B) 2.1
    C) 3.1
    D) 3.3
    E) None of the above

23. Solve the power equation

    $P = I^2R$ for R

    A) $R = EI$
    B) $R = I^2P$
    C) $R = PI$
    D) $R = P/I^2$
    E) $R = E/I$

24. The product of 3 kilo ohms times 3 micro ohms is

    A) 6×10^{-9} ohms
    B) 6×10^{-3} ohms
    C) 9×10^{3} ohms
    D) 9×10^{-6} ohms
    E) 9×10^{-3} ohms

In sample question 25 below, select the statement which is most nearly correct according to the paragraph.

"Prior to 1870, a conveyor that made use of rollers was developed for transporting clay. This construction substituted rolling friction at the idler bearing points for the sliding friction of the slider bed. A primitive type of troughing belt conveyor was developed about the same time for the handling of grain. This design was improved during the latter part of the century when the troughing idler was developed."

25. According to the above paragraph, which of the following statements is most nearly correct?

    A) The troughing belt conveyor was developed about 1870 to handle clay and grain.

    B) Rolling friction construction was replaced by sliding friction construction prior to 1870.

    C) In the late nineteenth century, conveyors were improved with the development of the troughing idler.

    D) The troughing idler, a significant design improvement for conveyors, was developed in the early nineteenth century.

    E) Conveyor belts were invented and developed in the 1800's.

26. A small crane was used to raise the heavy part. Raise MOST nearly means

    A) lift
    B) drag
    C) drop
    D) deliver
    E) guide

27. Short MOST nearly means

    A) tall
    B) wide
    C) brief
    D) heavy
    E) dark

For sample question 28 below, select from the drawings of objects on the right labeled A, B, C, and D, the one that would have the TOP, FRONT, and RIGHT views shown in the drawing at the left

28.

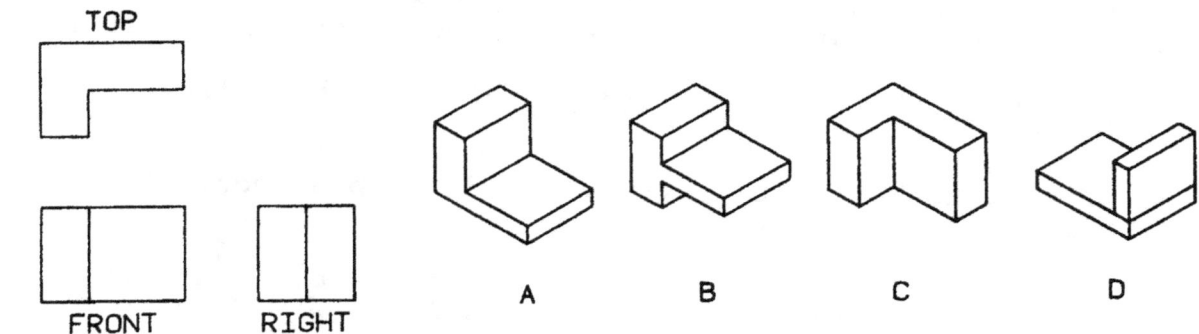

In sample question 29 below, there is, on the left, a drawing of a flat piece of paper and, on the right, four figures labeled A, B, C, and D. When the paper is bent on the dotted lines it will form one of the figures on the right. Decide which alternative can be formed from the flat piece.

29.

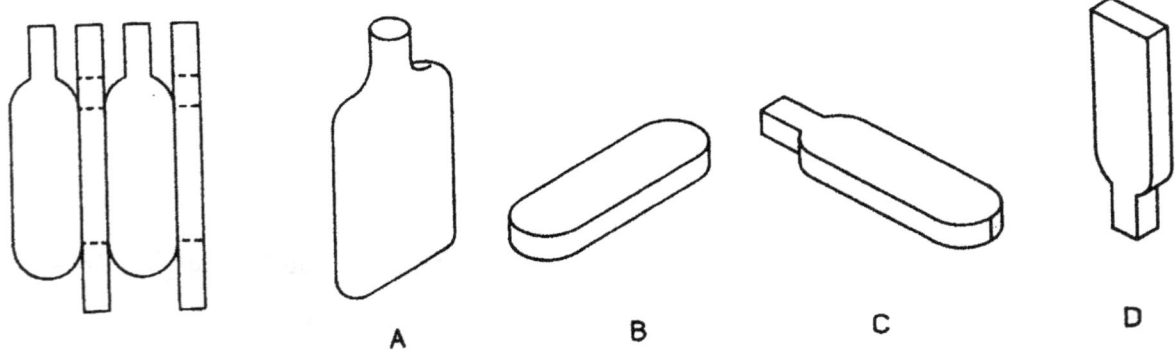

In each of the sample questions below, look at the symbols in the first two boxes. Something about the three symbols in the first box makes them alike; something about the two symbols in the other box with the question mark makes them alike. Look for some characteristic that is common to all symbols in the same box, yet makes them different from the symbols in the other box. Among dthe five answer choices, find the symbol that can best be substituted for the question mark, because it is <u>like</u> the symbols in the second box, and, <u>for the same reason</u>, different from those in the first box.

30.

In sample question 30 above, all the symbols in the first box are vertical lines. The second box has two lines, one broken and one solid. Their <u>likeness</u> to each other consists in their being horizontal; and their being horizontal makes them <u>different</u> from the vertical lines in the other box. The answer must be the only one of the five lettered choices that is a horizontal line, either broken or solid. NOTE: There is not supposed to be a series or progression in these symbol questions. If you look for a progression in the first box and the second box, you will be wasting time. Remember, look for a <u>likeness</u> within each box and a <u>difference</u> between the two boxes.

Now do sample questions 31 and 32.

31.

32.

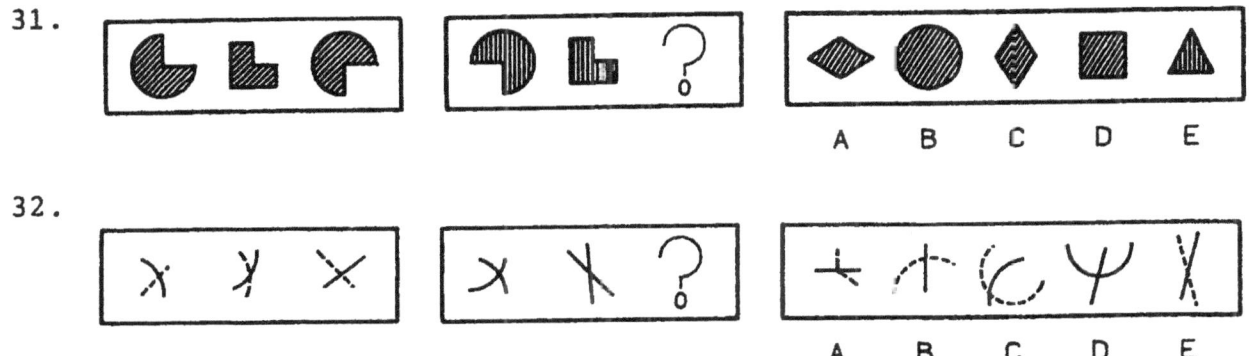

- 11 -

33. In Figure 3-8-6 below, what is the measurement of Dimension F? Drawing is not actual size.

A) 1 3/4 inches
B) 2 1/4 inches
C) 2 1/2 inches
D) 3 3/4 inches
E) None of the above

34. In Figure 160-57 below, what is the current flow through R_3 when:

$V = 50$ volts

$R_1 = 25$ ohms

$R_2 = 25$ ohms

$R_3 = 50$ ohms

$R_4 = 50$ ohms

$R_5 = 50$ ohms

and the current through the entire circuit totals one amp?

A) 0.5 amp
B) 5.0 amps
C) 5.0 milliamps
D) 50.0 milliamps
E) None of the above

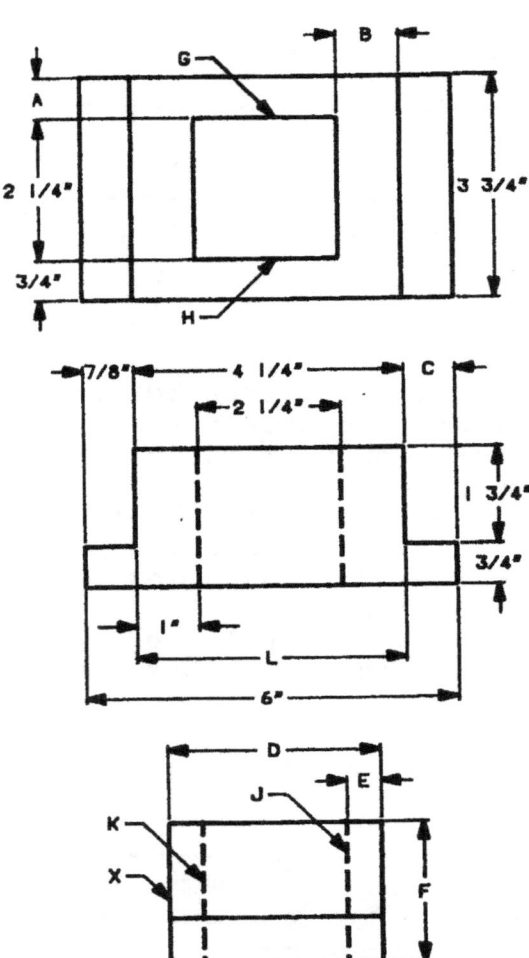

Figure 3-8-6

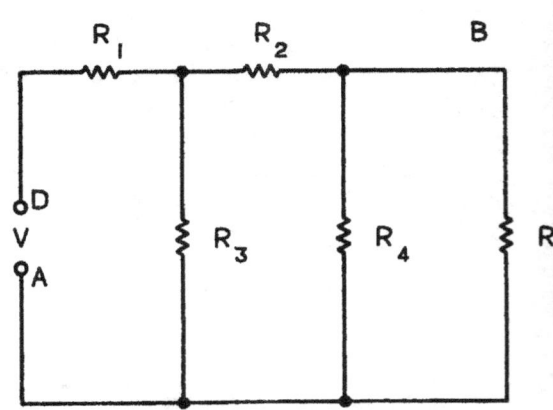

Figure 160-57

CORRECT ANSWERS TO SAMPLE QUESTIONS

1. C
2. D
3. D
4. D
5. A
6. A
7. A
8. E
9. E
10. D
11. A
12. E
13. A
14. E
15. B
16. D
17. E
18. C
19. D
20. C
21. B
22. B
23. D
24. E
25. C
26. A
27. C
28. C
29. C
30. C
31. E
32. D
33. C
34. A

EXHIBIT A

Test M/N 933 covers the following Knowledge, Skills and Abilities:

(1) Knowledge of basic mechanics refers to the theory of operation, terminology, usage, and characteristics of basic mechanical principles as they apply to such things as gears, pulleys, cams, pawls, power transmissions, linkages, fasteners, chains, sprockets, and belts; and including hoisting, rigging, roping, pneumatics, and hydraulic devices.

(2) Knowledge of basic electricity refers to the theory, terminology, usage, and characteristics of basic electrical principles such as Ohm's Law, Kirchoff's Law, and magnetism, as they apply to such things as AC-DC circuitry and hardware, relays, switches, and circuit breakers.

(3) Knowledge of basic electronics refers to the theory, terminology, usage, and characteristics of basic electronic principles concerning such things as solid state devices, vacuum tubes, coils, capacitors, resistors, and basic logic circuitry.

(5) Knowledge of safety procedures and equipment refers to the knowledge of industrial hazards (e.g., mechanical, chemical, electrical, electronic) and procedures and techniques established to avoid injuries to self and others such as lock-out devices, protective clothing, and waste disposal techniques.

(8) Knowledge of lubrication materials and procedures refers to the terminology, characteristics, storage, preparation, disposal, and usage techniques involved with lubrication materials such as oils, greases, and other types of lubricants.

(19) Ability to perform basic mathematical computations refers to the ability to perform basic calculations such as addition, subtraction, multiplication and division with whole numbers, fractions and decimals.

(20) Ability to perform more complex mathematics refers to the ability to perform calculations such as basic algebra, geometry, scientific notation, and number conversions, as applied to mechanical, electrical and electronic applications.

(21) <u>Ability to apply theoretical knowledge to practical applications</u> refers to mechanical, electrical and electronic maintenance applications such as inspection, troubleshooting equipment repair and modification, preventive maintenance, and installation of electrical equipment.

(22) <u>Ability to detect patterns</u> refers to the ability to observe and analyze qualitative factors such as number progressions, spatial relationships, and auditory and visual patterns. This includes combining information and determining how a given set of numbers, objects, or sounds are related to each other.

(23) <u>Ability to use written reference materials</u> refers to the ability to locate, read, and comprehend text material such as handbooks, manuals, bulletins, directives, checklists and route sheets.

(26) <u>Ability to follow instructions</u> refers to the ability to comprehend and execute written and oral instructions such as work orders, checklists, route sheets, and verbal directions and instructions.

(31) <u>Ability to use hand tools</u> refers to knowledge of, and proficiency with, various hand tools. This ability involves the safe and efficient use and maintenance of such tools as screwdrivers, wrenches, hammers, pliers, chisels, punches, taps, dies, rules, gauges, and alignment tools.

(32) <u>Ability to use portable power tools</u> refers to the knowledge of, and proficiency with, various power tools. This ability involves the safe and efficient use and maintenance of power tools such as drills, saws, sanders and grinders.

(35) <u>Ability to use technical drawings</u> refers to the ability to read and comprehend technical materials such as diagrams, schematics, flow charts, and blueprints.

(36) <u>Ability to use test equipment</u> refers to the knowledge of, and proficiency with, various types of mechanical, electrical and electronic test equipment such as VOMS, oscilloscopes, circuit tracers, amprobes, and tachometers.

(37) <u>Ability to solder</u> refers to the knowledge of, and the ability to safely and effectively apply, the appropriate soldering techniques.

EXHIBIT B

The following positions use Test M/N 933:

Position Title	Register Number
Maintenance Mechanic, MPE/06	M32
Maintenance Mechanic, MPE/07	M33
Overhaul Specialist	M34

HOW TO TAKE A TEST

I. YOU MUST PASS AN EXAMINATION

A. *WHAT EVERY CANDIDATE SHOULD KNOW*

Examination applicants often ask us for help in preparing for the written test. What can I study in advance? What kinds of questions will be asked? How will the test be given? How will the papers be graded?

As an applicant for a civil service examination, you may be wondering about some of these things. Our purpose here is to suggest effective methods of advance study and to describe civil service examinations.

Your chances for success on this examination can be increased if you know how to prepare. Those "pre-examination jitters" can be reduced if you know what to expect. You can even experience an adventure in good citizenship if you know why civil service exams are given.

B. *WHY ARE CIVIL SERVICE EXAMINATIONS GIVEN?*

Civil service examinations are important to you in two ways. As a citizen, you want public jobs filled by employees who know how to do their work. As a job seeker, you want a fair chance to compete for that job on an equal footing with other candidates. The best-known means of accomplishing this two-fold goal is the competitive examination.

Exams are widely publicized throughout the nation. They may be administered for jobs in federal, state, city, municipal, town or village governments or agencies.

Any citizen may apply, with some limitations, such as the age or residence of applicants. Your experience and education may be reviewed to see whether you meet the requirements for the particular examination. When these requirements exist, they are reasonable and applied consistently to all applicants. Thus, a competitive examination may cause you some uneasiness now, but it is your privilege and safeguard.

C. *HOW ARE CIVIL SERVICE EXAMS DEVELOPED?*

Examinations are carefully written by trained technicians who are specialists in the field known as "psychological measurement," in consultation with recognized authorities in the field of work that the test will cover. These experts recommend the subject matter areas or skills to be tested; only those knowledges or skills important to your success on the job are included. The most reliable books and source materials available are used as references. Together, the experts and technicians judge the difficulty level of the questions.

Test technicians know how to phrase questions so that the problem is clearly stated. Their ethics do not permit "trick" or "catch" questions. Questions may have been tried out on sample groups, or subjected to statistical analysis, to determine their usefulness.

Written tests are often used in combination with performance tests, ratings of training and experience, and oral interviews. All of these measures combine to form the best-known means of finding the right person for the right job.

II. HOW TO PASS THE WRITTEN TEST

A. NATURE OF THE EXAMINATION

To prepare intelligently for civil service examinations, you should know how they differ from school examinations you have taken. In school you were assigned certain definite pages to read or subjects to cover. The examination questions were quite detailed and usually emphasized memory. Civil service exams, on the other hand, try to discover your present ability to perform the duties of a position, plus your potentiality to learn these duties. In other words, a civil service exam attempts to predict how successful you will be. Questions cover such a broad area that they cannot be as minute and detailed as school exam questions.

In the public service similar kinds of work, or positions, are grouped together in one "class." This process is known as *position-classification*. All the positions in a class are paid according to the salary range for that class. One class title covers all of these positions, and they are all tested by the same examination.

B. FOUR BASIC STEPS

1) Study the announcement

How, then, can you know what subjects to study? Our best answer is: "Learn as much as possible about the class of positions for which you've applied." The exam will test the knowledge, skills and abilities needed to do the work.

Your most valuable source of information about the position you want is the official exam announcement. This announcement lists the training and experience qualifications. Check these standards and apply only if you come reasonably close to meeting them.

The brief description of the position in the examination announcement offers some clues to the subjects which will be tested. Think about the job itself. Review the duties in your mind. Can you perform them, or are there some in which you are rusty? Fill in the blank spots in your preparation.

Many jurisdictions preview the written test in the exam announcement by including a section called "Knowledge and Abilities Required," "Scope of the Examination," or some similar heading. Here you will find out specifically what fields will be tested.

2) Review your own background

Once you learn in general what the position is all about, and what you need to know to do the work, ask yourself which subjects you already know fairly well and which need improvement. You may wonder whether to concentrate on improving your strong areas or on building some background in your fields of weakness. When the announcement has specified "some knowledge" or "considerable knowledge," or has used adjectives like "beginning principles of..." or "advanced ... methods," you can get a clue as to the number and difficulty of questions to be asked in any given field. More questions, and hence broader coverage, would be included for those subjects which are more important in the work. Now weigh your strengths and weaknesses against the job requirements and prepare accordingly.

3) Determine the level of the position

Another way to tell how intensively you should prepare is to understand the level of the job for which you are applying. Is it the entering level? In other words, is this the position in which beginners in a field of work are hired? Or is it an intermediate or advanced level? Sometimes this is indicated by such words as "Junior" or "Senior" in the class title. Other jurisdictions use Roman numerals to designate the level – Clerk I, Clerk II, for example. The word "Supervisor" sometimes appears in the title. If the level is not indicated by the title, check the description of duties. Will you be working under very close supervision, or will you have responsibility for independent decisions in this work?

4) Choose appropriate study materials

Now that you know the subjects to be examined and the relative amount of each subject to be covered, you can choose suitable study materials. For beginning level jobs, or even advanced ones, if you have a pronounced weakness in some aspect of your training, read a modern, standard textbook in that field. Be sure it is up to date and has general coverage. Such books are normally available at your library, and the librarian will be glad to help you locate one. For entry-level positions, questions of appropriate difficulty are chosen – neither highly advanced questions, nor those too simple. Such questions require careful thought but not advanced training.

If the position for which you are applying is technical or advanced, you will read more advanced, specialized material. If you are already familiar with the basic principles of your field, elementary textbooks would waste your time. Concentrate on advanced textbooks and technical periodicals. Think through the concepts and review difficult problems in your field.

These are all general sources. You can get more ideas on your own initiative, following these leads. For example, training manuals and publications of the government agency which employs workers in your field can be useful, particularly for technical and professional positions. A letter or visit to the government department involved may result in more specific study suggestions, and certainly will provide you with a more definite idea of the exact nature of the position you are seeking.

III. KINDS OF TESTS

Tests are used for purposes other than measuring knowledge and ability to perform specified duties. For some positions, it is equally important to test ability to make adjustments to new situations or to profit from training. In others, basic mental abilities not dependent on information are essential. Questions which test these things may not appear as pertinent to the duties of the position as those which test for knowledge and information. Yet they are often highly important parts of a fair examination. For very general questions, it is almost impossible to help you direct your study efforts. What we can do is to point out some of the more common of these general abilities needed in public service positions and describe some typical questions.

1) General information

Broad, general information has been found useful for predicting job success in some kinds of work. This is tested in a variety of ways, from vocabulary lists to questions about current events. Basic background in some field of work, such as sociology or economics, may be sampled in a group of questions. Often these are principles which have become familiar to most persons through exposure rather than through formal training. It is difficult to advise you how to study for these questions; being alert to the world around you is our best suggestion.

2) Verbal ability

An example of an ability needed in many positions is verbal or language ability. Verbal ability is, in brief, the ability to use and understand words. Vocabulary and grammar tests are typical measures of this ability. Reading comprehension or paragraph interpretation questions are common in many kinds of civil service tests. You are given a paragraph of written material and asked to find its central meaning.

3) Numerical ability

Number skills can be tested by the familiar arithmetic problem, by checking paired lists of numbers to see which are alike and which are different, or by interpreting charts and graphs. In the latter test, a graph may be printed in the test booklet which you are asked to use as the basis for answering questions.

4) Observation

A popular test for law-enforcement positions is the observation test. A picture is shown to you for several minutes, then taken away. Questions about the picture test your ability to observe both details and larger elements.

5) Following directions

In many positions in the public service, the employee must be able to carry out written instructions dependably and accurately. You may be given a chart with several columns, each column listing a variety of information. The questions require you to carry out directions involving the information given in the chart.

6) Skills and aptitudes

Performance tests effectively measure some manual skills and aptitudes. When the skill is one in which you are trained, such as typing or shorthand, you can practice. These tests are often very much like those given in business school or high school courses. For many of the other skills and aptitudes, however, no short-time preparation can be made. Skills and abilities natural to you or that you have developed throughout your lifetime are being tested.

Many of the general questions just described provide all the data needed to answer the questions and ask you to use your reasoning ability to find the answers. Your best preparation for these tests, as well as for tests of facts and ideas, is to be at your physical and mental best. You, no doubt, have your own methods of getting into an exam-taking mood and keeping "in shape." The next section lists some ideas on this subject.

IV. KINDS OF QUESTIONS

Only rarely is the "essay" question, which you answer in narrative form, used in civil service tests. Civil service tests are usually of the short-answer type. Full instructions for answering these questions will be given to you at the examination. But in case this is your first experience with short-answer questions and separate answer sheets, here is what you need to know:

1) **Multiple-choice Questions**

Most popular of the short-answer questions is the "multiple choice" or "best answer" question. It can be used, for example, to test for factual knowledge, ability to solve problems or judgment in meeting situations found at work.

A multiple-choice question is normally one of three types—
- It can begin with an incomplete statement followed by several possible endings. You are to find the one ending which *best* completes the statement, although some of the others may not be entirely wrong.
- It can also be a complete statement in the form of a question which is answered by choosing one of the statements listed.

- It can be in the form of a problem – again you select the best answer.

Here is an example of a multiple-choice question with a discussion which should give you some clues as to the method for choosing the right answer:

When an employee has a complaint about his assignment, the action which will *best* help him overcome his difficulty is to
    A. discuss his difficulty with his coworkers
    B. take the problem to the head of the organization
    C. take the problem to the person who gave him the assignment
    D. say nothing to anyone about his complaint

In answering this question, you should study each of the choices to find which is best. Consider choice "A" – Certainly an employee may discuss his complaint with fellow employees, but no change or improvement can result, and the complaint remains unresolved. Choice "B" is a poor choice since the head of the organization probably does not know what assignment you have been given, and taking your problem to him is known as "going over the head" of the supervisor. The supervisor, or person who made the assignment, is the person who can clarify it or correct any injustice. Choice "C" is, therefore, correct. To say nothing, as in choice "D," is unwise. Supervisors have and interest in knowing the problems employees are facing, and the employee is seeking a solution to his problem.

2) True/False Questions

The "true/false" or "right/wrong" form of question is sometimes used. Here a complete statement is given. Your job is to decide whether the statement is right or wrong.

SAMPLE: A roaming cell-phone call to a nearby city costs less than a non-roaming call to a distant city.

This statement is wrong, or false, since roaming calls are more expensive.
This is not a complete list of all possible question forms, although most of the others are variations of these common types. You will always get complete directions for answering questions. Be sure you understand *how* to mark your answers – ask questions until you do.

V. RECORDING YOUR ANSWERS

Computer terminals are used more and more today for many different kinds of exams.
For an examination with very few applicants, you may be told to record your answers in the test booklet itself. Separate answer sheets are much more common. If this separate answer sheet is to be scored by machine – and this is often the case – it is highly important that you mark your answers correctly in order to get credit.
An electronic scoring machine is often used in civil service offices because of the speed with which papers can be scored. Machine-scored answer sheets must be marked with a pencil, which will be given to you. This pencil has a high graphite content which responds to the electronic scoring machine. As a matter of fact, stray dots may register as answers, so do not let your pencil rest on the answer sheet while you are pondering the correct answer. Also, if your pencil lead breaks or is otherwise defective, ask for another.

Since the answer sheet will be dropped in a slot in the scoring machine, be careful not to bend the corners or get the paper crumpled.

The answer sheet normally has five vertical columns of numbers, with 30 numbers to a column. These numbers correspond to the question numbers in your test booklet. After each number, going across the page are four or five pairs of dotted lines. These short dotted lines have small letters or numbers above them. The first two pairs may also have a "T" or "F" above the letters. This indicates that the first two pairs only are to be used if the questions are of the true-false type. If the questions are multiple choice, disregard the "T" and "F" and pay attention only to the small letters or numbers.

Answer your questions in the manner of the sample that follows:

32. The largest city in the United States is
    A. Washington, D.C.
    B. New York City
    C. Chicago
    D. Detroit
    E. San Francisco

1) Choose the answer you think is best. (New York City is the largest, so "B" is correct.)
2) Find the row of dotted lines numbered the same as the question you are answering. (Find row number 32)
3) Find the pair of dotted lines corresponding to the answer. (Find the pair of lines under the mark "B.")
4) Make a solid black mark between the dotted lines.

VI. BEFORE THE TEST

Common sense will help you find procedures to follow to get ready for an examination. Too many of us, however, overlook these sensible measures. Indeed, nervousness and fatigue have been found to be the most serious reasons why applicants fail to do their best on civil service tests. Here is a list of reminders:

- Begin your preparation early – Don't wait until the last minute to go scurrying around for books and materials or to find out what the position is all about.
- Prepare continuously – An hour a night for a week is better than an all-night cram session. This has been definitely established. What is more, a night a week for a month will return better dividends than crowding your study into a shorter period of time.
- Locate the place of the exam – You have been sent a notice telling you when and where to report for the examination. If the location is in a different town or otherwise unfamiliar to you, it would be well to inquire the best route and learn something about the building.
- Relax the night before the test – Allow your mind to rest. Do not study at all that night. Plan some mild recreation or diversion; then go to bed early and get a good night's sleep.
- Get up early enough to make a leisurely trip to the place for the test – This way unforeseen events, traffic snarls, unfamiliar buildings, etc. will not upset you.
- Dress comfortably – A written test is not a fashion show. You will be known by number and not by name, so wear something comfortable.

- Leave excess paraphernalia at home – Shopping bags and odd bundles will get in your way. You need bring only the items mentioned in the official notice you received; usually everything you need is provided. Do not bring reference books to the exam. They will only confuse those last minutes and be taken away from you when in the test room.
- Arrive somewhat ahead of time – If because of transportation schedules you must get there very early, bring a newspaper or magazine to take your mind off yourself while waiting.
- Locate the examination room – When you have found the proper room, you will be directed to the seat or part of the room where you will sit. Sometimes you are given a sheet of instructions to read while you are waiting. Do not fill out any forms until you are told to do so; just read them and be prepared.
- Relax and prepare to listen to the instructions
- If you have any physical problem that may keep you from doing your best, be sure to tell the test administrator. If you are sick or in poor health, you really cannot do your best on the exam. You can come back and take the test some other time.

VII. AT THE TEST

The day of the test is here and you have the test booklet in your hand. The temptation to get going is very strong. Caution! There is more to success than knowing the right answers. You must know how to identify your papers and understand variations in the type of short-answer question used in this particular examination. Follow these suggestions for maximum results from your efforts:

1) Cooperate with the monitor

The test administrator has a duty to create a situation in which you can be as much at ease as possible. He will give instructions, tell you when to begin, check to see that you are marking your answer sheet correctly, and so on. He is not there to guard you, although he will see that your competitors do not take unfair advantage. He wants to help you do your best.

2) Listen to all instructions

Don't jump the gun! Wait until you understand all directions. In most civil service tests you get more time than you need to answer the questions. So don't be in a hurry. Read each word of instructions until you clearly understand the meaning. Study the examples, listen to all announcements and follow directions. Ask questions if you do not understand what to do.

3) Identify your papers

Civil service exams are usually identified by number only. You will be assigned a number; you must not put your name on your test papers. Be sure to copy your number correctly. Since more than one exam may be given, copy your exact examination title.

4) Plan your time

Unless you are told that a test is a "speed" or "rate of work" test, speed itself is usually not important. Time enough to answer all the questions will be provided, but this does not mean that you have all day. An overall time limit has been set. Divide the total time (in minutes) by the number of questions to determine the approximate time you have for each question.

5) Do not linger over difficult questions

If you come across a difficult question, mark it with a paper clip (useful to have along) and come back to it when you have been through the booklet. One caution if you do this – be sure to skip a number on your answer sheet as well. Check often to be sure that you have not lost your place and that you are marking in the row numbered the same as the question you are answering.

6) Read the questions

Be sure you know what the question asks! Many capable people are unsuccessful because they failed to *read* the questions correctly.

7) Answer all questions

Unless you have been instructed that a penalty will be deducted for incorrect answers, it is better to guess than to omit a question.

8) Speed tests

It is often better NOT to guess on speed tests. It has been found that on timed tests people are tempted to spend the last few seconds before time is called in marking answers at random – without even reading them – in the hope of picking up a few extra points. To discourage this practice, the instructions may warn you that your score will be "corrected" for guessing. That is, a penalty will be applied. The incorrect answers will be deducted from the correct ones, or some other penalty formula will be used.

9) Review your answers

If you finish before time is called, go back to the questions you guessed or omitted to give them further thought. Review other answers if you have time.

10) Return your test materials

If you are ready to leave before others have finished or time is called, take ALL your materials to the monitor and leave quietly. Never take any test material with you. The monitor can discover whose papers are not complete, and taking a test booklet may be grounds for disqualification.

VIII. EXAMINATION TECHNIQUES

1) Read the general instructions carefully. These are usually printed on the first page of the exam booklet. As a rule, these instructions refer to the timing of the examination; the fact that you should not start work until the signal and must stop work at a signal, etc. If there are any *special* instructions, such as a choice of questions to be answered, make sure that you note this instruction carefully.

2) When you are ready to start work on the examination, that is as soon as the signal has been given, read the instructions to each question booklet, underline any key words or phrases, such as *least, best, outline, describe* and the like. In this way you will tend to answer as requested rather than discover on reviewing your paper that you *listed without describing*, that you selected the *worst* choice rather than the *best* choice, etc.

3) If the examination is of the objective or multiple-choice type – that is, each question will also give a series of possible answers: A, B, C or D, and you are called upon to select the best answer and write the letter next to that answer on your answer paper – it is advisable to start answering each question in turn. There may be anywhere from 50 to 100 such questions in the three or four hours allotted and you can see how much time would be taken if you read through all the questions before beginning to answer any. Furthermore, if you come across a question or group of questions which you know would be difficult to answer, it would undoubtedly affect your handling of all the other questions.

4) If the examination is of the essay type and contains but a few questions, it is a moot point as to whether you should read all the questions before starting to answer any one. Of course, if you are given a choice – say five out of seven and the like – then it is essential to read all the questions so you can eliminate the two that are most difficult. If, however, you are asked to answer all the questions, there may be danger in trying to answer the easiest one first because you may find that you will spend too much time on it. The best technique is to answer the first question, then proceed to the second, etc.

5) Time your answers. Before the exam begins, write down the time it started, then add the time allowed for the examination and write down the time it must be completed, then divide the time available somewhat as follows:
   - If 3-1/2 hours are allowed, that would be 210 minutes. If you have 80 objective-type questions, that would be an average of 2-1/2 minutes per question. Allow yourself no more than 2 minutes per question, or a total of 160 minutes, which will permit about 50 minutes to review.
   - If for the time allotment of 210 minutes there are 7 essay questions to answer, that would average about 30 minutes a question. Give yourself only 25 minutes per question so that you have about 35 minutes to review.

6) The most important instruction is to *read each question* and make sure you know what is wanted. The second most important instruction is to *time yourself properly* so that you answer every question. The third most important instruction is to *answer every question*. Guess if you have to but include something for each question. Remember that you will receive no credit for a blank and will probably receive some credit if you write something in answer to an essay question. If you guess a letter – say "B" for a multiple-choice question – you may have guessed right. If you leave a blank as an answer to a multiple-choice question, the examiners may respect your feelings but it will not add a point to your score. Some exams may penalize you for wrong answers, so in such cases *only*, you may not want to guess unless you have some basis for your answer.

7) Suggestions
   a. Objective-type questions
      1. Examine the question booklet for proper sequence of pages and questions
      2. Read all instructions carefully
      3. Skip any question which seems too difficult; return to it after all other questions have been answered
      4. Apportion your time properly; do not spend too much time on any single question or group of questions

5. Note and underline key words – *all, most, fewest, least, best, worst, same, opposite,* etc.
6. Pay particular attention to negatives
7. Note unusual option, e.g., unduly long, short, complex, different or similar in content to the body of the question
8. Observe the use of "hedging" words – *probably, may, most likely,* etc.
9. Make sure that your answer is put next to the same number as the question
10. Do not second-guess unless you have good reason to believe the second answer is definitely more correct
11. Cross out original answer if you decide another answer is more accurate; do not erase until you are ready to hand your paper in
12. Answer all questions; guess unless instructed otherwise
13. Leave time for review

  b. Essay questions
    1. Read each question carefully
    2. Determine exactly what is wanted. Underline key words or phrases.
    3. Decide on outline or paragraph answer
    4. Include many different points and elements unless asked to develop any one or two points or elements
    5. Show impartiality by giving pros and cons unless directed to select one side only
    6. Make and write down any assumptions you find necessary to answer the questions
    7. Watch your English, grammar, punctuation and choice of words
    8. Time your answers; don't crowd material

8) Answering the essay question

Most essay questions can be answered by framing the specific response around several key words or ideas. Here are a few such key words or ideas:

M's: manpower, materials, methods, money, management
P's: purpose, program, policy, plan, procedure, practice, problems, pitfalls, personnel, public relations

  a. Six basic steps in handling problems:
    1. Preliminary plan and background development
    2. Collect information, data and facts
    3. Analyze and interpret information, data and facts
    4. Analyze and develop solutions as well as make recommendations
    5. Prepare report and sell recommendations
    6. Install recommendations and follow up effectiveness

  b. Pitfalls to avoid
    1. *Taking things for granted* – A statement of the situation does not necessarily imply that each of the elements is necessarily true; for example, a complaint may be invalid and biased so that all that can be taken for granted is that a complaint has been registered

2. *Considering only one side of a situation* – Wherever possible, indicate several alternatives and then point out the reasons you selected the best one
3. *Failing to indicate follow up* – Whenever your answer indicates action on your part, make certain that you will take proper follow-up action to see how successful your recommendations, procedures or actions turn out to be
4. *Taking too long in answering any single question* – Remember to time your answers properly

IX. AFTER THE TEST

Scoring procedures differ in detail among civil service jurisdictions although the general principles are the same. Whether the papers are hand-scored or graded by machine we have described, they are nearly always graded by number. That is, the person who marks the paper knows only the number – never the name – of the applicant. Not until all the papers have been graded will they be matched with names. If other tests, such as training and experience or oral interview ratings have been given, scores will be combined. Different parts of the examination usually have different weights. For example, the written test might count 60 percent of the final grade, and a rating of training and experience 40 percent. In many jurisdictions, veterans will have a certain number of points added to their grades.

After the final grade has been determined, the names are placed in grade order and an eligible list is established. There are various methods for resolving ties between those who get the same final grade – probably the most common is to place first the name of the person whose application was received first. Job offers are made from the eligible list in the order the names appear on it. You will be notified of your grade and your rank as soon as all these computations have been made. This will be done as rapidly as possible.

People who are found to meet the requirements in the announcement are called "eligibles." Their names are put on a list of eligible candidates. An eligible's chances of getting a job depend on how high he stands on this list and how fast agencies are filling jobs from the list.

When a job is to be filled from a list of eligibles, the agency asks for the names of people on the list of eligibles for that job. When the civil service commission receives this request, it sends to the agency the names of the three people highest on this list. Or, if the job to be filled has specialized requirements, the office sends the agency the names of the top three persons who meet these requirements from the general list.

The appointing officer makes a choice from among the three people whose names were sent to him. If the selected person accepts the appointment, the names of the others are put back on the list to be considered for future openings.

That is the rule in hiring from all kinds of eligible lists, whether they are for typist, carpenter, chemist, or something else. For every vacancy, the appointing officer has his choice of any one of the top three eligibles on the list. This explains why the person whose name is on top of the list sometimes does not get an appointment when some of the persons lower on the list do. If the appointing officer chooses the second or third eligible, the No. 1 eligible does not get a job at once, but stays on the list until he is appointed or the list is terminated.

X. HOW TO PASS THE INTERVIEW TEST

The examination for which you applied requires an oral interview test. You have already taken the written test and you are now being called for the interview test – the final part of the formal examination.

You may think that it is not possible to prepare for an interview test and that there are no procedures to follow during an interview. Our purpose is to point out some things you can do in advance that will help you and some good rules to follow and pitfalls to avoid while you are being interviewed.

What is an interview supposed to test?

The written examination is designed to test the technical knowledge and competence of the candidate; the oral is designed to evaluate intangible qualities, not readily measured otherwise, and to establish a list showing the relative fitness of each candidate – as measured against his competitors – for the position sought. Scoring is not on the basis of "right" and "wrong," but on a sliding scale of values ranging from "not passable" to "outstanding." As a matter of fact, it is possible to achieve a relatively low score without a single "incorrect" answer because of evident weakness in the qualities being measured.

Occasionally, an examination may consist entirely of an oral test – either an individual or a group oral. In such cases, information is sought concerning the technical knowledges and abilities of the candidate, since there has been no written examination for this purpose. More commonly, however, an oral test is used to supplement a written examination.

Who conducts interviews?

The composition of oral boards varies among different jurisdictions. In nearly all, a representative of the personnel department serves as chairman. One of the members of the board may be a representative of the department in which the candidate would work. In some cases, "outside experts" are used, and, frequently, a businessman or some other representative of the general public is asked to serve. Labor and management or other special groups may be represented. The aim is to secure the services of experts in the appropriate field.

However the board is composed, it is a good idea (and not at all improper or unethical) to ascertain in advance of the interview who the members are and what groups they represent. When you are introduced to them, you will have some idea of their backgrounds and interests, and at least you will not stutter and stammer over their names.

What should be done before the interview?

While knowledge about the board members is useful and takes some of the surprise element out of the interview, there is other preparation which is more substantive. It *is* possible to prepare for an oral interview – in several ways:

1) Keep a copy of your application and review it carefully before the interview

This may be the only document before the oral board, and the starting point of the interview. Know what education and experience you have listed there, and the sequence and dates of all of it. Sometimes the board will ask you to review the highlights of your experience for them; you should not have to hem and haw doing it.

2) Study the class specification and the examination announcement

Usually, the oral board has one or both of these to guide them. The qualities, characteristics or knowledges required by the position sought are stated in these documents. They offer valuable clues as to the nature of the oral interview. For example, if the job involves supervisory responsibilities, the announcement will usually indicate that knowledge of modern supervisory methods and the qualifications of the candidate as a supervisor will be tested. If so, you can expect such questions, frequently in the form of a hypothetical situation which you are expected to solve. NEVER go into an oral without knowledge of the duties and responsibilities of the job you seek.

3) Think through each qualification required

Try to visualize the kind of questions you would ask if you were a board member. How well could you answer them? Try especially to appraise your own knowledge and background in each area, *measured against the job sought*, and identify any areas in which you are weak. Be critical and realistic – do not flatter yourself.

4) Do some general reading in areas in which you feel you may be weak

For example, if the job involves supervision and your past experience has NOT, some general reading in supervisory methods and practices, particularly in the field of human relations, might be useful. Do NOT study agency procedures or detailed manuals. The oral board will be testing your understanding and capacity, not your memory.

5) Get a good night's sleep and watch your general health and mental attitude

You will want a clear head at the interview. Take care of a cold or any other minor ailment, and of course, no hangovers.

What should be done on the day of the interview?

Now comes the day of the interview itself. Give yourself plenty of time to get there. Plan to arrive somewhat ahead of the scheduled time, particularly if your appointment is in the fore part of the day. If a previous candidate fails to appear, the board might be ready for you a bit early. By early afternoon an oral board is almost invariably behind schedule if there are many candidates, and you may have to wait. Take along a book or magazine to read, or your application to review, but leave any extraneous material in the waiting room when you go in for your interview. In any event, relax and compose yourself.

The matter of dress is important. The board is forming impressions about you – from your experience, your manners, your attitude, and your appearance. Give your personal appearance careful attention. Dress your best, but not your flashiest. Choose conservative, appropriate clothing, and be sure it is immaculate. This is a business interview, and your appearance should indicate that you regard it as such. Besides, being well groomed and properly dressed will help boost your confidence.

Sooner or later, someone will call your name and escort you into the interview room. *This is it*. From here on you are on your own. It is too late for any more preparation. But remember, you asked for this opportunity to prove your fitness, and you are here because your request was granted.

What happens when you go in?

The usual sequence of events will be as follows: The clerk (who is often the board stenographer) will introduce you to the chairman of the oral board, who will introduce you to the other members of the board. Acknowledge the introductions before you sit down. Do not be surprised if you find a microphone facing you or a stenotypist sitting by. Oral interviews are usually recorded in the event of an appeal or other review.

Usually the chairman of the board will open the interview by reviewing the highlights of your education and work experience from your application – primarily for the benefit of the other members of the board, as well as to get the material into the record. Do not interrupt or comment unless there is an error or significant misinterpretation; if that is the case, do not hesitate. But do not quibble about insignificant matters. Also, he will usually ask you some question about your education, experience or your present job – partly to get you to start talking and to establish the interviewing "rapport." He may start the actual questioning, or turn it over to one of the other members. Frequently, each member undertakes the questioning on a particular area, one in which he is perhaps most competent, so you can expect each member to participate in the examination. Because time is limited, you may also expect some rather abrupt switches in the direction the questioning takes, so do not be upset by it. Normally, a board member will not pursue a single line of questioning unless he discovers a particular strength or weakness.

After each member has participated, the chairman will usually ask whether any member has any further questions, then will ask you if you have anything you wish to add. Unless you are expecting this question, it may floor you. Worse, it may start you off on an extended, extemporaneous speech. The board is not usually seeking more information. The question is principally to offer you a last opportunity to present further qualifications or to indicate that you have nothing to add. So, if you feel that a significant qualification or characteristic has been overlooked, it is proper to point it out in a sentence or so. Do not compliment the board on the thoroughness of their examination – they have been sketchy, and you know it. If you wish, merely say, "No thank you, I have nothing further to add." This is a point where you can "talk yourself out" of a good impression or fail to present an important bit of information. Remember, *you close the interview yourself.*

The chairman will then say, "That is all, Mr. _____, thank you." Do not be startled; the interview is over, and quicker than you think. Thank him, gather your belongings and take your leave. Save your sigh of relief for the other side of the door.

How to put your best foot forward

Throughout this entire process, you may feel that the board individually and collectively is trying to pierce your defenses, seek out your hidden weaknesses and embarrass and confuse you. Actually, this is not true. They are obliged to make an appraisal of your qualifications for the job you are seeking, and they want to see you in your best light. Remember, they must interview all candidates and a non-cooperative candidate may become a failure in spite of their best efforts to bring out his qualifications. Here are 15 suggestions that will help you:

1) Be natural – Keep your attitude confident, not cocky

If you are not confident that you can do the job, do not expect the board to be. Do not apologize for your weaknesses, try to bring out your strong points. The board is interested in a positive, not negative, presentation. Cockiness will antagonize any board member and make him wonder if you are covering up a weakness by a false show of strength.

2) Get comfortable, but don't lounge or sprawl

Sit erectly but not stiffly. A careless posture may lead the board to conclude that you are careless in other things, or at least that you are not impressed by the importance of the occasion. Either conclusion is natural, even if incorrect. Do not fuss with your clothing, a pencil or an ashtray. Your hands may occasionally be useful to emphasize a point; do not let them become a point of distraction.

3) Do not wisecrack or make small talk

This is a serious situation, and your attitude should show that you consider it as such. Further, the time of the board is limited – they do not want to waste it, and neither should you.

4) Do not exaggerate your experience or abilities

In the first place, from information in the application or other interviews and sources, the board may know more about you than you think. Secondly, you probably will not get away with it. An experienced board is rather adept at spotting such a situation, so do not take the chance.

5) If you know a board member, do not make a point of it, yet do not hide it

Certainly you are not fooling him, and probably not the other members of the board. Do not try to take advantage of your acquaintanceship – it will probably do you little good.

6) Do not dominate the interview

Let the board do that. They will give you the clues – do not assume that you have to do all the talking. Realize that the board has a number of questions to ask you, and do not try to take up all the interview time by showing off your extensive knowledge of the answer to the first one.

7) Be attentive

You only have 20 minutes or so, and you should keep your attention at its sharpest throughout. When a member is addressing a problem or question to you, give him your undivided attention. Address your reply principally to him, but do not exclude the other board members.

8) Do not interrupt

A board member may be stating a problem for you to analyze. He will ask you a question when the time comes. Let him state the problem, and wait for the question.

9) Make sure you understand the question

Do not try to answer until you are sure what the question is. If it is not clear, restate it in your own words or ask the board member to clarify it for you. However, do not haggle about minor elements.

10) Reply promptly but not hastily

A common entry on oral board rating sheets is "candidate responded readily," or "candidate hesitated in replies." Respond as promptly and quickly as you can, but do not jump to a hasty, ill-considered answer.

11) Do not be peremptory in your answers

A brief answer is proper – but do not fire your answer back. That is a losing game from your point of view. The board member can probably ask questions much faster than you can answer them.

12) Do not try to create the answer you think the board member wants

He is interested in what kind of mind you have and how it works – not in playing games. Furthermore, he can usually spot this practice and will actually grade you down on it.

13) Do not switch sides in your reply merely to agree with a board member

Frequently, a member will take a contrary position merely to draw you out and to see if you are willing and able to defend your point of view. Do not start a debate, yet do not surrender a good position. If a position is worth taking, it is worth defending.

14) Do not be afraid to admit an error in judgment if you are shown to be wrong

The board knows that you are forced to reply without any opportunity for careful consideration. Your answer may be demonstrably wrong. If so, admit it and get on with the interview.

15) Do not dwell at length on your present job

The opening question may relate to your present assignment. Answer the question but do not go into an extended discussion. You are being examined for a *new* job, not your present one. As a matter of fact, try to phrase ALL your answers in terms of the job for which you are being examined.

Basis of Rating

Probably you will forget most of these "do's" and "don'ts" when you walk into the oral interview room. Even remembering them all will not ensure you a passing grade. Perhaps you did not have the qualifications in the first place. But remembering them will help you to put your best foot forward, without treading on the toes of the board members.

Rumor and popular opinion to the contrary notwithstanding, an oral board wants you to make the best appearance possible. They know you are under pressure – but they also want to see how you respond to it as a guide to what your reaction would be under the pressures of the job you seek. They will be influenced by the degree of poise you display, the personal traits you show and the manner in which you respond.

ABOUT THIS BOOK

This book contains tests divided into Examination Sections. Go through each test, answering every question in the margin. We have also attached a sample answer sheet at the back of the book that can be removed and used. At the end of each test look at the answer key and check your answers. On the ones you got wrong, look at the right answer choice and learn. Do not fill in the answers first. Do not memorize the questions and answers, but understand the answer and principles involved. On your test, the questions will likely be different from the samples. Questions are changed and new ones added. If you understand these past questions you should have success with any changes that arise. Tests may consist of several types of questions. We have additional books on each subject should more study be advisable or necessary for you. Finally, the more you study, the better prepared you will be. This book is intended to be the last thing you study before you walk into the examination room. Prior study of relevant texts is also recommended. NLC publishes some of these in our Fundamental Series. Knowledge and good sense are important factors in passing your exam. Good luck also helps. So now study this Passbook, absorb the material contained within and take that knowledge into the examination. Then do your best to pass that exam.

EXAMINATION SECTION

Following Oral Directions

DESCRIPTION OF THE TEST AND SAMPLE QUESTIONS

Since it is important that each employee does exactly as he is instructed, this test is used to make sure that each applicant can and will listen carefully and follow through without extra supervision.

The directions in the test are not hard to follow, but you must listen carefully and do exactly what you are told to do.

In order to do this practice section, you must have a friend who will read the directions to you. *Hints* for *Doing the Test of Following Oral Directions*
- Listen carefully to the directions.
- Do exactly what the examiner tells you to do.
- Do not try to get ahead of the examiner.
- If you missed an instruction, wait for the next one.
- Make sure that you darken only one box for each number on the answer sheet.

The material which you will use for practice on the Following Oral Directions Test is on pages 2-8.

Do not read the material on pages 9-13 yourself; because, if you do, you will lose the value of this practice.

Following Oral Directions-Sample Questions

The directions are to be read at the rate of 80 words per minute. Since not everybody speaks at this speed, your friend should practice reading the 1-minute practice on page 9 until he can read it in exactly 1 minute whenever he wants to. He will also need a watch with a second hand.

To do the sample questions tear out page 9 which has the 1-minute practice and the directions for the sample questions. Give it to your friend to use. (Each friend who is helping you will have to use it to practice, so don't throw it away.)

When your friend reads the directions to you, listen carefully and do what he says. If you fall behind and miss a direction, don't get excited. Let that one go and listen for the next one. Since B and D sound very much alike, he will say "B as in baker" when he means B and "D as in dog" when he means D.

He will tell you some things to do with the 5 sample questions below. Then, when he tells you to darken a box on the Sample Answer Sheet, use the one on this page.

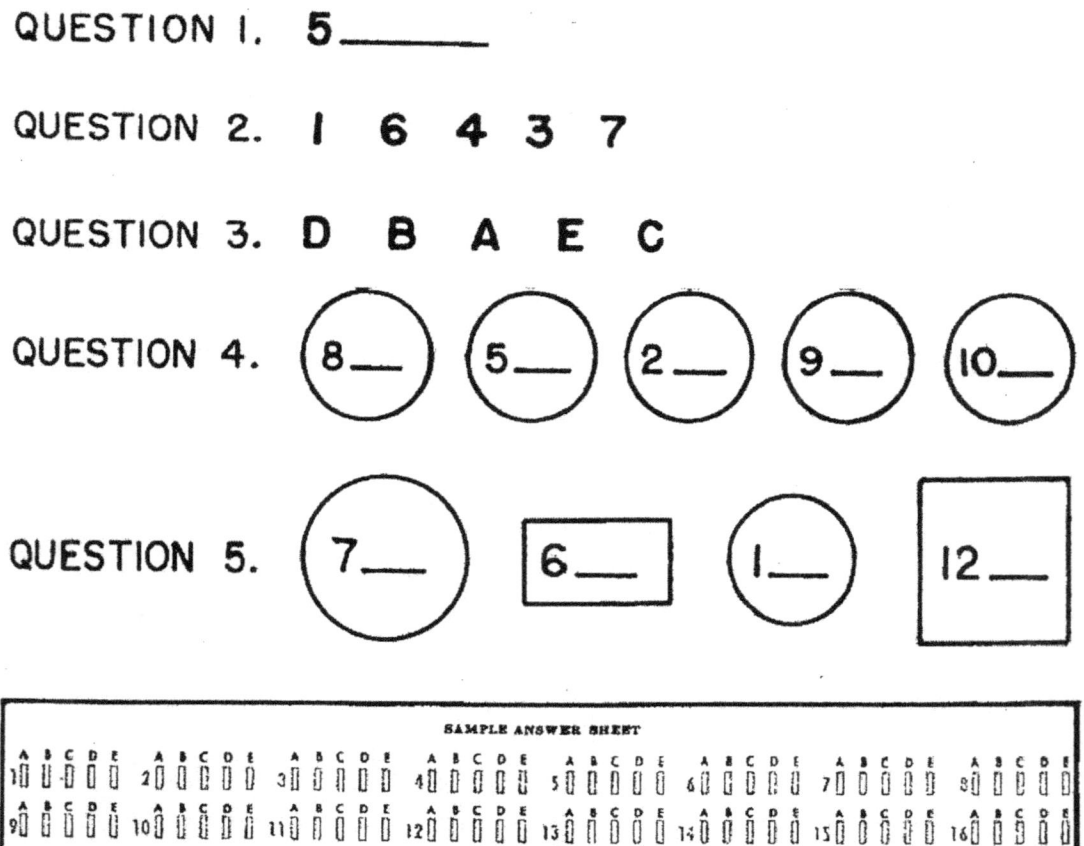

WORKSHEET FOR PRACTICE TEST 1

1. 45_____   43_____   83_____

2. |___A| |___E| |___C| |___B| |___D|

3. 69 87 50 54 25 47 20 80 27

4. (71__) (36__) (49__) (11__)

5. |42__| (44__) (14__) |56__|

6. (88__) (68__) (61__) (70__) (34__)

7. 28 67 29 77 26

8.
A	B	C
CHESTNUT STREET	HYDE PARK	PRUDENTIAL PLAZA
___	___	___

9. |85__| |86__| |63__| |39__|

Now check your answers by comparing your answers with the correct answers shown below.

Your Test Score on this Practice Test is the number you got right.

    Count how many you got right, and write that number on this line ————➤ _____

Meaning of Test Score

    If your Test Score is *15 or 16,* you have a Good score.

    If your Test Score is *13 or 14,* you have a Fair score.

    If your Test Score is *12 or less,* you are not doing too well.

        You may be working too slowly or you may not be doing exactly what you are told to do.

            You need more practice.

WORKSHEET FOR PRACTICE TEST 2

1. 40　85　17　87　52　55　56　45　75

2. | 65 __ | 37 __ | 12 __ | 4 __ |

3. X O O O X O O X X O X O X

4. | 78 __ |　(25 __)　| 27 __ |　(73 __)

5. 88　2　69　84　34

6. (63 __)　(38 __)　(76 __)　(53 __)　(57 __)

7. | 435 __B | 466 __C | 474 __E | 467 __A | 489 __D |

8. 79 _____　　39 _____

9. | __C | __E | __A | __D | __B |

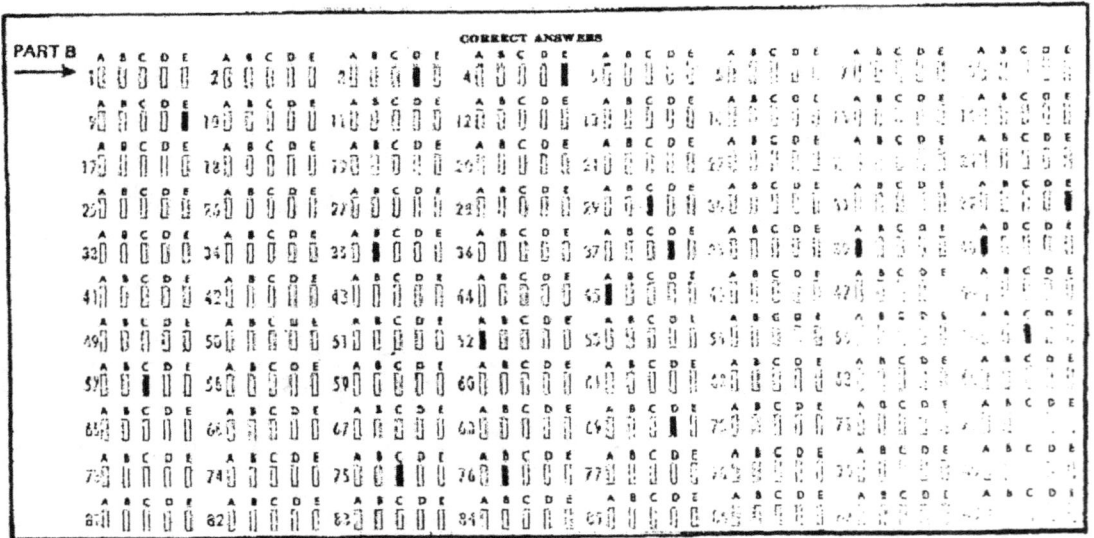

Now check your answers by comparing your answers with the correct answers shown below.

Your Test Score on this Practice Test is the number you got right.

    Count how many you got right, and write that number on this line ———————→ _____

Meaning of Test Score

    If your Test Score *is 15 or 16,* you have a Good score.

    If your Test Score is *13 or 14,* you have a Fair score.

    If your Test Score is *12 or less,* you are not doing too well.

      You may be working too slowly or you may not be doing exactly what you are told to do.

        You need more practice.

WORKSHEET FOR PRACTICE TEST 3

1. 59   35   62   58   8

2. (__C) (__A) (__D) (__E) (__B)

3. 15_____   20_____

4. [3__] [37__] [36__]   CURE   DAMP   BEAR

5. A C B A B D C E D

6. [48__] [28__] [22__] [43__]

7. 51_____   69_____   50_____

8. (65__) (13__) (87__) (31__) (17__)

9. [55__] [44__] [74__] [25__]

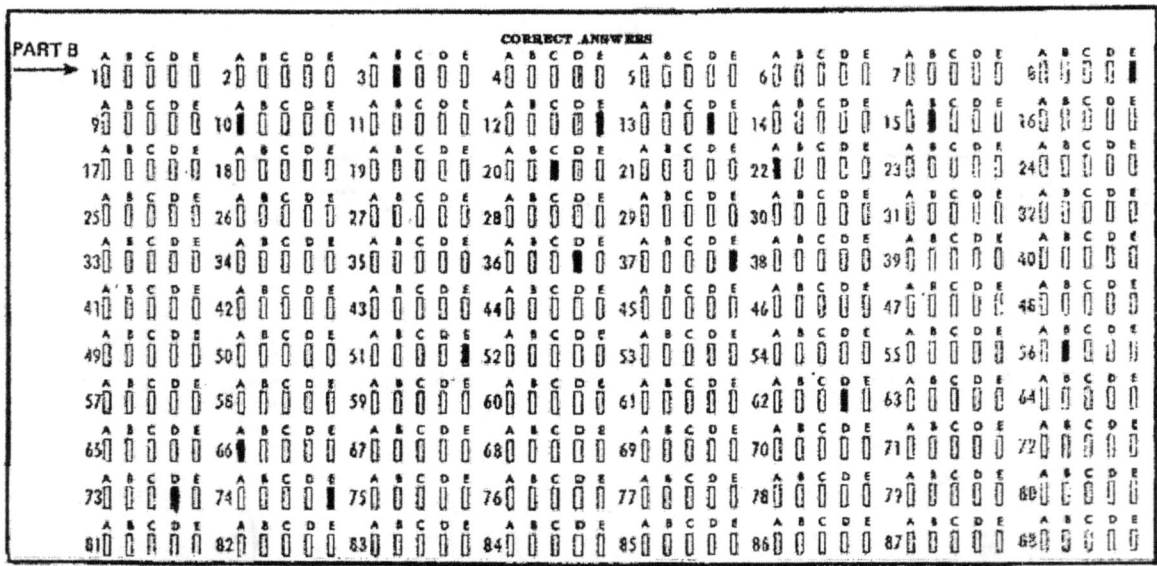

Your Test Score on this Practice Test is the number you got right.

    Count how many you got right, and write that number on this line ————→ _____

Meaning of Test Score

    If your Test Score is *15 or 16,* you have a Good score.

    If your Test Spore is *13 or 14,* you have a Fair score.

    If your Test Score is *12 or less,* you are not doing too well.

        You may be working too slowly or you may not be doing exactly what you are told to do.

            You need more practice.

For The Person Who Will Read The Following Oral Directions Test to You

The directions should be read at about 80 words per minute. Practice reading aloud the material in the box below until you can do it in exactly 1 minute. This will give you a feel for the way you should read the test material.

1-MINUTE PRACTICE
(This is for practice in reading aloud. It is not the sample test.)

> Look at line 20 in your work booklet. There are two circles and two boxes of different sizes with numbers in them. If 7 is less than 3 and if 2 is smaller than 4, write a G in the larger circle. Otherwise write B as in baker in the smaller box. Now on your Code Sheet darken the space for the number-letter combination in the box or circle.

DIRECTIONS: (The words in parentheses should *not* be read aloud. They tell you how long you should pause at the various spots. You should time the pauses with a watch with a second hand. The instruction "Pause slightly" means that you should stop long enough to take a breath.) You should not repeat any directions.

THIS IS THE SAMPLE.

> You are to follow the instructions that I read to you. I cannot repeat them.
>
> Look at the Sample Questions. Question 1 has a number and a line beside it. On the line write an A. (Pause 2 seconds.) Now on the Sample Answer Sheet, find number 5 (pause 2 seconds) and darken the box for the letter you just wrote on the line. (Pause 5 seconds.)
>
> Look at Question 2. (Pause slightly.) Draw a line under the third number. (Pause 2 seconds.) Now on the Sample Answer Sheet, find the number under which you just drew a line and darken box B as in baker for that number. (Pause 5 seconds.)
>
> Look at the letters in Question 3. (Pause slightly.) Draw a line under the third letter in the line. (Pause 2 seconds.) Now on your answer sheet, find number 9 (pause 2 seconds) and darken the box for the letter under which you drew a line. (Pause 5 seconds.)
>
> Look at the five circles in Question 4. (Pause slightly.) Each circle has a number and a line in it. Write D as in dog on the blank in the last circle. (Pause 2 seconds.) Now on the Sample Answer Sheet, darken the space for the number-letter combination that is in the circle you just wrote in. (Pause 5 seconds.)
>
> Look at Question 5. (Pause slightly.) There are two circles and two boxes of different sizes with numbers in them. (Pause slightly.) If 4 is more than 2 and if 5 is less than 3, write A in the smaller circle. (Pause slightly.) Otherwise write C in the larger box. (Pause 2 seconds.) Now on the Sample Answer Sheet, darken the space for the number-letter combination in the box or circle in which you just wrote. (Pause 5 seconds.)
>
> Now look at the Sample Answer Sheet. (Pause slightly.) You should have darkened spaces 4B, 5A, 9A, 10D, and 12C on the Sample Answer Sheet.

FOLLOWING ORAL DIRECTIONS-PRACTICE TEST 1

When you are ready to try Practice Test 1, tear this sheet out and give it to your friend who is helping you practice the Following Oral Directions Test.

*To the Person Who Is to Read the Directions*Directions are to be read at the rate of 80 words per minute. Do not read aloud the material which is in parentheses. Do not repeat any directions.

Read the following directions aloud.

For this practice test you are to use the worksheet that is on page 3 and the answer sheet which is on page 4 . (Pause until the person studying has turned to page 3)

Look at line 1 on your worksheet. (Pause slightly.) Next to the left-hand number write the letter E. (Pause 2 seconds.) Now on your answer sheet, find the space for the number beside which you wrote and darken box E. (Pause 5 seconds.)

Now look at line 2 on your worksheet. (Pause slightly.) There are 5 boxes. Each box has a letter. (Pause slightly.) In the fifth box write the answer to this question: Which of the following numbers is largest: 18, 9, 15, 19, 13? (Pause 5 seconds.) Now on your answer sheet, darken the space for the number-letter combination that is in the box you just wrote in. (Pause 5 seconds.) In the fourth box on the same line do nothing. In the third box write 5. (Pause 2'seconds.) Now on your answer sheet, darken the space for the number-letter combination that is in the box you just wrote in. (Pause 5 seconds.) In the second box, write the answer to this question: How many hours are there in a day? (Pause 2 seconds.) Now on your answer sheet, darken the space for the number-letter combination that is in the box you just wrote in. (Pause 5 seconds.)

Look at line 3 on your worksheet. (Pause slightly.) Draw a line under every number that is more than 50 but less than 85. (Pause 12 seconds.) Now on your answer sheet, for each number that you drew a line under, darken box D as in dog. (Pause 25 seconds.)

Look at line 4 on your worksheet. (Pause slightly.) Write a B as in baker in the third circle. (Pause 2 seconds.) Now on your answer sheet, find the number in that circle and darken box B for that number. (Pause 5 seconds.)

Look at line 4 again. (Pause slightly.) Write C in the first circle. (Pause 2 seconds.) Now on your answer sheet, find the number in that circle and darken box C for that number. (Pause 5 seconds.)

Look at line 5 on your worksheet. (Pause slightly.) There are two circles and two boxes of different sizes with numbers in them. (Pause slightly.) If 4 is more than 6 and if 9 is less than 7, write D as in dog in the smaller box. (Pause slightly.) Otherwise write A in the larger circle. (Pause 2 seconds.) Now on your answer sheet, darken the space for the number-letter combination for the box or circle you just wrote in. (Pause 5 seconds.)

Now look at line 6 on your worksheet. (Pause slightly.) Write an E in the second circle. (Pause 2 seconds.) Now on your answer sheet, find the number in that circle and darken box E for that number. (Pause 5 seconds.)

Now look at line 6 again. (Pause slightly.) Write a B as in baker in the middle circle. (Pause 2 seconds.) Now on your answer sheet, find the number in that circle and darken box B as in baker for that number. (Pause 5 seconds.)

Look at the numbers on line 7 on your worksheet. (Pause slightly.) Draw a line under the largest number in the line. (Pause 2 seconds.) Now on your answer sheet, find the space for that number and darken box C for that number. (Pause 5 seconds.)

Now look at line 7 again. (Pause slightly.) Draw a circle around the smallest number in the line. (Pause 2 seconds.) Now on your answer sheet, find the space for the number which you just drew a circle around and darken box A for that number. (Pause 5 seconds.)

(over)

Now look at line 8 on your worksheet. There are 3 boxes with words and letters in them. (Pause slightly.) Each box represents a station in a large city. Station A delivers mail in the Chestnut Street area, Station B delivers mail in Hyde Park, and Station C delivers mail in the Prudential Plaza. Mr. Adams lives in Hyde Park. Write the number 30 on the line inside the box which represents the station that delivers Mr. Adams' mail. (Pause 2 seconds.) Now on your answer sheet, find the space for number 30 and darken the box for the letter that is in the box you just wrote in. (Pause 5 seconds.)

Now look at line 9 on your worksheet. (Pause slightly.) Write a D as in dog in the second box. (Pause 2 seconds.) Now on your answer sheet, find the number that is in the box you just wrote in and darken box D as in dog for that number. (Pause 5 seconds.)

Now check your answers by comparing them with the correct answers on page 4.

FOLLOWING ORAL DIRECTIONS—PRACTICE TEST 2

When you are ready to try Practice Test 2, tear this sheet out and give it to your friend who is helping you practice the Following Oral Directions Test.

To the Person Who Is to Read the Directions The Directions are to be read at the rate of 80 words per minute. Do not read aloud the material which is in parentheses. Do not repeat any directions.

Read the following directions aloud.

For this practice test you are to use the worksheet that is on page 26 and the answer sheet which is on page 6 . (Pause until the person studying has turned to page 5 .)

Look at line 1 on your worksheet. (Pause slightly.) Draw a line under every number that is more than 35 but less than 55. (Pause 12 seconds.) Now on your answer sheet, for each number that you drew a line under darken box A. (Pause 25 seconds.)

Now look at line 1 on your worksheet again. (Pause slightly.) Draw two lines under every number that is more than 55 and less than 80. (Pause 12 seconds.) Now on your answer sheet for each number that you drew two lines under darken box C. (Pause 25 seconds.)

Look at line 2 on your worksheet. (Pause slightly.) Write an E in the last box. (Pause 2 seconds.) Now on your answer sheet, find the number in that box and darken box E for that number. (Pause 5 seconds.)

Now look at line 2 on your worksheet again. (Pause slightly.) Write a D as in dog in the second box. (Pause 2 seconds.) Now on your answer sheet, find the number in that box and darken box D as in dog for that number. (Pause 5 seconds.)

Look at line 3 on your worksheet. (Pause slightly.) Draw a line under every "X" in the line. (Pause 5 seconds.) Count the number of lines that you have drawn, add 3, and write that number at the end of the line. (Pause 5 seconds.) Now on your answer sheet, find that number and darken space E for that number. (Pause 5 seconds.)

Look at line 4 on your worksheet. (Pause slightly.) If the number in the right-hand box is larger than the number in the left-hand circle, add 4 to the number in the left-hand circle, and change the number in the circle to this number. (Pause 8 seconds.) Then write C next to the new number. (Pause slightly.) Otherwise, write A next to the number in the smaller box. (Pause 3 seconds.) Now on your answer sheet, darken the space for the number-letter combination that is in the box or circle you just wrote in. (Pause 5 seconds.)

Now look at line 5 on your worksheet. (Pause slightly.) Draw a line under the middle number in the line. (Pause 2 seconds.) Now on your answer sheet, find the number under which you just drew the line and darken box D as in dog for that number. (Pause 5 seconds.)

Now look at line 6 on your worksheet. (Pause slightly.) Write a B as in baker in the third circle. (Pause 2 seconds.) Now on your answer sheet, find the number in that circle and darken box B as in baker for that number. (Pause 5 seconds.)

Now look at line 6 again. (Pause slightly.) Write a C in the last circle. (Pause 2 seconds.) Now on your answer sheet, find the number in that circle and darken box C for that number. (Pause 5 seconds.)

Look at the drawings on line 7 on your worksheet. The number in each box is the number of employees in a post office. (Pause slightly.) In the box for the post office with the smallest number of employees, write on the line the last two figures of the number of employees. (Pause 5 seconds.) Now on your answer sheet, darken the space for the number-letter combination that is in the box you just wrote in. (Pause 5 seconds.)

Now look at line 8 on your worksheet. (Pause slightly.) Write an A on the line next to the right-hand number. (Pause 2 seconds.) Now on your answer sheet find the space for the number next to which you just wrote and darken box A. (Pause 5 seconds.)

Look at line 9 on your worksheet. (Pause slightly.) In the fourth box, write the answer to this question: How many feet are in a yard? (Pause 2 seconds.) Now on your answer sheet darken the space for the number-letter combination that is in the box you just wrote in. (Pause 5 seconds.)

Look at line 9 again. (Pause slightly.) In the second box, write the number 32, (Pause 2 seconds.) Now on your answer sheet, find the number-letter combination that is in the box you just wrote in. (Pause 5 seconds.)

Now check your answers by comparing them with the Correct Answers on page 6.

FOLLOWING ORAL DIRECTIONS—PRACTICE TEST 3

When you are ready to try Practice Test 3, tear this sheet out and give it to your friend who is helping you practice the Following Oral Directions Test.

To the Person Who Is to Read the Directions—The Directions are to be read at the rate of 80 words per minute. Do not read the material which is in parentheses aloud. Do not repeat any directions.

Read the following directions aloud.

For this practice test you are to use the worksheet that is on page 28 and the answer sheet that is on page 29. (Pause until the person preparing for the examination has turned to page 28.)

Look at line 1 on your worksheet. (Pause slightly.) Draw a line under the largest number in the line. (Pause 2 seconds.) Now on your answer sheet, find the number under which you just drew a line and darken box D as in dog for that number. (Pause 5 seconds.)

Look at line 1 on your worksheet again. (Pause slightly.) Draw two lines under the smallest number in the line. (Pause 2 seconds.) Now on your answer sheet, find the number under which you just drew two lines and darken box E. (Pause 5 seconds.)

Look at the circles in line 2 on your worksheet. (Pause slightly.) In the second circle, write the answer to this question: How much is 6 plus 4? (Pause 8 seconds.) In the third circle, write the answer to this question: Which of the following numbers is largest: 67, 48, 15, 73, 61? (Pause 5 seconds.) In the fourth circle, write the answer to this question: How many months are there in a year? (Pause 2 seconds:) Now, .on your answer sheet, darken the number-letter combinations that are in the circles you wrote in. (Pause 10 seconds.)

Now look at line 3 on your worksheet. (Pause slightly.) Write the letter C on the blank next to the right-hand number. (Pause 2 seconds.) Now on your answer sheet, find the space for the number beside which you wrote and darken box C. (Pause 5 seconds.)

Now look at line 3 on your worksheet again. (Pause slightly.) Write the letter B as in baker on the blank next to the left-hand number. (Pause 2 seconds.) Now on your answer sheet, find the space for the number beside which you just wrote and darken box B as in baker. (Pause 5 seconds.)

Look at the boxes and words in line 4 on your worksheet. (Pause slightly.) Write the first letter of the second word in the third box. (Pause 2 seconds.) Write the last letter of the first word in the second box. (Pause 2 seconds.) Write the first letter of the third word in the first box. (Pause 2 seconds.) Now on your answer sheet, darken the spaces for the number-letter combinations that are in the three boxes you just wrote in. (Pause 10 seconds.)

Look at the letters on line 5 on your worksheet. (Pause slightly.) Draw a line under the fifth letter in the line. (Pause 2 seconds.) Now on your answer sheet, find the number 56 (pause 2 seconds) and darken the space for the letter under which you drew a line. (Pause 5 seconds.)

Look at the letters on line 5 on your worksheet again. (Pause slightly.) Draw two lines under the fourth letter in the line. (Pause 2 seconds.) Now on your answer sheet, find the number 66 (pause 2 seconds) and darken the space for the letter under which you drew two lines. (Pause 5 seconds.)

Look at the drawings on line 6 on your worksheet. (Pause slightly.) The four boxes indicate the number of buildings in four different carrier routes. In the box for the route with the fewest number of buildings, write an A. (Pause 2 seconds.) Now on your answer sheet, darken the space for the number-letter combination that is in the box you just wrote in. (Pause 5 seconds.)

Now look at line 7 on your worksheet. (Pause slightly.) If fall comes before summer, write the letter B as in baker on the line next to the middle number. (Pause slightly.) Otherwise, write an E on the blank next to the left-hand number. (Pause 5 seconds.) Now on your answer sheet, darken the space for the number-letter combination that you hare just written. (Pause 5 seconds.)

Now look at line 8 on your worksheet. (Pause slightly.) Write a D as in dog in the circle with the lowest number. (Pause 2 seconds.) Now on your answer sheet, darken the space for the number-letter combination that is in the circle you just wrote in. (Pause 5 seconds.)

Look at the drawings in line 9 on your worksheet. The four boxes are planes for carrying mail. (Pause slightly.) The plane with the highest number is to be loaded first. Write an E in the box with the highest number. (Pause 2 seconds.) Now on your answer sheet, darken the space for the number-letter combination that is in the box you just wrote in. (Pause 5 seconds.)

Now check your answers by comparing them with the Correct Answers on page 8.

EXAMINATION SECTION
TEST 1

DIRECTIONS: Each question or incomplete statement is followed by several suggested answers or completions. Select the one that BEST answers the question or completes the statement. *PRINT THE LETTER OF THE CORRECT ANSWER IN THE SPACE AT THE RIGHT.*

1. Soft iron is MOST suitable for use in a

    A. permanent magnet
    B. natural magnet
    C. temporary magnet
    D. magneto

    1._____

2. Static electricity is MOST often produced by

    A. pressure B. magnetism C. heat D. friction

    2._____

3. A fundamental law of electricity is that the current in a circuit is

    A. inversely proportional to the voltage
    B. equal to the voltage
    C. directly proportional to the resistance
    D. directly proportional to the voltage

    3._____

4. A substance is classed as a magnet if it has

    A. the ability to conduct lines of force
    B. the property of high permeability
    C. the property of magnetism
    D. a high percentage of iron in its composition

    4._____

5. If a compass is placed at the center of a bar magnet, the compass needle

    A. *points* to the geographic south pole
    B. *points* to the geographic north pole
    C. *alines* itself parallel to the bar
    D. *alines* itself perpendicular to the bar

    5._____

6. When electricity is produced by heat in an iron-and-copper thermocouple, electrons move from

    A. north to south
    B. the hot junction, through the copper, across the cold junction to the iron, and then to the hot junction
    C. the hot junction, through the iron, across the cold junction to the copper, and then return through the copper to the hot junction
    D. east to west

    6._____

7. The four factors affecting the resistance of a wire are its

    A. length, material, diameter, and temperature
    B. size, length, material, and insulation
    C. length, size, relative resistance, and material
    D. size, insulation, relative resistance, and material

    7._____

8. Electricity in a battery is produced by

   A. chemical action
   B. chemical reaction
   C. a chemical acting upon metallic plates
   D. all of the above

9. Resistance is ALWAYS measured in

   A. coulombs   B. henrys   C. ohms   D. megohms

10. The magnetic pole that points northward on a compass

    A. is called the north pole
    B. is actually a south magnetic pole
    C. points to the north magnetic pole of the earth
    D. indicates the direction of the north geographic pole

11. Of the six methods of producing a voltage, which is the LEAST used?

    A. Chemical action   B. Heat
    C. Friction   D. Pressure

12. As the temperature of carbon is increased, its resistance will

    A. increase   B. decrease
    C. remain constant   D. double

13. Around a magnet, the external lines of force

    A. leave the magnet from the north pole and enter the south pole
    B. often cross one another
    C. leave the magnet from the south pole and enter the north pole
    D. may be broken by a piece of iron shielding

14. When a voltage is applied to a conductor, free electrons

    A. are forced into the nucleus of their atom
    B. are impelled along the conductor
    C. unite with protons
    D. cease their movement

15. When the molecules of a substance are altered, the action is referred to as

    A. thermal   B. photoelectric
    C. electrical   D. chemical

16. When matter is separated into individual atoms, it

    A. has undergone a physical change only
    B. has been reduced to its basic chemicals
    C. retains its original characteristics
    D. has been reduced to its basic elements

17. MOST permanent magnets and all electro-magnets are 17.____

    A. classed as natural magnets
    B. manufactured in various shapes from lodestone
    C. classed as artificial magnets
    D. manufactured in various shapes from magnetite

18. When a conductor moves across a magnetic field, 18.____

    A. a voltage is induced in the conductor
    B. a current is induced in the conductor
    C. both current and voltage are induced in the conductor
    D. neither a voltage nor a current is induced

19. The nucleus of an atom contains 19.____

    A. electrons and neutrons
    B. protons and neutrons
    C. protons and electrons
    D. protons, electrons, and neutrons

20. An alnico artificial magnet is composed of 20.____

    A. magnetite, steel, and nickel
    B. cobalt, nickel, and varnish
    C. aluminum, copper, and cobalt
    D. aluminum, nickel, and cobalt

21. A material that acts as an insulator for magnetic flux is 21.____

    A. glass   B. aluminum
    C. soft iron   D. unknown today

22. The force acting through the distance between two dissimilarly-charged bodies 22.____

    A. is a chemical force
    B. is referred to as a magnetic field
    C. constitutes a flow of ions
    D. is referred to as an electrostatic field

23. An atom that has lost or gained electrons 23.____

    A. is negatively charged   B. has a positive charge
    C. is said to be ionized   D. becomes electrically neutral

24. Which of the following is considered to be the BEST conductor? 24.____

    A. Zinc   B. Copper   C. Aluminum   D. Silver

25. As the temperature increases, the resistance of most conductors also increases. 25.____
    A conductor that is an EXCEPTION to this is

    A. aluminum   B. carbon   C. copper   D. brass

KEY (CORRECT ANSWERS)

1. C
2. D
3. D
4. C
5. C

6. B
7. A
8. D
9. C
10. A

11. C
12. B
13. A
14. B
15. D

16. D
17. C
18. A
19. B
20. D

21. D
22. D
23. C
24. D
25. B

TEST 2

DIRECTIONS: Each question or incomplete statement is followed by several suggested answers or completions. Select the one that BEST answers the question or completes the statement. *PRINT THE LETTER OF THE CORRECT ANSWER IN THE SPACE AT THE RIGHT.*

1. The dry cell battery is a _____ cell. 1._____

    A. secondary   B. polarized   C. primary   D. voltaic

2. The electrolyte of a lead-acid wet cell is 2._____

    A. sal ammoniac   B. manganese dioxide
    C. sulfuric acid   D. distilled water

3. A battery which can be restored after discharge is a _____ cell. 3._____

    A. primary   B. galvanic   C. dry   D. secondary

4. Lead-acid battery plates are held together by a 4._____

    A. glass wool mat   B. wood separator
    C. grid work   D. hard rubber tube

5. When mixing electrolyte, ALWAYS pour 5._____

    A. water into acid
    B. acid into water
    C. both acid and water into vat simultaneously
    D. first acid, then water into vat

6. When charging a battery, the electrolyte should NEVER exceed a temperature of 6._____

    A. 125° F.   B. 113° F.   C. 80° F.   D. 40° F.

7. The plates of a lead-acid battery are made of 7._____

    A. lead and lead dioxide   B. lead and lead oxide
    C. silver and peroxide   D. lead and lead peroxide

8. A battery is receiving a normal charge. It begins to gas freely. The charging current should 8._____

    A. be increased
    B. be decreased
    C. be cut off and the battery allowed to cool
    D. remain the same

9. A hydrometer reading is 1.265 at 92° F. The CORRECTED reading is 9._____

    A. 1.229   B. 1.261   C. 1.269   D. 1.301

10. In the nickel-cadmium battery, KOH is 10._____

    A. the positive plate   B. the negative plate
    C. the electrolyte   D. none of the above

21

11. When sulfuric acid, H_2SO_4, and water, H_2O, are mixed together, they form a

   A. gas
   B. compound
   C. mixture
   D. hydrogen solution

12. How many No. 6 dry cells are required to supply power to a load requiring 6 volts if the cells are connected in series?

   A. Two   B. Four   C. Five   D. Six

13. The ordinary 6-volt lead-acid storage battery consists of how many cells?

   A. Two   B. Three   C. Four   D. Six

14. A fully-charged aircraft battery has a specific gravity reading of

   A. 1.210 to 1.220
   B. 1.250 to 1.265
   C. 1.285 to 1.300
   D. 1.300 to 1.320

15. What is the ampere-hour rating of a storage battery that can deliver 20 amperes continuously for 10 hours?
    _____ ampere-hour.

   A. 20   B. 40   C. 200   D. 400

16. The normal cell voltage of a fully-charged nickel-cadmium battery is _____ volts.

   A. 2.0   B. 1.5   C. 1.4   D. 1.0

17. The electrolyte in a mercury cell is

   A. sulfuric acid
   B. KOH
   C. potassium hydroxide, zincate, and mercury
   D. potassium hydroxide, water, and zincate

18. Concentrated sulfuric acid has a specific gravity of

   A. 1.285   B. 1.300   C. 1.830   D. 2.400

19. The number of negative plates in a lead-acid cell is ALWAYS _____ of positive plates.

   A. one greater than the number
   B. equal to the number
   C. one less than the number
   D. double the number

20. A lead-acid battery is considered fully charged when the specific gravity readings of all cells taken at half-hour intervals show no change for _____ hour(s).

   A. four   B. three   C. two   D. one

KEY (CORRECT ANSWERS)

1. C
2. C
3. D
4. C
5. B

6. A
7. D
8. B
9. C
10. C

11. C
12. B
13. B
14. C
15. C

16. C
17. D
18. C
19. A
20. A

TEST 3

DIRECTIONS: Each question or incomplete statement is followed by several suggested answers or completions. Select the one that BEST answers the question or completes the statement. *PRINT THE LETTER OF THE CORRECT ANSWER IN THE SPACE AT THE RIGHT.*

1. In which direction does current flow in an electrical circuit?

    A. - to + externally, + to - internally
    B. + to - externally, + to - internally
    C. - to + externally, - to + internally
    D. + to - externally, - to + internally

2. Given the formula $P = E^2/R$, solve for E.

    A. $E = \sqrt{ER}$ B. $E = \sqrt{PR}$ C. $E = IR$ D. $E = \sqrt{P/R}$

3. Resistance in the power formula equals

    A. $R = \sqrt{I/P}$ B. $R = E/I$ C. $R = \sqrt{P \times I}$ D. $R = E^2/P$

4. One joule is equal to

    A. 1 watt second
    B. 10 watt seconds
    C. 1 watt minute
    D. 10 watt minutes

5. A lamp has a source voltage of 110 v. and a current of 0.9 amps. What is the resistance of the lamp?

    A. 12.22 Ω   B. 122.2 Ω   C. 0.008 Ω   D. 0.08 Ω

6. In accordance with Ohm's law, the relationship between current and voltage in a simple circuit is that the

    A. current varies inversely with the resistance if the voltage is held constant
    B. voltage varies as the square of the applied e.m.f.
    C. current varies directly with the applied voltage if the resistance is held constant
    D. voltage varies inversely as the current if the resistance is held constant

7. The current needed to operate a soldering iron which has a rating of 600 watts at 110 volts is

    A. 0.182 a.   B. 5.455 a.   C. 18.200 a.   D. 66.000 a.

8. In electrical circuits, the time rate of doing work is expressed in

    A. volts   B. amperes   C. watts   D. ohms

9. If the resistance is held constant, what is the relationship between power and voltage in a simple circuit?

    A. Resistance must be varied to show a true relationship.
    B. Power will vary as the square of the applied voltage.
    C. Voltage will vary inversely proportional to power.
    D. Power will vary directly with voltage.

10. How many watts are there in 1 horsepower?

    A. 500   B. 640   C. 746   D. 1,000

11. What formula is used to find watt-hours?

    A. E x T   B. E x I x T   C. E x I x $\sqrt{\theta}$ D. E x I²

12. What is the resistance of the circuit shown at the right?

    A. 4.8 Ω
    B. 12.0 Ω
    C. 48 Ω
    D. 120 Ω

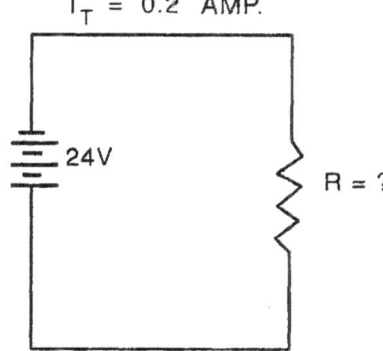

13. In the figure at the right, solve for I_T.

    A. 0.5 a.
    B. 1 a.
    C. 13 a.
    D. 169 a.

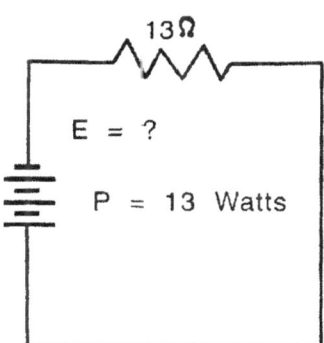

14. A simple circuit consists of one power source,

    A. and one power consuming device
    B. one power consuming device, and connecting wiring
    C. protective device, and control device
    D. one power consuming device, and protective device

15. The device used in circuits to prevent damage from overloads is called a

    A. fuse   B. switch   C. resistor   D. connector

16. What happens in a series circuit when the voltage remains constant and the resistance increases?
    Current

    A. increases   B. decreases
    C. remains the same   D. increases by the square

17. Other factors remaining constant, what would be the effect on the current flow in a given circuit if the applied potential were doubled?
It would

    A. double
    B. remain the same
    C. be divided by two
    D. be divided by four

18. Which of the following procedures can be used to calculate the resistance of a load?

    A. *Multiply* the voltage across the load by the square of the current through the load
    B. *Divide* the current through the load by the voltage across the load
    C. *Multiply* the voltage across the load by the current through the load
    D. *Divide* the voltage across the load by the current through the load

19. A cockpit light operates from a 24-volt d-c supply and uses 72 watts of power. The current flowing through the bulb is _____ amps.

    A. 0.33   B. 3   C. 600   D. 1,728

20. If the resistance is held constant, what happens to power if the current is doubled?
Power is

    A. doubled
    B. multiplied by 4
    C. halved
    D. divided by 4

KEY (CORRECT ANSWERS)

1.	A	11.	B
2.	B	12.	D
3.	D	13.	B
4.	A	14.	B
5.	B	15.	A
6.	C	16.	B
7.	B	17.	A
8.	C	18.	D
9.	B	19.	B
10.	C	20.	B

TEST 4

DIRECTIONS: Each question or incomplete statement is followed by several suggested answers or completions. Select the one that BEST answers the question or completes the statement. *PRINT THE LETTER OF THE CORRECT ANSWER IN THE SPACE AT THE RIGHT.*

1. If a circuit is constructed so as to allow the electrons to follow only one possible path, the circuit is called a(n) _____ circuit.   1.____

   A. series-parallel
   B. incomplete
   C. series
   D. parallel

2. According to Kirchhoff's Law of Voltages, the algebraic sum of all the voltages in a series circuit is equal to   2.____

   A. zero
   B. source voltage
   C. total voltage drop
   D. the sum of the IR drop of the circuit

3. In a series circuit, the total current is   3.____

   A. always equal to the source voltage
   B. determined by the load only
   C. the same through all parts of the circuit
   D. equal to zero at the positive side of the source

4.   4.____

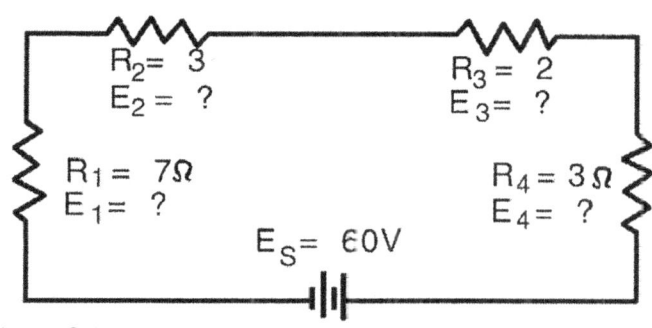

   The CORRECT voltage equation for the circuit above is

   A. $E_S + E_1 + E_2 + E_3 + E_4 = 0$
   B. $E_S - E_1 - E_2 - E_3 - E_4 = 0$
   C. $E_S = -E_1 - E_2 - E_3 - E_4$
   D. $-E_S = E_1 + E_2 + E_3 + E_4$

5. Referring to the circuit shown in Question 4 above, after expressing the voltage drops around the circuit in terms of current and resistance and the given values of source voltage, the equation becomes   5.____

   A. $-60 - 7I - 3I - 2I - 3I = 0$
   B. $-60 + 7I + 3I + 2I + 3I = 0$
   C. $60 - 7I - 3I - 2I - 3I = 0$
   D. $60 + 7I + 3I + 2I + 3I = 0$

6. By the use of the correct equation, it is found that the current (I) in the circuit shown in Question 4 is of positive value. This indicates that the

   A. assumed direction of current flow is correct
   B. assumed direction of current flow is incorrect
   C. problem is not solvable
   D. battery polarity should be reversed

7.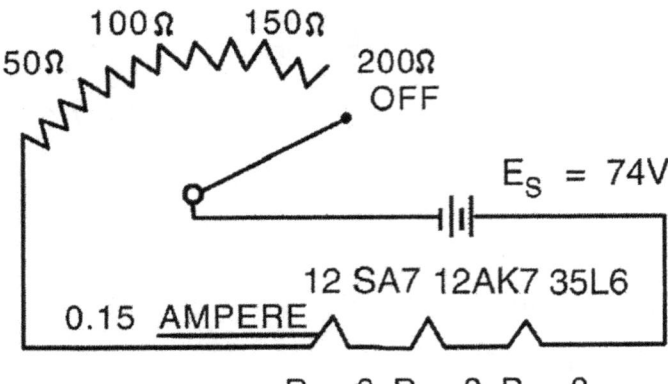

   $R_1 = ?$ $R_2 = ?$ $R_3 = ?$

   In what position would the variable rheostat in the circuit above be placed in order that the filaments of the tubes operate properly with a current flow of 0.15 ampere? _____ position.

   A. 50 Ω   B. 100 Ω   C. 150 Ω   D. 200 Ω

8. The power absorbed by the variable rheostat in the circuit used in Question 7 above, when placed in its proper operating position, would be _____ watts.

   A. 112.50   B. 2.25   C. 337.50   D. 450.00

9.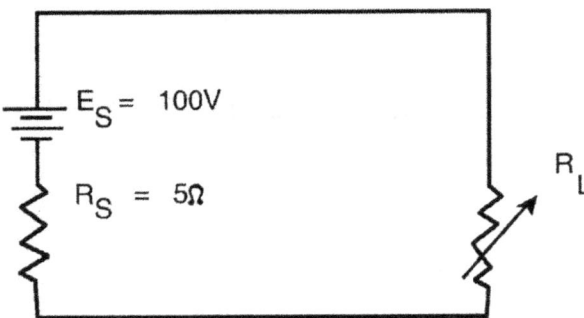

   In the circuit above, maximum power would be transferred from the source to the load (R_L) if R_L were set at _____ ohms.

   A. 2   B. 5   C. 12   D. 24

10.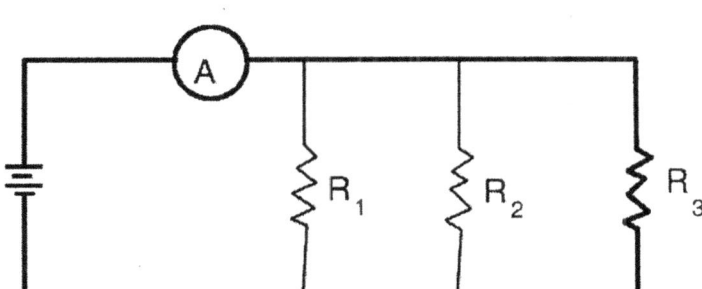

In the circuit above, if an additional resistor were placed in parallel to R_3, the ammeter reading would

A. increase
B. decrease
C. remain the same
D. drop to zero

11. In a parallel circuit containing a 4-ohm, 5-ohm, and 6-ohm resistor, the current flows

A. *highest* through the 4-ohm resistor
B. *lowest* through the 4-ohm resistor
C. *highest* through the 6-ohm resistor
D. *equal* through all three resistors

12. Three resistors of 2, 4, and 6 ohms respectively, are connected in parallel. Which resistor would absorb the GREATEST power?

A. The 2-ohm resistor
B. The 4-ohm resistor
C. The 6-ohm resistor
D. It will be the same for all resistors

13. If three lamps are connected in parallel with a power source, connecting a fourth lamp in parallel will

A. *decrease* E_T
B. *decrease* I_T
C. *increase* E_T
D. *increase* I_T

14.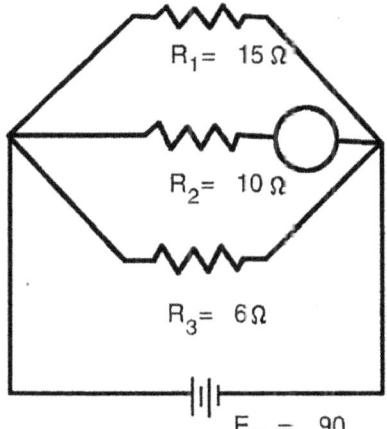

What is the current flow through the ammeter in the circuit shown above?
_____ amps.

A. 4
B. 9
C. 15
D. 28

15.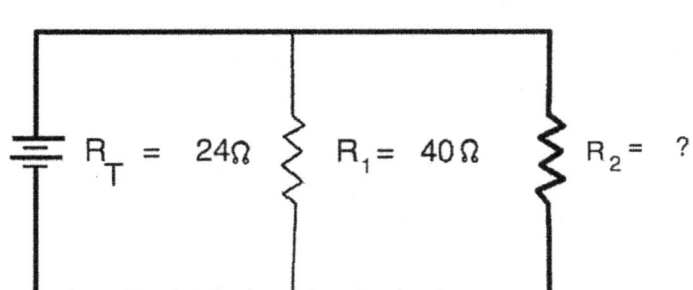

In the circuit shown above, the TOTAL resistance is 24 ohms. What is the value of R_2?
_____ ohms.

A. 16   B. 40   C. 60   D. 64

16.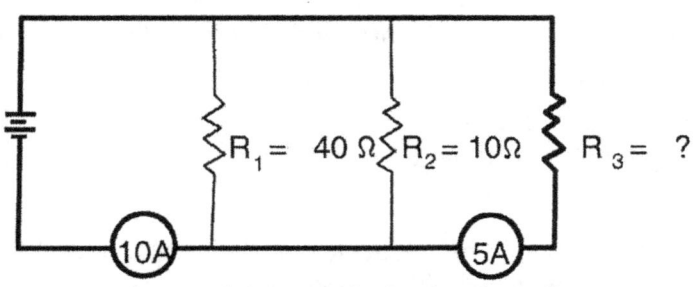

What is the source voltage of the circuit shown above?
_____ volts.

A. 40   B. 50   C. 100   D. 500

17. What is the value of R_3 in the circuit shown in Question 16 above?
_____ ohms.

A. 8   B. 10   C. 20   D. 100

18.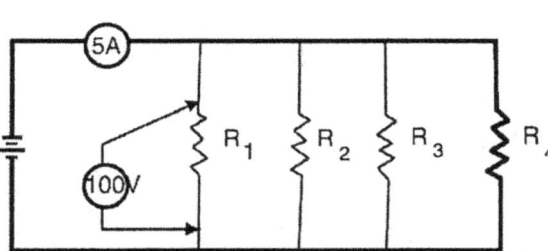

If all 4 resistors in the circuit above are of equal ohmic resistances, what is the value of R_3?
_____ ohms.

A. 5   B. 20   C. 60   D. 80

19.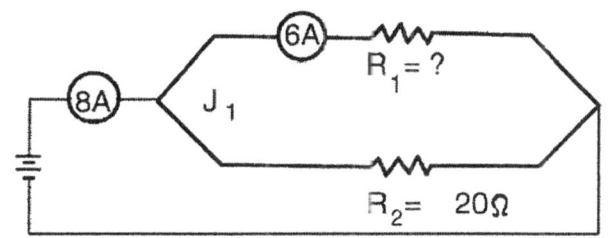

What is the value of the source voltage in the circuit above?
_____ volts

A. 20 B. 40 C. 120 D. 160

20.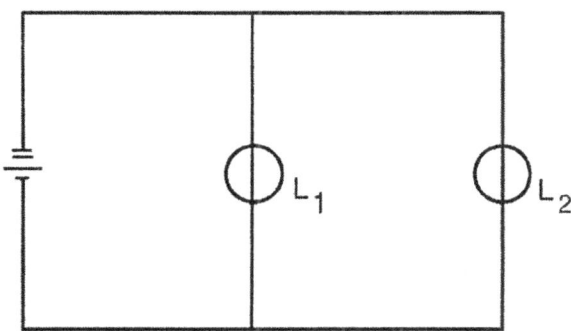

If Lamp L_2 in the circuit above should suddenly burn out, which of the statements below is CORRECT?

A. More current would flow through lamp L_1.
B. Source voltage would decrease.
C. The filament resistance of lamp L_1 would decrease.
D. Lamp L_1 would still burn normal.

21. When referring to a circuit's conductance, you visualize the degree to which the circuit

A. *permits* or conducts voltage
B. *opposes* the rate of voltage changes
C. *permits* or conducts current flow
D. *opposes* the rate of current flow

22.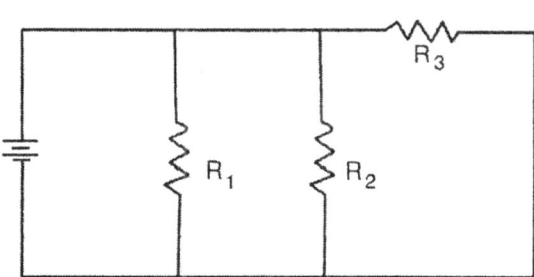

The TOTAL conductance of the circuit above would be solved by which of the equations?

A. $G_T - G_1 - G_2 - G_3 = 0$
B. $G_T + G_1 + G_2 + G_3 = 0$
C. $G_T = G_1 - G_2 - G_3$
D. $G_T = G_1 + G_2 + G_3$

23.

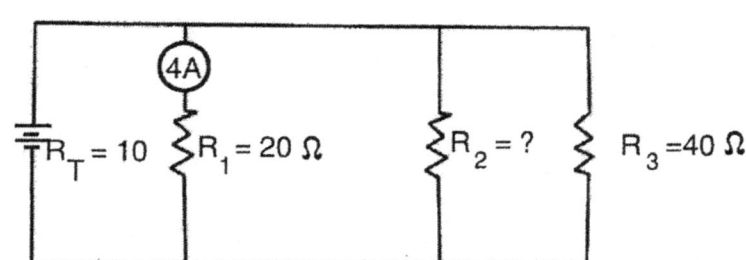

If the resistors in the circuit above are all rated at 250 watts, which resistor or resistors would overheat?

A. R_1 B. R_2 C. R_3 D. All

24.

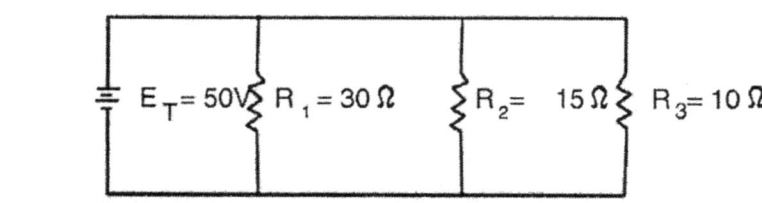

The TOTAL conductance of the circuit above is

A. 0.15G   B. 0.20G   C. 0.50G   D. 0.75G

KEY (CORRECT ANSWERS)

1. C
2. A
3. C
4. B
5. C

6. A
7. B
8. B
9. B
10. A

11. A
12. A
13. D
14. B
15. C

16. A
17. A
18. D
19. B
20. D

21. C
22. D
23. A
24. B

TEST 5

DIRECTIONS: Each question or incomplete statement is followed by several suggested answers or completions. Select the one that BEST answers the question or completes the statement. *PRINT THE LETTER OF THE CORRECT ANSWER IN THE SPACE AT THE RIGHT.*

1. The MINIMUM number of resistors in a compound circuit is (are)

   A. four   B. three   C. two   D. one

   1._____

2.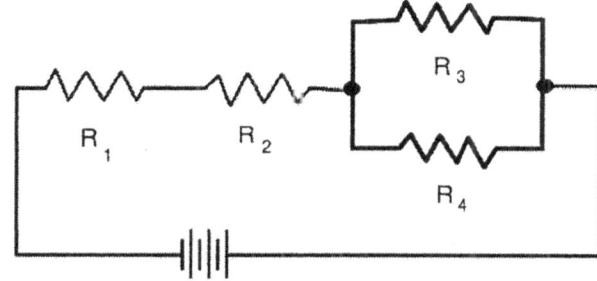

   Total resistance of the circuit shown is determined by the formula

   A. $R_1R_2 + \dfrac{R_3R_4}{R_4+R_3}$

   B. $R_1+R_2 + \dfrac{R_3+R_4}{R_3R_4}$

   C. $R_1+R_2 + \dfrac{R_3R_4}{R_3+R_4}$

   D. $R_1+R_2 + (\dfrac{R_3R_4}{R_3+R_4})$

   2._____

3.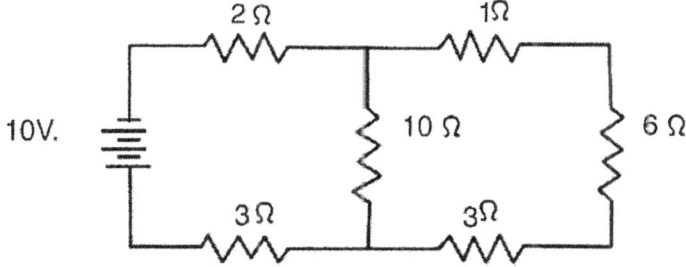

   In the circuit above, what is the value of I_t?

   $I_t =$ _____ amp.

   A. 1.14   B. 0.4   C. 0.667   D. 1

   3._____

4. In the circuit in Question 3 above, how much power is consumed by the 6-ohm resistor? _____ watts.

   A. 15   B. 1.5   C. 60   D. 6

   4._____

5. A voltage divider is used to

   A. provide different voltage values for multiple loads from a single source
   B. provide several voltage drops in parallel
   C. increase the voltage to the load at several taps
   D. provide tap points to alter power supplied

   5._____

6. The total power supplied to the entire circuit by a voltage divider and 4 loads is the

   A. sum of the 4 loads
   B. voltage divider minus 4 loads
   C. voltage divider plus the 4 loads
   D. voltage divider only

7. The total voltage of a voltage divider is the

   A. input voltage minus the load's voltages
   B. the load's voltages only
   C. sum of the input and load voltage
   D. sum of the voltages across the divider

8. An attenuator is

   A. a network of resistors used to reduce power, voltage, or current
   B. a network of resistors to change the input voltage
   C. also called a pad
   D. used in every power circuit

9. In an attenuator, the resistors are

   A. adjusted separately
   B. connected in parallel with the load
   C. connected in series with the load
   D. ganged

10. What two conditions may be observed in a bridge circuit?

    A. T and L network characteristics
    B. No-load and full-load bridge current
    C. Unequal potential and unequal current
    D. Balance and unbalance

11.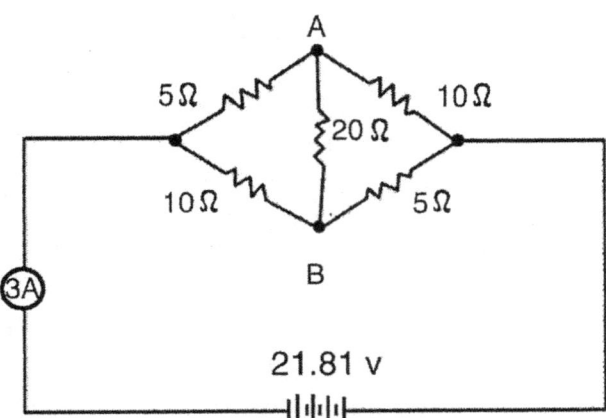

In the circuit above, how much current flows in the resistor and what is its direction?

   A. 26 a.; B to A
   B. Ia.; A to B
   C. 0.273 a.; A to B
   D. Ia.; B to A

12. In a three-wire distribution system, an unbalanced situation is indicated by the

   A. potential of the positive wire being equal to the negative wire
   B. positive wire carrying more amperage than the negative wire
   C. current in the neutral wire
   D. neutral wire carrying the total current

13.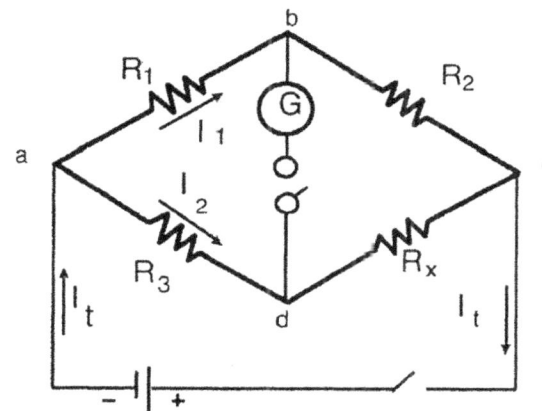

SCHEMATIC WHEATSTONE-BRIDGE CIRCUIT

In the figure above, the galvanometer will show zero deflection when

A. $\dfrac{R_1}{R_2} + \dfrac{R_3}{R_x}$

B. $R_x = \dfrac{R_1 R_3}{R_2}$

C. $\dfrac{I_1 R_1}{I_2 R_x} = \dfrac{I_2 R_3}{I_1 R_2}$

D. $R_x = \dfrac{R_1 R_2}{R_3}$

14. In the Wheatstone Bridge type circuit shown at the right, the bridge current is toward Point A.
The resistance of R_x is

   A. 30Ω
   B. greater than 45Ω
   C. 20Ω
   D. less than 15Ω

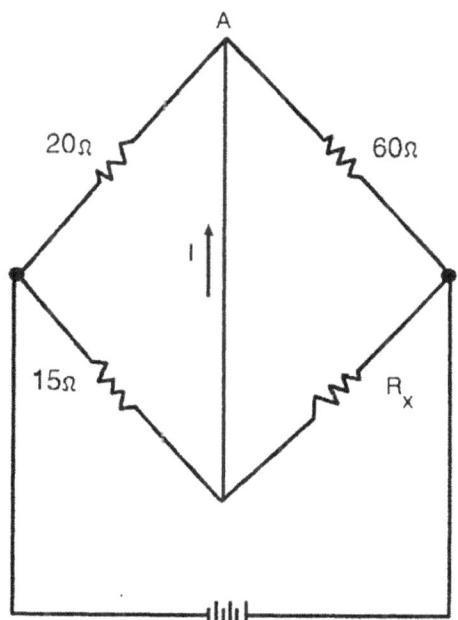

15.

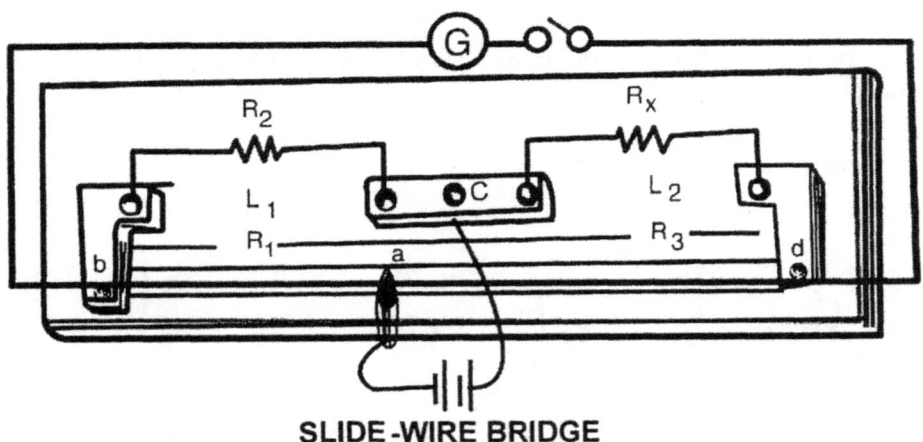

SLIDE-WIRE BRIDGE

In the slide-wire bridge shown above, L_1 is equal to

A. $L_1 = \dfrac{R_2 L_2}{R_1}$

B. $L_1 = \dfrac{R_1 + L_2}{R_2}$

C. $\dfrac{R_2}{R_1 L_2} = L_1$

D. $\dfrac{R_2 L_2}{R_x} = L_1$

16.

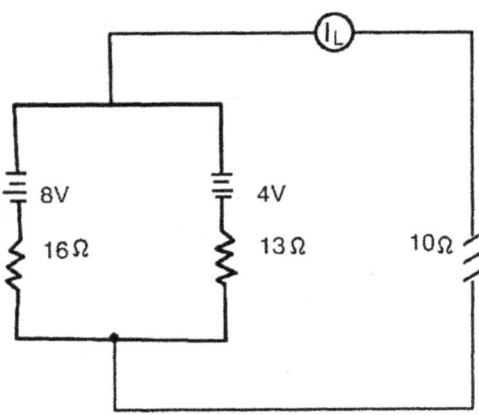

In the circuit above, I line is

A. 4.44 a.   B. 0.444 a.   C. 0.337 a.   D. 5.22 a.

17. When checking a 3-wire distribution circuit going against the direction of current flow, the IR drop is ALWAYS

A. negative
B. positive
C. not used
D. always in direction of current flow

18.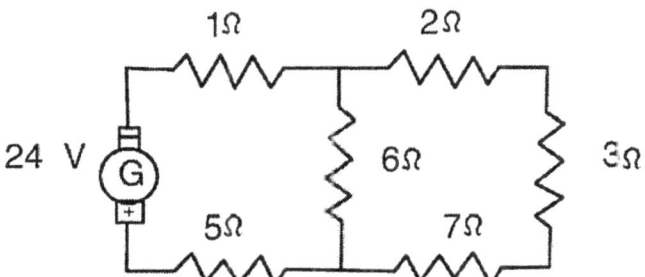

In the circuit above, the voltage drop across the 3-ohm resistor is _____ volts.

A. 2.4   B. 24   C. 9.6   D. 0.96

19. The resistance of the wire is taken into consideration in the 2- and 3-wire distribution systems because the

A. source and load are very close
B. resistance of the wire is the same throughout
C. load and source are at a considerable distance from each other
D. load must be decreased in order to determine accurate circuit values

20. What is Kirchhoff's second law as applied to 3-wire distribution circuits?

A. Sum of all the voltages is zero.
B. Algebraic sum of all the voltages about closed path is zero.
C. Algebraic sum of all voltage is zero.
D. All IR drops in the circuit are negative.

KEY (CORRECT ANSWERS)

1.	B	11.	C
2.	C	12.	C
3.	D	13.	A
4.	B	14.	B
5.	A	15.	D
6.	C	16.	C
7.	D	17.	B
8.	A	18.	A
9.	D	19.	C
10.	D	20.	B

TEST 6

DIRECTIONS: Each question or incomplete statement is followed by several suggested answers or completions. Select the one that BEST answers the question or completes the statement. *PRINT THE LETTER OF THE CORRECT ANSWER IN THE SPACE AT THE RIGHT.*

1. A mil is what part of an inch?

    A. 1/10
    B. 1/100
    C. 1/1000
    D. 1/1,000,000

2. The discharge (electrical leakage) that MIGHT occur from a wire carrying a high potential is called

    A. arcing
    B. sparking
    C. static discharge
    D. corona

3. Bare wire ends are spliced by the

    A. western union method
    B. rat-tail joint method
    C. fixture joint method
    D. all of the above

4. What is a unit conductor called that has a length of one foot and a cross-sectional area of one circular mil?

    A. Square mil
    B. Circular mil
    C. Circular mil foot
    D. Square mil foot

5. The induction-type soldering iron is commonly known as the

    A. soldering copper
    B. pencil iron
    C. soldering gun
    D. resistance gun

6. All good quality soldering irons operate at what temperature?

    A. 400 - 500° F.
    B. 500 - 600° F.
    C. 600 - 700° F.
    D. 300 - 600° F.

7. A No. 12 wire has a diameter of 80.81 mils.
   What is the area in circular mils?
   _____ cm.

    A. 6,530
    B. 5,630
    C. 4,530
    D. 3,560

8. Dielectric strength is the

    A. opposite of potential difference
    B. ability of a conductor to carry large amounts of current
    C. ability of an insulator to withstand a potential difference
    D. strength of a magnetic field

9. To readily transfer the heat from the soldering iron tip, it FIRST should be

    A. tinned with solder
    B. allowed to form an oxide film
    C. cleaned with carbon tetrachloride
    D. allowed to heat for 25 minutes

10. A No. 12 wire has a diameter of 80.81 mils.
    What is the area in square mils?
    _____ square mils.

    A. 2,516.8   B. 5,128.6   C. 6,530   D. 8,512.6

11. Varnished cambric insulation is used to cover conductors carrying voltages above _____ volts.

    A. 1,000   B. 1,500   C. 15,000   D. 5,000

12. The solder splicer is used to

    A. prevent the waste of rosin core solder
    B. connect together small lengths of solder
    C. connect two conductors together
    D. none of the above

13. The conductance of a conductor is the ease with which current will flow through it. It is measured in

    A. ohms   B. mhos   C. henrys   D. amperes

14. Asbestos insulation loses its insulating properties when it becomes

    A. overaged
    B. overheated
    C. used over a long period of time
    D. wet

15. How are solderless connectors installed on conductors?

    A. Bolted on   B. Chemical compound
    C. Crimped on   D. All of the above

16. The factor(s) governing the selection of wire size is (are)

    A. (I^2R loss) in the line
    B. (IR drop) in the line
    C. current-carrying ability of the line
    D. all of the above

17. Enamel insulated conductors are USUALLY called

    A. magnet wire   B. high voltage wire
    C. low voltage wire   D. transmission lines

18. The advantage of solderless connectors over soldered-type connectors is that they are

    A. mechanically stronger B. easier to install
    C. free of corrosion   D. all of the above

19. The basic requirement of any splice is that it be

   A. soldered
   B. mechanically and electrically as strong as the conductor that is spliced
   C. made with a splicer
   D. taped

20. The type of tape that is used for electrical circuits having a temperature of 175° F. or above is

   A. glass cloth
   B. plastic
   C. synthetic rubber compound
   D. impregnated cloth

KEY (CORRECT ANSWERS)

1.	C	11.	C
2.	D	12.	C
3.	D	13.	B
4.	C	14.	D
5.	A	15.	C
6.	B	16.	D
7.	A	17.	A
8.	C	18.	B
9.	A	19.	B
10.	B	20.	A

EXAMINATION SECTION
TEST 1

DIRECTIONS: Each question or incomplete statement is followed by several suggested answers or completions. Select the one that BEST answers the question or completes the statement. *PRINT THE LETTER OF THE CORRECT ANSWER IN THE SPACE AT THE RIGHT.*

1. The one of the following items which is used to test the electrolyte of a battery is a(n) 1._____

    A. manometer   B. hydrometer   C. electrometer   D. hygrometer

2. The one of the following instruments which CANNOT be used to measure the current in both a.c. circuits and d.c. circuits *without* additional equipment is a(n) 2._____

    A. D'Arsonval galvanometer
    B. hot wire ammeter
    C. iron vane ammeter
    D. electro-dynamometer type ammeter

3. A growler is *commonly* used to test 3._____

    A. relays   B. armatures   C. cable joints   D. rectifiers

4. In cutting a large stranded copper cable with a hacksaw, the PRIMARY reason for using a blade with fine teeth rather than one with coarse teeth is 4._____

    A. that using a coarse blade overheats the copper
    B. to avoid making too wide a cut
    C. that the coarse blade bends too easily
    D. to avoid snagging or pulling the strands

5. Toggle bolts are MOST commonly used to fasten an outlet box to a 5._____

    A. solid brick wall   B. solid concrete wall
    C. plaster or tile wall   D. wooden partition wall

6. Laminated sheet steel is *usually* used to make up transformer cores in order to minimize 6._____

    A. copper loss   B. weight
    C. hysterisis loss   D. eddy current loss

Questions 7-9.

DIRECTIONS: Questions 7 to 9, inclusive, refer to the diagram below.

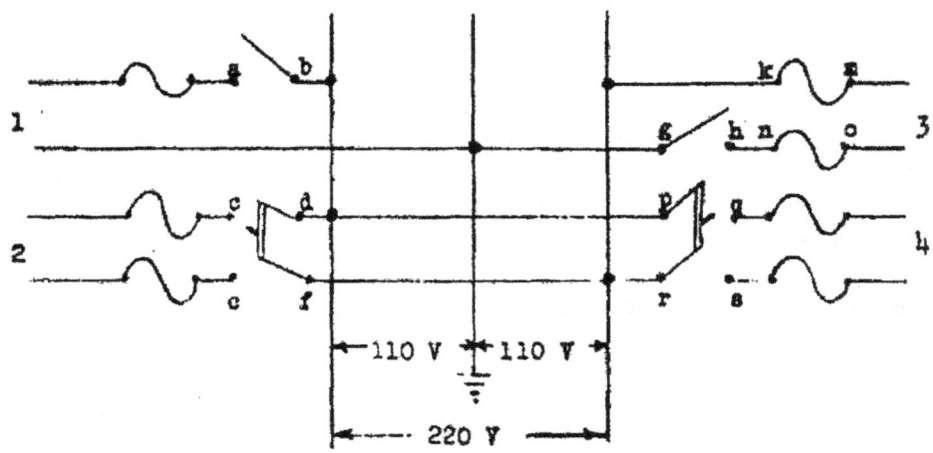

7. Circuit No. 3 in the above diagram

   A. supplies 220 volts to the load
   B. would be correctly wired if there were a direct connection instead of a fuse between points k and m
   C. would be correctly wired if there were a direct connection instead of a fuse between points n and o
   D. would be correctly wired if the switch and fuse were eliminated and replaced by a direct connection between g and o

8. Circuit No. 4 in the above diagram

   A. is not properly fused as it should have only one fuse in the hot leg
   B. supplies 220 volts to the load
   C. is grounded if, with the switch open, test lamps light when placed between points p and r
   D. is shorted if, with the switch open, test lamps light when placed between points p and r

9. Circuit No. 1 in the above diagram

   A. supplies 220 volts to the load
   B. is grounded if a pair of test lamps light when placed between point b and ground
   C. is not properly fused as it should have a fuse in each leg
   D. is shorted if, with the switch open, a pair of test lamps light when placed between points a and b

10. An ideal transformer which has 1 ampere in the primary and 10 amperes in the secondary MUST have

    A. 10 volt amperes in the primary
    B. a ratio of primary turns to secondary turns of 1 to 10
    C. 10 volt amperes in the secondary
    D. a ratio of primary turns to secondary turns of 10 to 1

11. In soldering electric wires, rosin is used in preference to acid as a flux PRIMARILY because rosin is

    A. a dry powder
    B. non-conducting
    C. non-corrosive
    D. a strong electrolyte

12. The one of the following items which should be used to test whether a circuit is a.c. or d.c. is a

    A. pair of test lamps
    B. hot wire ammeter
    C. psychrometer
    D. neon light

13. An ideal transformer has 200 volts impressed across its primary. If the primary current is 10 amperes,

    A. the ratio of primary turns to secondary turns is 20 to 1
    B. the ratio of primary turns to secondary turns is 1 to 20
    C. there are approximately 2 KVA in the secondary
    D. the secondary voltage is 20 volts

14. To control a lamp independently from five locations, the one of the following groups of switches which is required is:

    A. Four 3-way switches and one 4-way switch
    B. Three 3-way and two 4-way switches
    C. Two 3-way and three 4-way switches
    D. Two single-pole, single throw switches and three 4-way switches

Questions 15-20.

DIRECTIONS: Questions 15 to 20, inclusive, refer to the terms listed below which are defined in the electrical code.

1. Appliance
2. Branch Circuit
3. Connected load
4. Concealed
5. Computed load
6. Device
7. Demand factor
8. Intermittent duty
9. Periodic duty
10. Short time duty
11. Varying duty
12. Enclosed
13. Equipment
14. Feeder
15. Isolated
16. Mains
17. Service
18. Service cable
19. Service conductor
20. Service drop
21. Service Entrance conductors
22. Sub-feeder
23. Scalable
24. Rating

15. The one term in the above which is defined as a unit of an electrical system, other than a conductor, which is intended to carry but not consume electrical energy, is numbered

    A. 1   B. 6   C. 13   D. 19

16. The one term in the above which is defined as that portion of the wiring system extending beyond the final overcurrent device protecting the circuit, is numbered

    A. 2   B. 14   C. 16   D. 22

17. The one term in the above which is defined as that portion of the overhead service conductors between the last pole and the first point of attachment to the building, is numbered

    A. 17   B. 18   C. 20   D. 21

18. The one term in the above which is defined as rendered inaccessible by the structure or finish of the building, is numbered

    A. 4   B. 12   C. 15   D. 23

19. The one term in the above which is defined as a requirement of service that demands operation at loads, and for intervals of time, both of which may be subject to wide variation, is numbered

    A. 8   B. 9   C. 10   D. 11

20. The one term in the above which is defined as the sum of the continuous ratings of the load consuming apparatus connected to the system or part of the system under consideration, is numbered

    A. 3   B. 5   C. 7   D. 24

21. In electrical tests, a megger is calibrated to read

    A. amperes   B. ohms   C. volts   D. watts

22. Metal cabinets for lighting circuits are grounded in order to

    A. save insulating material
    B. provide a return for the netural current
    C. eliminate short circuits
    D. minimize the possibility of shock

23. In an a.c. circuit containing only resistance, the power factor will be

    A. zero   B. 50% lagging   C. 50% leading   D. 100%

24. The size of fuse for a two-wire lighting circuit using No. 14 wire should NOT exceed

    A. 15 amperes   B. 20 amperes
    C. 25 amperes   D. 30 amperes

25. When working near acid storage batteries, extreme care should be taken to guard against sparks MAINLY because a spark may

    A. cause an explosion
    B. set fire to the electrolyte
    C. short-circuit a ceil
    D. ignite the battery case

KEY (CORRECT ANSWERS)

1. B
2. A
3. B
4. D
5. C

6. D
7. D
8. B
9. D
10. D

11. C
12. D
13. C
14. C
15. B

16. A
17. C
18. A
19. D
20. A

21. B
22. D
23. D
24. A
25. A

TEST 2

DIRECTIONS: Each question or incomplete statement is followed by several suggested answers or completions. Select the one that BEST answers the question or completes the statement. *PRINT THE LETTER OF THE CORRECT ANSWER IN THE SPACE AT THE RIGHT.*

1. If a blown fuse in an existing lighting circuit is replaced by another of the same rating which also blows, the PROPER maintenance procedure is to

    A. use a higher rating fuse
    B. cut out some of the outlets in the circuit
    C. check the circuit for grounds or shorts
    D. install a renewable fuse

2. The number of fuses required in a three-phase, four-wire branch circuit with grounded neutral is

    A. one   B. two   C. three   D. four

3. The electrodes of the common dry cell are carbon *and*

    A. zinc   B. lead   C. steel   D. tin

4. An electrician's hickey is used to

    A. strip insulation off wire
    B. pull cable through conduits
    C. thread metallic conduit
    D. bend metallic conduit

5. A group of wire sizes that is CORRECTLY arranged in the order of increasing current-carrying capacity is:

    A. 6; 12; 3/0   B. 12; 6; 3/0   C. 3/0; 12; 6   D. 3/0; 6; 12

6. The metal which is the BEST conductor of electricity is

    A. silver   B. copper   C. aluminum   D. nickel

7. If the two supply wires to a d.c. series motor are reversed, the motor will

    A. run in the opposite direction
    B. not run
    C. run in the same direction
    D. become a generator

8. Before doing work on a motor, to prevent accidental starting, you should

    A. short-circuit the motor leads
    B. remove the fuses
    C. block the rotor
    D. ground the frame

9. The material *commonly* used for brushes on d.c. motors is

    A. copper   B. carbon   C. brass   D. aluminum

10. The conductors of a two-wire No. 12 armored cable used in an ordinary lighting circuit are _____ insulated.

    A. stranded and rubber
    B. solid and rubber
    C. stranded and cotton
    D. solid and cotton

46

11. The rating, 125V.-10A.; 250V.-5A., commonly applies to a   11._____

    A. snap switch   B. lamp   C. conductor   D. fuse

12. Commutators are found on   12._____

    A. alternators   B. d.c. motors
    C. transformers   D. circuit breakers

13. A proper *use* for an electrician's knife is to   13._____

    A. cut wires
    B. pry out a small cartridge fuse
    C. mark the place where a conduit is to be cut
    D. skin wires

14. A d.c. device taking one milliampere at one kilovolt takes a *total* power of one   14._____

    A. milliwatt   B. watt   C. kilowatt   D. megawatt

15. In connection with electrical work, it is GOOD practice to   15._____

    A. scrape the silvery coating from a wire before soldering
    B. nick a wire in several places before bending it around a terminal
    C. assume that a circuit is alive
    D. open a switch to check the load

16. Mica is *commonly* used as an insulation   16._____

    A. for cartridge fuse cases
    B. between commutator bars
    C. between lead acid battery plates
    D. between transformer steel laminations

17. The function of a step-down transformer is to *decrease* the   17._____

    A. voltage   B. current   C. power   D. frequency

18. A conduit run is MOST often terminated in a(n)   18._____

    A. coupling   B. elbow   C. bushing   D. outlet box

19. In long conduit runs, pull boxes are *sometimes* installed at intermediate points to   19._____

    A. avoid using couplings
    B. support the conduit
    C. make use of short lengths of conduit
    D. facilitate pulling wire

20. A rheostat would LEAST likely be used in connection with the operation of   20._____

    A. transformers   B. motors
    C. generators   D. battery charging M.G. sets

21. The fiber bushing inserted at the end of a piece of flexible metallic conduit prevents

    A. moisture from entering the cable
    B. the rough edges from cutting the insulation
    C. the wires from touching each other
    D. the wires from slipping back into the armor

21._____

22. Portable lamp cord is MOST likely to have

    A. paper insulation
    B. solid wire
    C. armored wire
    D. stranded wire

22._____

23. Thermal relays are used in motor circuits to protect a-gainst

    A. reverse current
    B. overspeed
    C. overvoltage
    D. overload

23._____

24. It is GOOD practice to connect the ground wire for a building electrical system to a

    A. vent pipe
    B. steam pipe
    C. cold water pipe
    D. gas pipe

24._____

25. The MOST practical way to determine in the field the *approximate* length of insulated wire in a large coil is to

    A. unreel the wire and measure it with a 6-foot rule
    B. find another coil with the length marked on it and compare
    C. count the turns and multiply by the average circumference
    D. weigh the coil and compare it with a 1000-ft. coil

25._____

KEY (CORRECT ANSWERS)

1. C
2. C
3. A
4. D
5. B

6. A
7. C
8. B
9. B
10. B

11. A
12. B
13. D
14. B
15. C

16. B
17. A
18. C
19. C
20. A

21. B
22. D
23. D
24. C
25. C

TEST 3

DIRECTIONS: Each question or incomplete statement is followed by several suggested answers or completions. Select the one that BEST answers the question or completes the statement. *PRINT THE LETTER OF THE CORRECT ANSWER IN THE SPACE AT THE RIGHT.*

1. The property of an electric circuit tending to prevent the flow of current and, at the same time, causing electric energy to be converted into heat energy, is called   1.____

    A. conductance
    B. inductance
    C. resistance
    D. reluctance

2. If a certain length of copper wire is elongated by stretching and its volume does not change, it then can be said that, for a fixed volume, the resistance of this conductor varies *directly* as   2.____

    A. the square of its length
    B. its length
    C. the cube of its length
    D. the square root of its length

3. The property of a circuit or of a material which tends to permit the flow of an electric current is called   3.____

    A. conductance
    B. inductance
    C. resistance
    D. reluctance

4. The equivalent resistance in ohms of a circuit having four resistances, respectively, 1, 2, 3, and 4 ohms in parallel, is   4.____

    A. 14.8   B. 10   C. 4.8   D. .48

5. The area in square inches of one circular mil is   5.____

    A. $(\pi/4)(0.001)^2$
    B. $4\pi(.01)$
    C. $(0.001)^2$
    D. $(0.01)^2$

6. The current through a field rheostat is 5 amperes and its resistance is 10 ohms. The power lost as heat in the rheostat is, *approximately,*   6.____

    A. 500 watts   B. 250 watts   C. 125 watts   D. 50 watts

7. A d.c. motor takes 30 amps at 220 volts and has an efficiency of 80%. The horsepower available at the pulley is, *approximately,*   7.____

    A. 10   B. 7   C. 5   D. 2

8. A tap is a tool *commonly* used to   8.____

    A. remove broken screws
    B. cut internal threads
    C. cut external threads
    D. smooth the ends of conduit

9. Lead covering is used on conductors for   9.____

    A. heat prevention
    B. explosion protection
    C. grounding
    D. moisture proofing

10. The one of the following tools which is run through a conduit to clear it before wire is pulled through is a(n)   10._____

    A. auger   B. borer   C. stop   D. mandrel

11. A pothead as used in the trade is a   11._____

    A. pot to heat solder
    B. cable terminal
    C. protective device used for cable splicing
    D. type of fuse

12. Resistance measurements show that an electro-magnet coil consisting of 90 turns of wire having an average diameter of 8 inches is shorted. The length of wire, in feet, required to rewind this coil is, *approximately*,   12._____

    A. 110   B. 190   C. 550   D. 2280

13. An inexpensive and portable instrument *commonly* used for detecting the presence of static electricity is the   13._____

    A. neon-tube electrical circuit tester   B. gauss meter
    C. photo-electric cell   D. startometer

14. A coil of wire is connected to an a.c. source of supply. If an iron bar is placed in the center of this coil, it will affect the magnetic circuit in such a way that the   14._____

    A. inductance of the coil will increase
    B. power taken by the coil will increase
    C. coil will draw more current
    D. impedance of the coil will decrease

15. The electrolyte used with the Edison nickel-iron-alkaline cell is   15._____

    A. sulphuric acid   B. nitric acid
    C. potassium hydroxide   D. lead peroxide

16. The D'Arsonval galvanometer principle used in sensitive current-measuring instruments is *nothing more than*   16._____

    A. the elongation of a wire due to the flow of current
    B. two coils carrying current reacting from one another
    C. the dynamic reaction of an aluminum disc due to eddy currents
    D. a coil turning in a magnetic field

17. With reference to armature windings, lap windings are *often* called   17._____

    A. series windings   B. cascade windings
    C. multiple or parallel windings   D. ring windings

18. With reference to armature windings, wave windings are *often* called   18._____

    A. series windings   B. cascade windings
    C. multiple or parallel windings   D. ring windings

19. Polarization in a dry cell causes the reduction in the current capacity of the cell after it has delivered current for some time. A remedy for polarization is to bring oxidizing agents into intimate contact with the cell cathode. A chemical agent *commonly* used for this purpose is

    A. potash
    B. manganese dioxide
    C. lead carbonate
    D. acetylene

20. The e.m.f. inducted in a coil is GREATEST where the magnetic field within the coil is

    A. constant
    B. increasing
    C. decreasing
    D. changing most rapidly

21. The BRIGHTNESS of incandescent lamps is *commonly* rated in

    A. foot candles   B. kilowatts   C. lumens   D. watts

22. The effect of eddy currents in a.c. magnetic circuits may be *reduced* by

    A. laminating the iron used
    B. making the magnet core of solid steel
    C. making the magnet core of solid cast iron
    D. inserting brass rings around the magnet core

23. The direction of rotation of a single-phase repulsion induction motor can be *reversed* by

    A. reversing two supply leads
    B. shifting the position of the brushes
    C. changing the connections to the field
    D. changing the connections to the armature

24. Underexciting the d.c. field of a synchronous motor will cause it to

    A. slow down
    B. speed up
    C. draw lagging current
    D. be unable to carry full normal load

25. A certain 6-pole 60-cycle induction motor has a slip of 5% when operating at a certain load. The *actual* speed of this motor under these conditions is, *most nearly*,

    A. 1200 rpm   B. 1140 rpm   C. 570 rpm   D. 120 rpm

KEY (CORRECT ANSWERS)

1. C
2. A
3. A
4. D
5. A

6. B
7. B
8. B
9. D
10. D

11. B
12. B
13. A
14. A
15. C

16. D
17. C
18. A
19. B
20. D

21. C
22. A
23. B
24. C
25. B

TEST 4

DIRECTIONS: Each question or incomplete statement is followed by several suggested answers or completions. Select the one that BEST answers the question or completes the statement. *PRINT THE LETTER OF THE CORRECT ANSWER IN THE SPACE AT THE RIGHT.*

Questions 1-4.

DIRECTIONS: Questions 1 to 4, inclusive, refer to the diagram below.

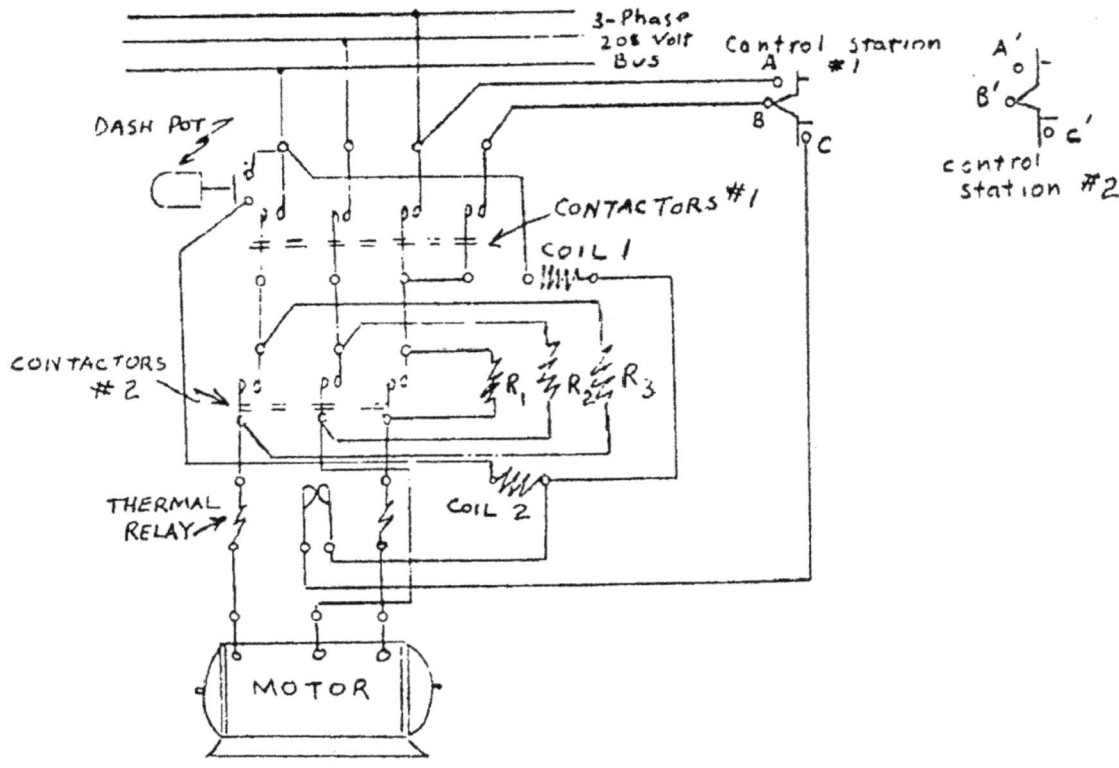

The above is a wiring diagram of a resistance starting controller for a.c. motors. This type of starter limits the starting current by means of equal resistances in each line wire leading to the motor. These resistances are automatically shunted out after the motor has gained full speed connecting the motor directly across the lines.

Station #2 may be added to Station #1 by connecting the start buttons in parallel and the stop buttons in series.

1. When the starting button is pressed,   1.____

   A. contactor coil #1 is immediately energized, causing contactors #1 to close
   B. contactor coil #2 is immediately energized, causing contactors #2 to close

54

C. contactor coil #1 is energized, but contactors #1 close only after contactors #2 close
D. both contactors #1 and contactors #2 close at the same time

2. The motor shown in the above diagram is a 3-phase   2._____

   A. wound rotor induction motor
   B. squirrel-cage induction motor
   C. capacitor-type induction motor
   D. synchronous motor

3. When the motor current becomes excessive, the thermal relay will actuate and cause   3._____

   A. contactors #1 to open first
   B. contactors #2 to open first
   C. contactors #1 and contactors #2 to open simultaneously
   D. the dash pot to energize coil #2

4. To add control station #2 to the circuit,   4._____

   A. A is connected to A^1, lead to C is disconnected and connected to C^1, and C is connected to B^1
   B. A is connected to A^1, C to C, and B to B^1
   C. lead to B is disconnected and connected to B^1, A^1 to B, and C to C^1
   D. A is connected to B^1, A^1 to B, and C to C^1

Questions 5-12.

DIRECTIONS: Questions 5 to 12, inclusive, refer to the electric wiring plan below.

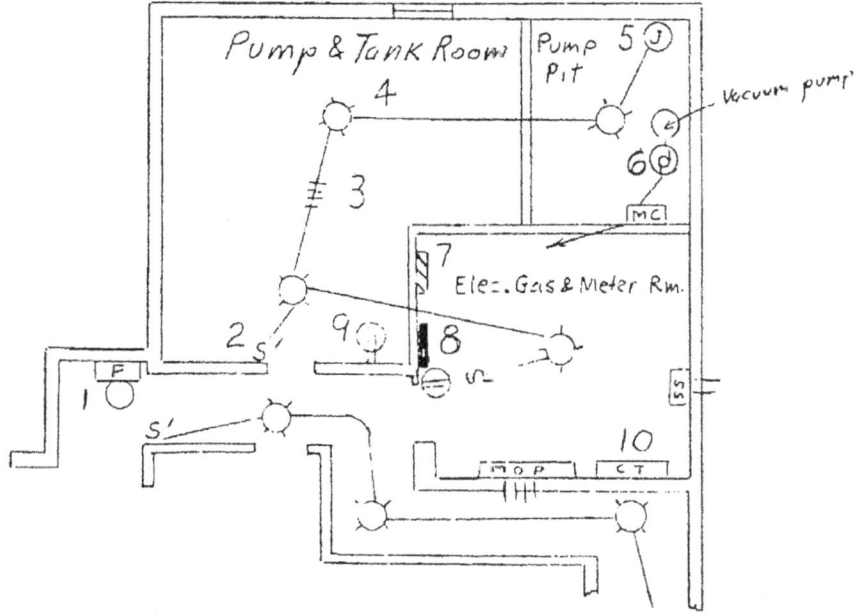

PART OF BUILDING CELLAR PLAN

5. Symbol numbered 1 represents a

   A. local fire alarm gong
   B. bell
   C. buzzer
   D. local fire alarm station

6. Symbol numbered 2 represents a

   A. 3-way switch
   B. 2-way switch
   C. single pole switch
   D. push button switch and pilot

7. Symbol numbered 3 represents a

   A. flexible conduit
   B. the number of phases
   C. the number of conductors in the conduit
   D. the size of wire in the conduit

8. Symbol numbered 4 represents a

   A. drop cord
   B. lamp holder
   C. floor outlet
   D. ceiling outlet

9. Symbol numbered 5 represents a

   A. telephone jack
   B. junction box
   C. Jandus fixture
   D. convenience outlet

10. Symbol numbered 6 represents a

    A. doorbell   B. drop cord   C. transformer   D. motor

11. Symbol numbered 7 represents a(n)

    A. power panel
    B. telephone box
    C. interconnection cabinet
    D. voltmeter

12. Symbol numbered 8 represents a(n)

    A. meter panel
    B. interconnection cabinet
    C. lighting panel
    D. underfloor duct

Questions 13-16.

DIRECTIONS: Questions 13 to 16, inclusive, refer to the diagram below.

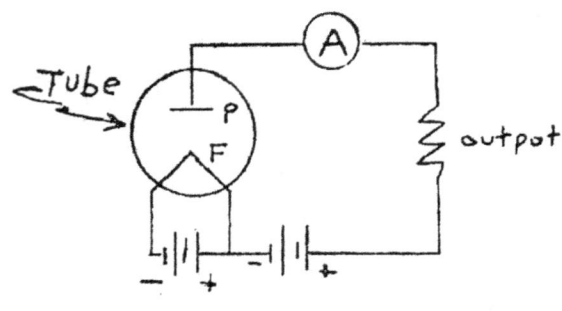
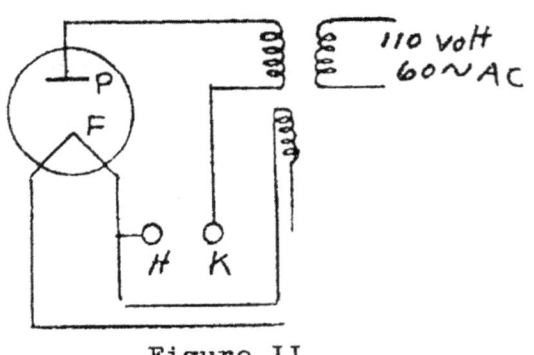

Figure I   Figure II

13. With reference to Figure I, the flow of electrons is 13._____

    A. blocked by the negative filament
    B. blocked by the negative plate
    C. from F to P
    D. from P to F

14. Figure II represents the diagram of a(n) 14._____

    A. rectifier   B. amplifier
    C. oscillator   D. voltage doubler

15. With reference to Figure II, under normal operating conditions, terminal 15._____

    A. H is negative
    B. H is alternately plus or minus
    C. K is positive
    D. H is positive

16. The tube in the above diagram (Figure I) is a *commonly* used symbol for a 16._____

    A. tetrode   B. heptode   C. pentode   D. diode

17. A 10" pulley revolving at 950 rpm is belted to a 20" pulley. The rpm of the 20" pulley is, *most nearly*, 17._____

    A. 1900   B. 1425   C. 950   D. 475

18. A battery composed of 5 cells, each having an e.m.f. of 1.5 volts and an internal resistance of .1 ohm, is connected to a .5 ohm resistance. If the cells are all in parallel, the current in amperes drawn from the battery is, *most nearly*, 18._____

    A. 2.88   B. 3.00   C. 12.50   D. 14.50

19. The MAXIMUM power delivered by a battery is obtained when the external resistance of the battery is made 19._____

    A. two times as large as its internal resistance
    B. one-half as large as its internal resistance
    C. one-quarter as large as its internal resistance
    D. equal to its internal resistance

20. A voltmeter is connected across the terminals of a certain battery. The difference between the open-circuit voltage and the voltage when current is taken from the battery is the 20._____

    A. internal voltage drop in the battery
    B. external voltage drop of the battery
    C. emf of the battery
    D. drop in voltage across the load resistance

Questions 21-22.

DIRECTIONS: According to the electrical code, the number of wires, running through or terminating in an outlet or junction box, shall be limited according to the free space within the box and the size of the wires. For combinations NOT found in a table provided for the selection of junction boxes, the code gives the following table:

Size of Conductor	Free Space Within Box for Each Conductor
No. 14	2 cubic inches
No. 12	2.25 cubic inches
No. 10	2.5 cubic inches
No. 8	3 cubic inches

21. In accordance with the above information, the MINIMUM size of box, in inches, for nine No. 12 wires is

    A. 1 1/2 X 4 square
    B. 1 1/2 X 3 square
    C. 2 X 3 square
    D. 2 X 4 square

22. With reference to the above information, the MINIMUM size of box, in inches, for four No. 8 wires and four No. 10 wires is

    A. 1 1/2 X 4 square
    B. 1 1/2 X 3 square
    C. 2 X 3 square
    D. 2 X 4 square

23. The current, in amperes, drawn from a battery cell having an e.m.f. of 3 volts and an internal resistance of 0.02 ohm when connected to an external resistance of 0.28 ohm is, *most nearly,*

    A. 5   B. 10   C. 15   D. 20

24. The term OPEN CIRCUIT means that

    A. the wiring is exposed
    B. the fuse is located outdoors
    C. the circuit has one end exposed
    D. all parts of the circuit (or path) are not in contact

25. The direction of rotation of a 3-phase wound rotor induction motor can be *reversed* by

    A. interchanging the connections to any two rotor terminals
    B. interchanging the connections to any two stator terminals
    C. interchanging the connections to the field
    D. shifting the position of the brushes

KEY (CORRECT ANSWERS)

1. A
2. B
3. C
4. A
5. A

6. C
7. C
8. D
9. B
10. D

11. A
12. C
13. C
14. A
15. D

16. D
17. D
18. A
19. D
20. A

21. A
22. A
23. B
24. D
25. B

TEST 5

DIRECTIONS: Each question or incomplete statement is followed by several suggested answers or completions. Select the one that BEST answers the question or completes the statement. *PRINT THE LETTER OF THE CORRECT ANSWER IN THE SPACE AT THE RIGHT.*

Questions 1-4.

DIRECTIONS: Questions 1 through 4, inclusive, refer to the diagram below.

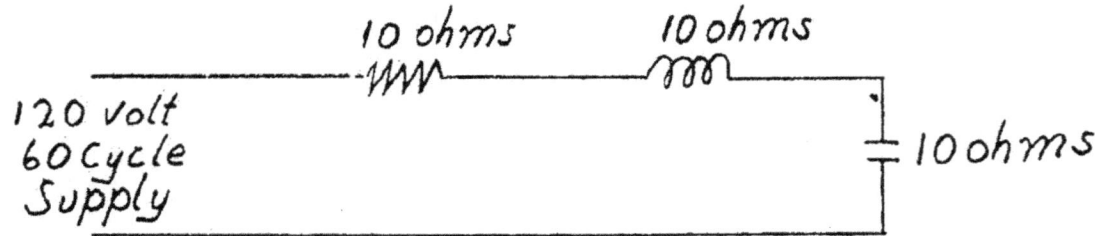

1. The value of the impedance, in ohms, of the above circuit is, *most nearly,* 1._____
   A. 30   B. 10   C. 3.33   D. 1.73

2. The current, in amperes, flowing in the above circuit is, *most nearly,* 2._____
   A. 4   B. 6   C. 12   D. 18

3. The power, in watts, consumed in the above circuit is, *most nearly,* 3._____
   A. 480   B. 635   C. 720   D. 1440

4. The voltage drop across the 10-ohm resistance is, *most nearly,* 4._____
   A. 10V   B. 40V   C. 60V   D. 120V

Questions 5-6.

DIRECTIONS: Questions 5 and 6 are to be answered in accordance with the information in the paragraph below.

    In the year 1914, a circuit was produced in which an electric current showed no diminution in strength 5 hours after the e.m.f. was removed. The current was induced magnetically in a short-circuited coil of lead wire at -270°C, produced by liquid helium, and the inducing source was removed. This experiment indicates that the resistance of lead was practically zero at this extremely low temperature.

5. In accordance with the above paragraph, the current in the short-circuited lead wire MUST have been 5._____

    A. electro-static current   B. induced current
    C. leading current   D. lagging current

6. According to the above paragraph, the resistance of lead 6._____

   A. is practically zero at -270°C
   B. is practically infinity at -270°C

7. A form of metal *suitable* for carrying electrical current, such as a wire or cable, is called 7._____
   a(n)

   A. raceway   B. trough   C. conductor   D. appliance

8. In accordance with the electrical code, the MINIMUM size of the wire used on a 15- 8._____
   ampere circuit is

   A. No. 16   B. No. 14   C. No. 12   D. No. 10

9. In cutting conduit, the pressure applied on a hacksaw should be on 9._____

   A. the forward stroke only
   B. the return stroke only
   C. the forward and return strokes equally
   D. either the forward or return stroke, depending on the material

10. To measure the diameter of wire most accurately, it is BEST to use a 10._____

    A. wire gauge   B. depth gauge
    C. micrometer   D. microtome

11. To measure the speed of an armature directly in rpm, it is BEST to use a 11._____

    A. tachometer   B. chronometer
    C. bolometer   D. manometer

12. The PRIMARY purpose for the use of oil in certain transformers is 12._____

    A. for lubrication
    B. to reduce the permeability
    C. to provide insulation and aid in cooling
    D. as a rust inhibitor

13. A single-throw switch should be mounted in such a way that, to open the switch, the blade 13._____
    MUST move

    A. to the right   B. upward
    C. to the left   D. downward

14. Of the following, the metal MOST commonly used as a filament in electric lamps is 14._____

    A. platinum   B. tungsten   C. mangarin   D. constantin

15. Of the following tools, the one MOST commonly used to cut holes in masonry is the 15._____

    A. star drill   B. auger   C. router   D. reamer

16. Resistance coils having a small resistance temperature coefficient, are made with a wire 16._____
    of a metal alloy called

    A. mallacca   B. massicot   C. manganin   D. malachite

17. For lead-acid type storage batteries, the *normal* battery potential is calculated on the basis of

    A. 12 volts per cell
    B. 6 volts per cell
    C. 3 volts per cell
    D. 2 volts per cell

18. Fluorescent lamps, while designed for alternating-current operation, can be used on a direct-current circuit if a specially designed d.c. auxiliary *and*

    A. parallel condenser of currect value are employed
    B. series condenser of correct value are employed
    C. parallel resistance of correct value are employed
    D. series resistance of correct value are employed

19. A transformer bank composed of three single-phase transformers is to be connected delta-delta. The primary side is first connected, but, before making the last secondary connection, the transformer should be tested for

    A. an open-circuit
    B. a grounded-circuit
    C. a cross-circuit
    D. the proper phase relation

20. As a safety measure, water should not be used to extinguish fires involving electrical equipment. The MAIN reason is that water

    A. is ineffective on electrical fires
    B. may transmit current and shock to the user
    C. may destroy the insulation property of wire
    D. may short-circuit the equipment

21. The SMALLEST number of wires necessary to carry 3-phase current is

    A. 2 wires   B. 3 wires   C. 4 wires   D. 5 wires

22. A 5-ampere d.c. ammeter may be *safely* used on a 50-ampere circuit provided the

    A. correct size current transformer is used
    B. proper size shunt is used
    C. proper circuit series resistance is used
    D. proper size multiplier is used

23. As used in the electrical code, the term "device" refers to

    A. an electrical appliance which does not have moving parts
    B. a unit of an electrical system other than a conductor which is intended to carry but not consume electrical energy
    C. current consuming equipment
    D. an accessory which is intended primarily to perform a mechanical rather than an electrical function

24. The difference of electrical potential between two wires of a circuit is its

    A. voltage   B. resistance   C. amperage   D. wattage

25. On long straight horizontal conduit runs, it is GOOD practice to use

    A. expansion joints
    B. universal joints
    C. isolation joints
    D. insulation joints

KEY (CORRECT ANSWERS)

1. B
2. C
3. D
4. D
5. B

6. A
7. C
8. C
9. A
10. C

11. A
12. C
13. D
14. B
15. A

16. C
17. D
18. D
19. D
20. B

21. B
22. B
23. B
24. A
25. A

TEST 6

DIRECTIONS: Each question or incomplete statement is followed by several suggested answers or completions. Select the one that BEST answers the question or completes the statement. *PRINT THE LETTER OF THE CORRECT ANSWER IN THE SPACE AT THE RIGHT.*

1. A circular mil is a measure of

    A. area   B. length   C. volume   D. weight

2. In electrical tests, a megger is calibrated to read

    A. amperes   B. ohms   C. volts   D. watts

3. Metal cabinets for lighting circuits are grounded in order to

    A. save insulating material
    B. provide a return for the neutral current
    C. eliminate short circuits
    D. minimize the possibility of shock

4. In an a.c. circuit containing only resistance, the power factor will be

    A. zero   B. 50% lagging   C. 50% leading   D. 100%

5. The size of fuse for a two-wire lighting circuit using No. 14 wire should NOT exceed

    A. 15 amperes
    B. 20 amperes
    C. 25 amperes
    D. 30 amperes

6. When working near acid storage batteries, extreme care should be taken to guard against sparks MAINLY because a spark may

    A. cause an explosion
    B. set fire to the electrolyte
    C. short-circuit a cell
    D. ignite the battery case

7. If a blown fuse in an existing lighting circuit is replaced by another of the same rating which also blows, the PROPER maintenance procedure is to

    A. use a higher rating fuse
    B. cut out some of the outlets in the circuit
    C. check the circuit for grounds or shorts
    D. install a renewable fuse

8. The number of fuses required in a three-phase, four-wire, branch circuit, with grounded neutral, is

    A. one   B. two   C. three   D. four

9. The electrodes of the common dry cell are carbon *and*

    A. zinc   B. lead   C. steel   D. tin

10. An electrician's hickey is used to 10.____

    A. strip insulation off wire
    B. pull cable through conduits
    C. thread metallic conduit
    D. bend metallic conduit

11. A group of wire sizes that is *correctly* arranged in the order of INCREASING current-car- 11.____
    rying capacity is:

    A. 6;12;3/0   B. 12;6;3/0   C. 3/0;12;6   D. 3/0;6;12

Questions 12-19.

DIRECTIONS: Questions 12 to 19 inclusive refer to the figures below. Each question gives the proper figure to use with that question.

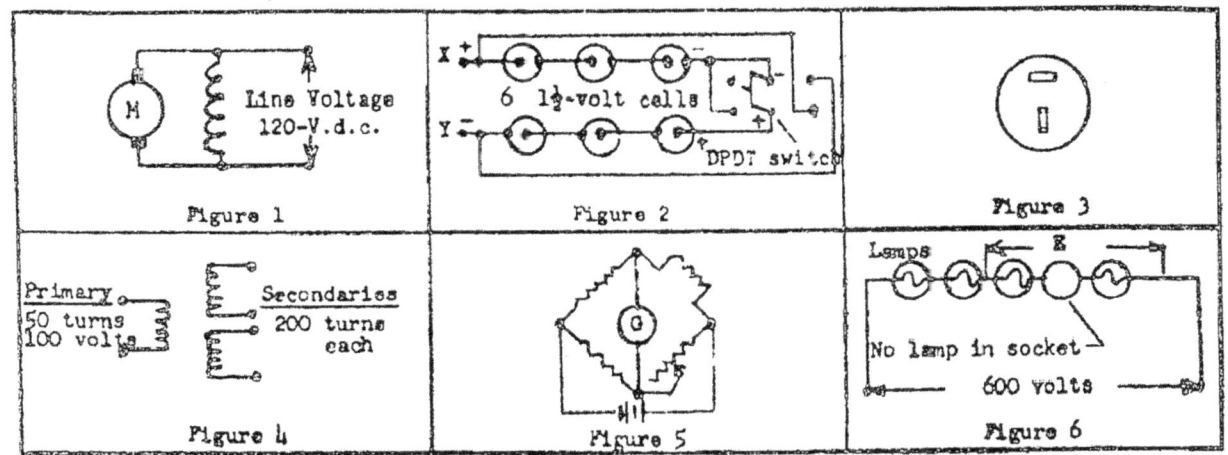

12. Figure 1 shows the standard diagram for a(n) 12.____

    A. synchronous motor   B. shunt motor
    C. series motor   D. induction motor

13. In Figure 1, if the line current is 5 amperes, the energy consumed by the motor if in con- 13.____
    tinuous operation for 3 hours, is _____ watthours.

    A. 200   B. 600   C. 1800   D. 9000

14. In Figure 2, with the DPDT switch closed to the right, the voltage between X and Y is 14.____

    A. 0   B. 1 1/2   C. 4 1/2   D. 9

15. In Figure 2, with the DPDT closed to the left, the voltage between X and Y is 15.____

    A. 9   B. 4 1/2   C. 1 1/2   D. 0

16. The convenience outlet shown in Figure 3 is used, particularly, for a device which 16.____

    A. is polarized   B. is often disconnected
    C. takes a heavy current   D. vibrates

3 (#6)

17. In Figure 4, the MAXIMUM secondary voltage possible by the interconnecting the secondaries is _____ volts.

    A. 50   B. 200   C. 400   D. 800

18. Figure 5 shows a Wheatstone bridge which is used to measure

    A. voltage   B. resistance   C. current   D. power

19. In Figure 6, with one of the five good lamps removed from its socket as indicated, the voltage E is *nearest* to

    A. 240   B. 0   C. 600   D. 360

20. The metal which is the BEST conductor of electricity is

    A. silver   B. copper   C. aluminum   D. nickel

21. If the two supply wires to a d.c. series motor are reversed, the motor will

    A. run in the opposite direction   B. not run
    C. run in the same direction   D. become a generator

22. Before doing work on a motor, to prevent accidental starting you *should*

    A. short circuit the motor leads   B. remove the fuses
    C. block the rotor   D. ground the frame

23. The material *commonly* used for brushes on d.c. motors is

    A. copper   B. carbon   C. brass   D. aluminum

24. The conductors of a two-wire, No.12, armored cable used in an ordinary lighting circuit are

    A. stranded and rubber insulated
    B. solid and rubber insulated
    C. stranded and cotton insulated
    D. solid and cotton insulated

25. The rating, 125C.-10A,; 250V.-5A., *commonly* applies to a

    A. snap switch   B. lamp   C. conductor   D. fuse

KEY (CORRECT ANSWERS)

1. A
2. B
3. D
4. D
5. A

6. A
7. C
8. C
9. A
10. D

11. B
12. B
13. C
14. C
15. A

16. A
17. D
18. E
19. C
20. A

21. C
22. B
23. B
24. B
25. A

EXAMINATION SECTION
TEST 1

DIRECTIONS: Each question or incomplete statement is followed by several suggested answers or completions. Select the one that BEST answers the question or completes the statement. *PRINT THE LETTER OF THE CORRECT ANSWER IN THE SPACE AT THE RIGHT.*

1. For a given level of illumination, the cost of electrical energy with fluorescent lighting fixtures as compared with incandescent lighting fixtures is   1.____

    A. less
    B. the same
    C. more
    D. dependent on the utility rate

2. The initial current of an incandescent lamp (tungsten) as compared with its normal operating current is   2.____

    A. less
    B. the same
    C. more
    D. dependent on the system frequency

3. According to the electrical code, fixtures in which the wiring may be exposed to temperatures in excess of 140° F (60° C)   3.____

    A. are prohibited
    B. shall be wired with type AF fixture wires
    C. shall be so designed or ventilated and installed to operate at temperatures which will not cause deterioration of the wiring
    D. shall have suitable thermal insulation between the fixture and any adjacent combustible material

4. The direction of rotation of a d.c. shunt motor can be reversed by   4.____

    A. reversing the line terminals
    B. reversing the field and armature
    C. reversing the field or armature
    D. flashing the field

5. A starting device which will limit the starting current of a d.c. motor is generally required because   5.____

    A. the counter e.m.f. is maximum at standstill
    B. the inertia of the driven load causes excessive starting current
    C. the counter e.m.f. is zero at standstill
    D. decreased starting current increases the starting torque

6. According to the electrical code, motor disconnecting means shall be located   6.____

    A. within 10 feet of the motor
    B. within sight of the controller
    C. within 15 feet of the motor
    D. where convenient

7. According to the electrical code, the controller for an a.c. motor shall be capable of interrupting

   A. twice the full load current of the motor
   B. three times the full load current of the motor
   C. five times the full load current of the motor
   D. the stalled rotor current

8. According to the electrical code, motor disconnecting means shall have a continuous duty rating, in percent, of the name plate current rating of the motor of AT LEAST

   A. 100%   B. 115%   C. 150%   D. 200%

9. The lumens per watt taken by a lamp varies with the type and size of lamp. Given that a one candle power light source emits 12.57 lumens, the lumens per watt taken by a 75 candle power lamp drawing 40 watts is *approximately*

   A. 1.9   B. 6.7   C. 23.6   D. 240

10. A 230-volt, 25-cycle magnetic brake coil is to be rewound to operate properly on 60 cycles at the same voltage. Assuming that the coil at 25 cycles has 1800 turns, at 60 cycles the number of turns should be

    A. *reduced* to 750
    B. *increased* to 2400
    C. *reduced* to 420
    D. *increased* to 3000

11. Nichrome wire having a resistance of 200 ohms per 100 feet is to be used for a heater requiring a total resistance of 10 ohms.
    The length, in feet, of wire required is

    A. 5   B. 15   C. 25   D. 50

12. The MAIN reason for grounding conduit is to prevent the conduit from becoming

    A. corroded by electrolysis
    B. magnetized
    C. a source of radio interference
    D. accidentally energized at a higher potential than ground

13. A feeder consisting of a positive and a negative wire supplies a motor load. The feeder is connected to bus-bars having a constant potential of 230 volts. The feeder is 500 feet long and consists of two 250,000 circular-mil conductors. The maximum load on the feeder is 170 amps. Assume that the resistance of 1000 feet of this cable is 0.0431 ohm.
    The voltage, at the motor terminals, is MOST NEARLY

    A. 201 V   B. 209 V   C. 213 V   D. 217 V

14. With reference to question 13 above, the efficiency of transmission, in percent, is MOST NEARLY

    A. 83%   B. 87%   C. 91%   D. 97%

15. With reference to a.c. motors, in addition to overload, many other things cause fuses to blow. The fuse will blow if, in starting an a.c. motor, the operator throws the starting switch of the compensator to the running position

A. too slowly
B. too quickly
C. with main switch in open position
D. with main switch in close position

16. A change in speed of a d.c. motor of 10 to 15 percent can USUALLY be made by

   A. rewinding the armature
   B. rewinding the field
   C. decreasing the number of turns in the field coils
   D. increasing or decreasing the gap between the armature and field

17. In order to check the number of poles in a 3-phase wound rotor induction motor, it is necessary to check the no-load speed. The no-load speed is obtained by running the motor with load disconnected and with the rotor resistance

   A. short-circuited   B. all in
   C. half in   D. one-third in

18. A group of industrial oil burners are equipped with several electric preheaters which can be used singly or in combination to heat the #6 oil for the burners. Electric preheater "A" alone can heat a certain quantity of oil from 70° to 160° in 15 minutes and preheater "B" alone can do the same job in 30 minutes. If both preheaters are used together, they will do the job in _____ minutes.

   A. 12   B. 11   C. 10   D. 9

19. With reference to armature windings, in a wave winding, regardless of the number of poles, ONLY _____ brushes are necessary.

   A. two   B. four   C. six   D. eight

20. The MINIMUM number of overload devices required for a 3-phase a.c. motor connected to a 120/208 volt, 3-phase, 4 wire system is

   A. 1   B. 2   C. 3   D. 4

21. According to the electrical code, an externally operable switch may be used as the starter for a motor of not over 2 horsepower (and not over 300 volts) provided it has a rating of AT LEAST

   A. 2 times the stalled rotor current of the motor
   B. 2 times the full load current of the motor
   C. 115% of the full load current of the motor
   D. 150% of the stalled rotor current of the motor

22. According to the electrical code, a single disconnecting means may serve a group of motors provided

   A. all motors are 1/2 HP or less
   B. all motors are within a short distance from each other
   C. all motors are located within a single room and within sight of the disconnecting means
   D. one-half of the motors are located within a single room and within sight of the disconnecting means

23. In a 3-phase system with 3 identical loads connected in delta, if the line voltage is 4160 volts, the line to neutral voltage is

    A. indeterminate
    B. 7200 volts
    C. 2400 volts
    D. 2000 volts

24. If the current in each line is 100 amperes, the currents in each of the individual loads is (under the conditions as set forth in question 23)

    A. indeterminate
    B. 57.7 amps
    C. 173 amps
    D. 50.0 amps

25. In a 3-phase system with 3 identical loads connected in wye, if the line to neutral voltage is 115 volts, the line voltage is

    A. indeterminate
    B. 208 volts
    C. 200 volts
    D. 220 volts

26. A circuit composed of a 6-ohm resistance, a 10-ohm capacitative reactance, and an 18-ohm inductive reactance connected in series is energized by a 120 volt a.c. supply. The current, in amperes, flowing in this circuit is

    A. 0   B. 12   C. 35   D. 20

27. With reference to question 26 above, the power, in watts, used in this circuit is

    A. 0   B. 1440   C. 420   D. 864

28. With reference to question 26 above, the power factor, in percent, is

    A. 100   B. 60   C. 80   D. 90

29. With reference to question 26 above, the total impedance, in ohms, of the circuit is

    A. 10   B. 34   C. 14   D. 28

30. A triode does NOT have a

    A. cathode
    B. screen grid
    C. control grid
    D. plate

31. An industrial plant utilizes acetone as a solvent in one area. All wiring in this area must be

    A. vaportight
    B. watertight
    C. explosionproof
    D. of normal construction

32. In an area where explosionproof wiring is required, each conduit entering an enclosure containing apparatus which may produce arcs, sparks, or high temperatures shall be provided with

    A. insulating bushings
    B. a cable terminator
    C. an approved sealing compound
    D. double locknuts

33. Decreasing the bias voltage on the control grid of a triode (making it less negative with respect to the cathode) causes the plate current to

   A. not change
   B. increase
   C. decrease
   D. oscillate

Questions 34-46.

DIRECTIONS: The following questions 34 to 46 inclusive are to be answered in accordance with the provisions of the electrical code.

34. The MINIMUM size of wire for signaling systems is

   A. #14AWG　　B. #16AWG　　C. #18AWG　　D. #19AWG

35. The MINIMUM size of service entrance conductors is

   A. #2AWG　　B. #4AWG　　C. #6AWG　　D. #8AWG

36. The MAXIMUM number of individual sets of service equipment which can be supplied from one set of service entrance conductors is

   A. 1　　B. 2　　C. 4　　D. 6

37. Service switches of ratings larger than 1,200 amperes

   A. are prohibited
   B. shall be of the pressure contact type
   C. shall be of the air circuit breaker type
   D. shall be remotely operable

38. The rating of service switches shall be less than

   A. the computed load current
   B. twice the computed load current
   C. one and a half times the computed load current
   D. one and a quarter times the computed load current

39. The allowable current carrying capacity of conductors in raceway or cable

   A. is independent of the number of conductors
   B. shall be reduced to 70% of table values if more than three conductors are contained within the raceway or cable
   C. shall be reduced to 50% of the table values if more than six conductors are contained in the raceway or cable
   D. shall be reduced to 80% for 4-6 conductors and to 70% for 7-9 conductors in the same raceway or cable

40. The MAXIMUM number of conductors for general light and power in a single raceway is

   A. 6　　B. 9　　C. 15　　D. unlimited

41. The number of signal wires in a conductor raceway shall be

   A. the same as for lighting and power conductors
   B. such that their total cross-sectional area shall not exceed 50% of the cross-sectional area of the conduit or raceway
   C. the maximum number which can be easily installed
   D. such that their total cross-sectional area shall not exceed 40% of the cross-sectional area of the conduit or raceway

42. Lightning arrestors for receiving station antennas shall operate at a voltage of NOT more than _____ volts.

   A. 100   B. 200   C. 500   D. 1000

43. The MINIMUM size of copper ground connection to lightning arrestors for receiving antennas shall be

   A. #14AWG   B. #10AWG   C. #6AWG   D. #16AWG

44. Only motor generator sets having a generated voltage of 65 volts or less may be protected by

   A. one protective device in the generator armature circuit
   B. a protective device in each armature lead
   C. the over current protective devices in the motor circuit set to trip when the generators are delivering not more than 150% of their full load rated current
   D. the motor running protective devices of the motor

45. Single pole protective devices for direct current generators MUST be activated by

   A. the total generated current, including all field current
   B. total current except that in the shunt field
   C. separate elements in each brush lead
   D. separate elements in each line lead

46. Motor control equipment for hazardous locations MUST

   A. not produce sparks
   B. be contained in an enclosure which is vaportight
   C. be capable of withstanding an external explosion
   D. be of a type specifically approved for the installation

47. A room is 20 feet wide and is to be provided with 4 rows of lighting outlets symmetrically spaced. The distance from the wall to the center line of the first fixture row will be

   A. 5'0"   B. 10'0"   C. 7'6"   D. 2'6"

48. A fixture mounting height of 9'6" is specified for a room with a ceiling height of 12'0", utilizing fixtures with a height of 6". The size of stem required is MOST NEARLY

   A. 3'0"   B. 2'6"   C. 2'0"   D. 1'6"

49. Specifications for a project require that 40W, T-12, RS/CW lamps be installed in a given group of fixtures. The type of lamp required is

    A. 40 watt, type 12, reflector spot, clear white, incandescent
    B. 40 watt, single pin, relay start, code white, fluorescent
    C. 40 watt, bi-pin, rapid start, cool white, fluorescent
    D. type 12, medium base, recessed spot, clear white, incandescent

49.____

50. Specifications for a project require the use of indirect type of lighting fixtures. The one of the following types that will meet this requirement is

    A. RCM dome fixture
    B. concentric ring fixture with silverbowl lamp
    C. downlight with par 38 spot
    D. opal glass bowl

50.____

KEY (CORRECT ANSWERS)

1. A	11. D	21. B	31. C	41. D
2. C	12. D	22. C	32. C	42. C
3. C	13. D	23. C	33. B	43. A
4. C	14. D	24. B	34. D	44. C
5. C	15. B	25. C	35. B	45. B
6. B	16. D	26. B	36. D	46. D
7. D	17. A	27. D	37. B	47. D
8. B	18. C	28. B	38. D	48. C
9. C	19. A	29. A	39. D	49. C
10. A	20. B	30. B	40. B	50. B

TEST 2

DIRECTIONS: Each question or incomplete statement is followed by several suggested answers or completions. Select the one that BEST answers the question or completes the statement. *PRINT THE LETTER OF THE CORRECT ANSWER IN THE SPACE AT THE RIGHT.*

1. The list of symbols for the plans for a project gives and defines the following symbol: 1.____
   0_{A5C} - Incandescent lighting fixture, letters, and number indicate fixture type per specifications, circuit number and controlling switch, respectively.
   The symbol for a fixture connected to circuit 8, controlled by a switch designated "e" and conforming to the requirements of a type D fixture would be

   A. 0_{E8d} B. 0_{d8E} C. 0_{D8e} D. $0_{8eD}{}^{o}$

Questions 2-5.

DIRECTIONS: The questions numbered 2 to 5 inclusive shall be answered in accordance with the diagram which appears below.

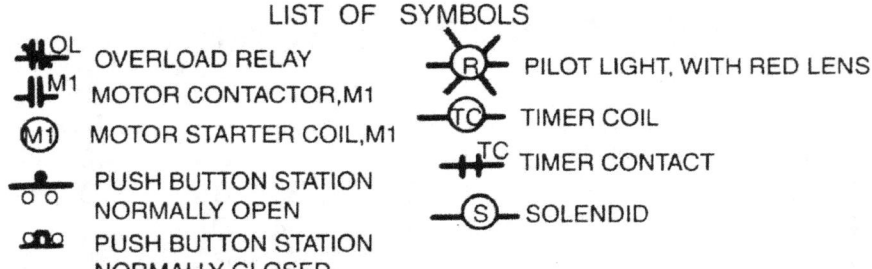

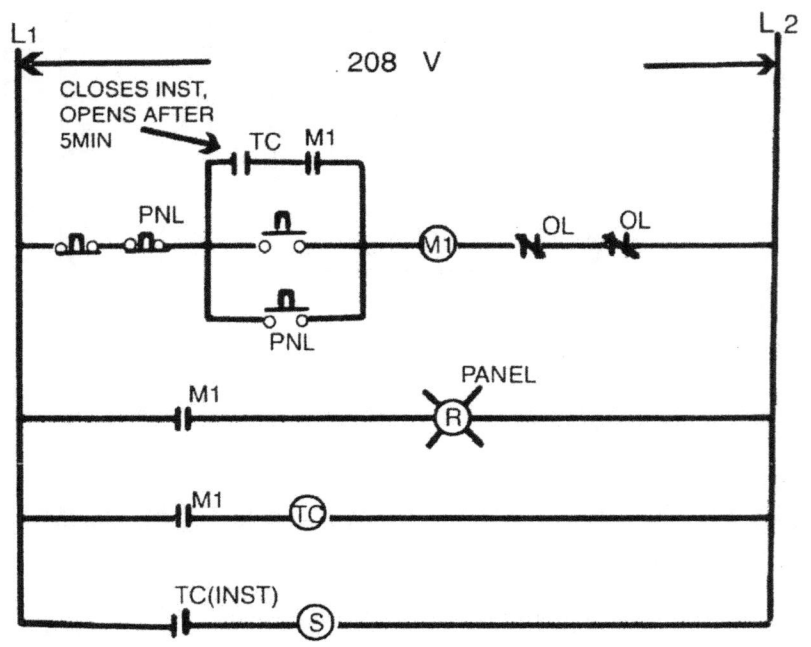

76

2. The above schematic diagram indicates a desired control scheme for a pump motor. The number of locations the motor can be started from is (are)

   A. 1   B. 2   C. 3   D. 4

2.____

3. Of the following, the one which contains the most complete and correct list of possible operations which will cause the already started motor to stop is

   A. pressing of stop PB after 5 minutes have elapsed since motor started, or operation of OL
   B. a lapse of 5 minutes since starting of motor, or pressing of stop PB, or operation of OL
   C. the passing of 5 minutes from the time of starting, or pressing, of stop PB, or operation of OL, or loss of voltage
   D. loss of voltage after 5 minutes have elapsed since starting motor, or operation of OL

3.____

4. The solenoid will be energized

   A. as long as the motor starter is energized
   B. only as long as the start PB is depressed
   C. for five minutes
   D. until the stop PB is depressed

4.____

5. If the timer fails to close its associated contact, the motor

   A. cannot run
   B. will run only as long as the start PB is depressed
   C. will run continuously
   D. will run for five minutes

5.____

Questions 6-8.

DIRECTIONS: The following questions 6 to 8 inclusive should be answered in accordance with the diagram below.

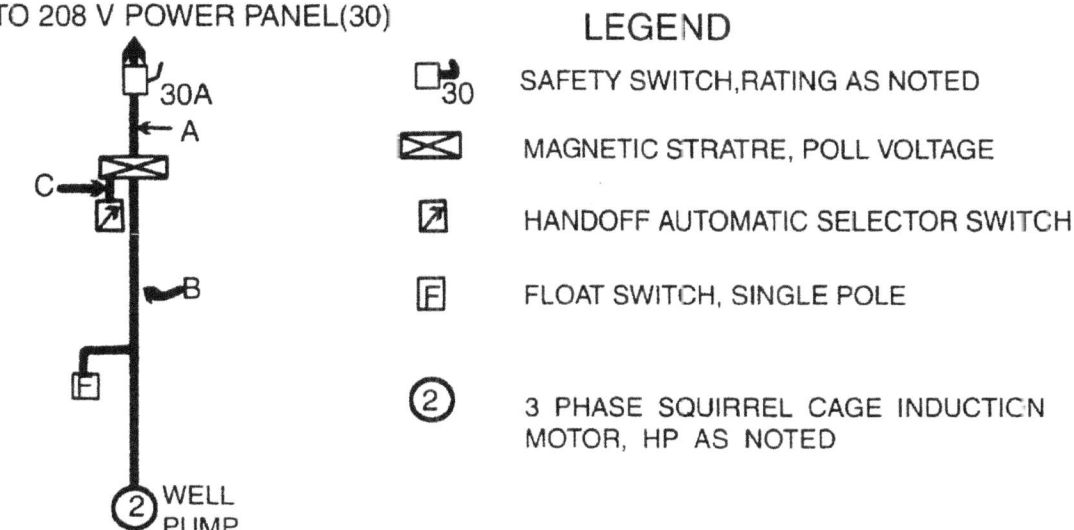

6. The required number of conductors at point "A" is
   A. 2   B. 3   C. 4   D. 5

7. The required number of conductors at point "B" is
   A. 2   B. 3   C. 4   D. 5

8. The required number of conductors at point "C" is
   A. 2   B. 3   C. 4   D. 5

9. The LEAST number of single-phase wattmeters that can be be used to measure the power in an unbalanced 3-phase, 4-wire a.c. circuit is
   A. 1   B. 2   C. 3   D. 4

10. A note on a plan states: "All runs shall be 3/4" conduit with 2#12AWG conductors or number of #12 conductors indicated by hatchmarks unless otherwise designated." A run is shown as follows: ─/─/─/
    This run consists of
    A. 2#12, 1/2"C   B. 3#12, 1/2"C
    C. 3#12, 3/4"C   D. 2#12, 3/4"C

11. Specifications for a particular project call for a system of empty conduits and outlet boxes for public telephones, with a galvanized steel wire installed in each conduit. The one of the following reasons for providing this wire which is MOST acceptable is to
    A. ensure that the conduit is clear
    B. permit pulling in of wire at a later date
    C. ground the system
    D. limit corrosion of the interior surfaces of the conduit

12. An interior auxiliary fire alarm system to be installed in a building is to be of the coded city connected shunt-trip type. The one of the following which BEST describes the operation of this system is operating any station
    A. sounds a coded signal on all bells and uses local power to trip a city box
    B. operates the city box only
    C. trips a city box using municipal system power and simultaneously sounds a coded signal on interior bells
    D. operates interior gongs only

13. A magnetic motor starter is to be controlled with momentary start-stop pushbuttons at two locations. The number of control wires required, respectively, in the conduit between the controller and the first station and in the conduit between the two stations is
    A. 3 and 3   B. 4 and 4
    C. 3 and 4   D. 2 and 4

14. If the voltage on a 3-phase squirrel cage induction motor is reduced to 90% of its rating, the starting current
    A. increases slightly   B. is unchanged
    C. decreases 10%   D. decreases 20%

15. If the voltage on a 3-phase squirrel cage induction motor is reduced to 90% of its rating, the full load current

    A. decreases slightly
    B. is unchanged
    C. increases 10%
    D. increases 20%

16. A 3-conductor cable is used to provide a "hot" leg, switch leg and neutral between two outlets. The individual conductors are MOST commonly connected as follows: red is

    A. hot, white is neutral, black is switch
    B. switch, white is hot, black is neutral
    C. neutral, white is switch, black is hot
    D. switch, white is neutral, black is hot

17. To obtain a.c. current from a d.c. source of supply, it is BEST to use a(n)

    A. inverter
    B. diode
    C. rectifier
    D. shunt generator

18. Insulation resistance is commonly measured by means of a(n)

    A. ammeter
    B. varmeter
    C. capacitance bridge
    D. megger

19. A specification requires the installation of five pole, four wire, grounded 250 volt, 15 amp receptacles for 120/208 volt 3 ϕ 4 wire service, with matching plug and 15 foot #14AWG portable heavy duty cord. The number of conductors which the required cord MUST have is

    A. 3
    B. 4
    C. 5
    D. not clearly specified

Questions 20-21.

DIRECTIONS: The following questions 20 and 21 are to be answered in accordance with the information given below.

To get equivalent delta from wye

$$A = \frac{ab+bc+ac}{a}$$

$$B = \frac{ab+bx+ac}{b}$$

$$C = \frac{ab+bx+ac}{c}$$

To get equivalent wye from delta

$$a = \frac{BC}{A+B+C}$$

$$b = \frac{AC}{A+B+C}$$

$$c = \frac{AB}{A+B+C}$$

NOTE: The above formula indicates the relationship between equivalent wye and delta net works.

20. If, in a delta, the branches are resistors such that A=5 ohms, B=10 ohms, and C=10 ohms, the resistor of branch "a" of the equivalent wye is _____ ohms.

    A. 5 B. 10 C. 2 D. 4

21. In the problem 20 above, the resistor of branch "b" of the equivalent wye is _____ ohms.

    A. 10 B. 4 C. 2 D. 5

Questions 22-23.

DIRECTIONS: The following questions 22 and 23 should be answered in accordance with the paragraph below.

Insulation resistance tests are best made with a direct-reading Megger. These tests can also be made with a high-resistance voltmeter and a source of d.c. supply. Assume that a direct reading instrument is not available but you have on hand a 100-volt voltmeter having a sensitivity of 5000 ohms per volt and a 100-volt battery. The battery is connected in series with the voltmeter. One free battery lead is connected to the wire whose insulation resistance is to be measured, and the other free lead to the grounded circuit. With this hookup, the voltmeter reads 50 volts.

22. The insulation resistance, in ohms, of the above conductor is

    A. 500 B. 5,000 C. 250,000 D. 500,000

23. The resistance, in ohms, of the above-mentioned voltmeter is

    A. 500 B. 5,000 C. 250,000 D. 500,000

24. An ammeter and voltmeter are connected through instrument transformers to measure the KVA of a balanced three phase load connected to a 2400 volt, 3-phase, 3 wire system. The PT is rated 2400/120 volts, and the CT is rated 200/5 amperes.
    If the ammeter reads 4 amps and the voltmeter 100 volts, the load, in KVA, is APPROXIMATELY

    A. 0.4 B. 6.8 C. 320 D. 555

25. A note on a lighting plan states: "All fluorescent fixtures shall be symmetrically spaced and oriented so that the major axis of the fixture is parallel to the major axis of the room."
    For a room 20' long by 16' wide, with four-four foot fixtures, the desired arrangement is:
    Fixtures parallel with and centered

    A. 4' from 20' wall, 5' from 16' wall
    B. 5' from 20' wall, 4' from 16' wall
    C. 4' from 16' wall, 5' from 20' wall
    D. 5' from 16' wall, 4' from 20' wall

Questions 26-31.

DIRECTIONS: The following questions 26 to 31 inclusive are to be answered in accordance with the provisions of the electrical code.

26. Individual conductors of multi-conductor control cables shall be   26._____

    A. color coded   B. clearly tagged at each end
    C. identified by painting   D. stranded

27. Terminals of motor-starting rheostats shall be   27._____

    A. suitable for solderless external connections only
    B. clearly marked to indicate wire to which they are to be connected
    C. equipped with barriers
    D. brought out to a suitable terminal block

28. Incandescent lamps can be used for control resistors   28._____

    A. under no circumstances
    B. as protective resistances provided they do not carry the main current
    C. for loads less than 1000 watts
    D. if mounted in porcelain receptacles

29. Wiring in battery rooms shall   29._____

    A. utilize lead covered cable
    B. be installed in rigid steel conduit
    C. be installed in Greenfield
    D. be enclosed in non-corrodible conduit or be exposed

30. Control switches for emergency lights in a theater shall be located   30._____

    A. where convenient to operating personnel
    B. in the lobby where accessible to authorized persons
    C. on the stage switchboard
    D. in the projection booth

31. Signal wires of sizes #18 or #16 shall be considered as properly protected by fuses rated   31._____
    at _____ amps.

    A. 15   B. 20   C. 25   D. 30

32. If the voltage of a 3-phase squirrel cage induction motor is reduced to 90% of its rating,   32._____
    the power factor

    A. increases slightly   B. is unchanged
    C. decreases slightly   D. decreases 10 points

33. To reverse the direction of rotation of a wound rotor 3-phase induction motor, interchange   33._____

    A. all line wires   B. all rotor connections
    C. any 2 rotor connections   D. any 2-line wires

Questions 34-36.

DIRECTIONS: The following questions 34 to 36 inclusive relate to the diagram appearing on the following page.

LEGEND

1° ALARM CONTACT, NORMALLY OPEN    NORMALLY CLOSED CONTACT RELAY R1

HORN   PUSH BUTTON STATION NORMALLY OPEN

RELAY COIL R1   RED ALARM LIGHT

 NORMALLY OPEN CONTACT, RELAY R1

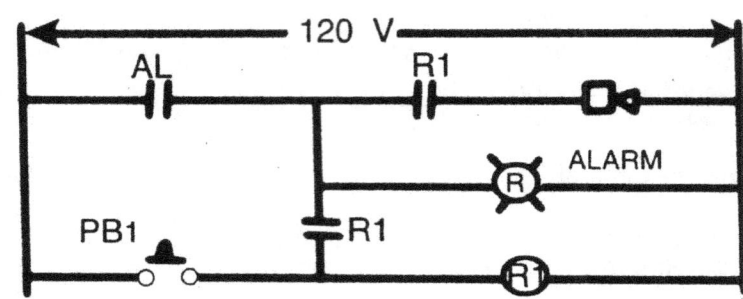

NOTE: The above diagram represents a simple alarm panel. Note that closing of the alarm contact causes the horn to sound and alarm lamp to light.

34. Assume that the alarm contact has closed. Then, pressing the PB

　　A. causes the red alarm light to go out only as long as the button is depressed
　　B. causes the horn to be silenced until the alarm contact opens and closes again
　　C. tests the alarm light
　　D. tests the alarm horn

35. The alarm light is illuminated

　　A. only when the pushbutton is depressed
　　B. only after the horn is silenced
　　C. as long as the alarm contact is closed
　　D. continuously

36. The relay R_1 has the following contacts:

　　A. 2 N.O.　　　　　　　　　　　　B. 2 N.C.
　　C. 1 N.O. and 1N.C.　　　　　　 D. 2 N.O. and 1 N.C.

37. A blind hickey is used

　　A. to cap a spare conduit
　　B. in lieu of a fixture stud
　　C. in lieu of a fixture extension
　　D. to hang a lighting fixture on a gas outlet

Questions 38-41.

DIRECTIONS: The following questions 38 to 41 inclusive are to be answered in accordance with the diagram below.

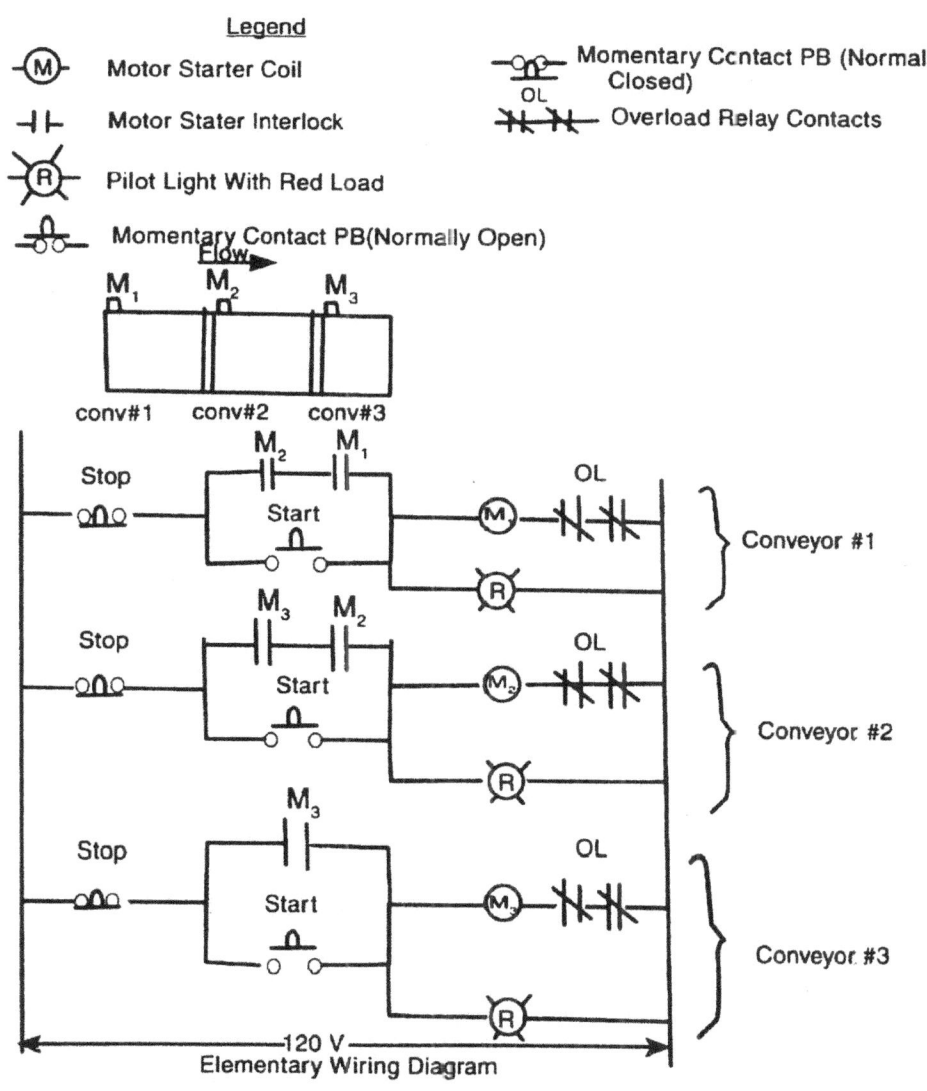

38. For continuous operation of all conveyors,

    A. conveyor #1 must be started first
    B. conveyor #2 must be started first
    C. conveyor #3 must be started first
    D. conveyors can be started in any order

    38.____

39. Stopping of conveyor #3 will

    A. not affect other conveyors
    B. stop conveyor #2
    C. stop conveyor #1
    D. stop conveyors #1 and #2

    39.____

40. Momentarily depressing the start PB of conveyor #2 before starting conveyor #3 or #1 will

   A. start conveyors #1 and #2
   B. start conveyor #2 and permit it to run continuously
   C. start conveyor #2 for only the time the button is depressed
   D. have no effect

41. When the thermal overload relays of conveyor #2 open,

   A. motor #2 only stops
   B. motors #1 and #2 will stop
   C. motor #1, #2, and #3 will stop
   D. an alarm will sound

42. An Erickson coupling is used

   A. to join sections of EMT
   B. to connect EMT to flexible conduit
   C. to connect two sections of rigid conduit when one section cannot be turned
   D. as a substitute for all thread

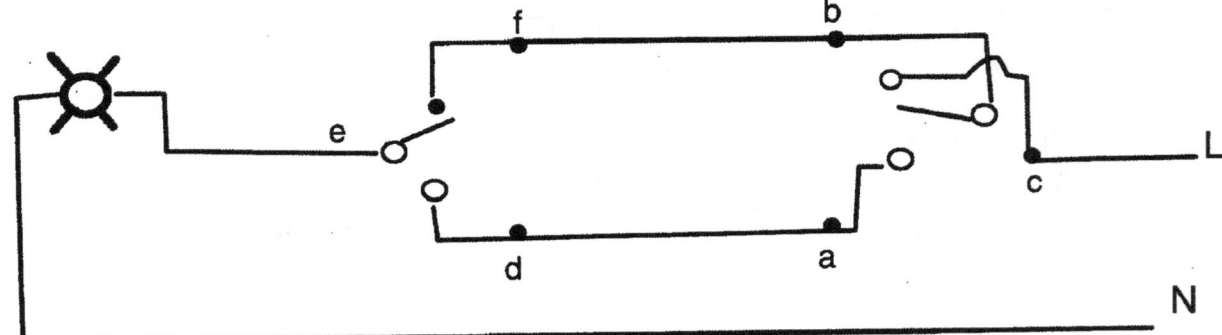

43. A light is to be controlled from two locations. It is connected with two 3-way switches as shown above and does not work properly.
   To correct the wiring, the following changes should be made: Interchange connections

   A. e and f B. b and c C. a and b D. a and c

44. Proper and economical control of lighting fixtures from three locations without the use of relays

   A. cannot be done
   B. requires a 3-way switch at each location
   C. requires two 3-way switches and one 4-way switch
   D. requires two 4-way switches and one 3-way switch

45. The outside diameter of a certain rigid steel conduit is measured to be approximately 2" (to the nearest 1/8 inch). The NOMINAL trade size is

   A. 2" B. 1 1/2" C. 1 1/4" D. 2 1/2"

46. Electrical equipment can be secured to concrete walls by means of

   A. toggle bolts
   B. wooden plugs and screws
   C. cut nails
   D. lead shields

47. Continuity of an electrical circuit can conveniently be determined in the field by means of a(n)

   A. smoke test
   B. bell and battery set
   C. ammeter
   D. Wheatstone Bridge

48. The speed of a motor can be measured by means of a

   A. potentiometer
   B. megger
   C. tachometer
   D. thermocouple

49. A test for transformer polarity is made on a transformer rated 2400-240 volts by applying a voltage V_1=120 volts to the high voltage terminals H_1 and H_2 and measuring the voltage between terminals H_2 and X_2. (See diagram to the right.) If the transformer is of subtractive polarity, the voltmeter will read APPROXIMATELY _____ volts.

   A. 132 B. 12 C. 108 D. 0

50. An ammeter connected to the secondary of an energized metering transformer requires repairs.
Before disconnecting the instrument, the electrician should

   A. open the secondary circuit
   B. short circuit the transformer secondary terminals
   C. short circuit the transformer primary terminals
   D. remove the transformer secondary fuses

KEY (CORRECT ANSWERS)

1. C	11. B	21. C	31. A	41. B
2. B	12. C	22. D	32. A	42. C
3. C	13. C	23. D	33. D	43. B
4. A	14. C	24. D	34. B	44. C
5. B	15. C	25. A	35. C	45. B
6. B	16. D	26. A	36. C	46. D
7. D	17. A	27. B	37. D	47. B
8. B	18. D	28. B	38. C	48. C
9. C	19. C	29. D	39. D	49. C
10. C	20. D	30. B	40. C	50. B

EXAMINATION SECTION
TEST 1

DIRECTIONS: Each question or incomplete statement is followed by several suggested answers or completions. Select the one that BEST answers the question or completes the statement. *PRINT THE LETTER OF THE CORRECT ANSWER IN THE SPACE AT THE RIGHT.*

1. Two lamps need 50V and 2 amp each in order to operate at a desired brilliancy. If they are to be connected in series across a 120V line, the resistance, in ohms, of the rheostat that must be placed in series with the lamps needs to be

    A. 4   B. 10   C. 20   D. 100

2. The Kelvin Bridge is BASICALLY a device for measuring

    A. low resistance   B. high resistance
    C. high emf   D. low emf

3. If a capacitance of 250 Mf, connected to an AC line, has a capacitive reactance measured at 10.6 ohms, the AC line has a frequency, in c/sec, of

    A. 30   B. 60   C. 90   D. 120

4. Of the following, the one that is NOT normally used as a component of some electronic oscillator circuits is the

    A. lighthouse tube   B. pitot tube
    C. klystron   D. magnetron

5. The term *magnetostriction* refers to the

    A. strict conditions that determine magnetic polarity
    B. change in dimensions when a substance is magnetized
    C. Curie point
    D. magnetic properties near absolute zero

6. In a three-phase alternator, the armature is Y-connected and three terminals are brought out.
   If the voltage per armature phase is 200V, the line voltage is CLOSEST to which one of the following?

    A. 140V   B. 170V   C. 340V   D. 400V

7. If a charged capacitor loses one-half its charge by leakage, it has lost what fraction of its store of energy?

    A. 1/8   B. 1/4   C. 1/2   D. 3/4

8. An electrical current flows through an iron wire connected in series with another iron wire of equal length but one-half its cross-section area.
   If the voltage drop across the thicker wire is 8 volts, the drop across the thinner wire, in volts, is CLOSEST to

    A. 2   B. 4   C. 8   D. 16

9. Of the following connections, the one which may be used to convert a galvanometer into a voltmeter is that of a _____-ohm resistor in _____.

   A. .005; series
   B. .005; parallel
   C. 5000; series
   D. 5000; parallel

10. A pivoted compass needle placed directly beneath a horizontal wire carrying an electrical current will orient itself so that its

    A. long axis is parallel to the wire
    B. long axis is perpendicular to the wire
    C. north pole will point downward
    D. north pole will point upward

11. The element of an n-p-n transistor which is analogous to the grid of a vacuum tube is the

    A. base
    B. collector
    C. emitter
    D. suppressor

12. An example of a transducer is a

    A. transistor
    B. telephone transmitter
    C. transformer
    D. thermionic tube

13. In a parallel electrical circuit, the device with the LOWEST resistance has the

    A. least heating effect
    B. highest wattage
    C. lowest current
    D. lowest voltage drop

14. A device known as a transducer is used to convert

    A. AC to DC and back again
    B. a light beam into sound
    C. heat waves into sound pressure and back again
    D. sound pressure to electric signals and back again

15. Two resistances of 6 and 24 ohms are connected in series to a 120-volt source. The voltage drop across the 6 ohm resistor is

    A. 4   B. 18   C. 24   D. 96

16. Four capacitors, each of 10 microfarads capacity, are fully charged when connected in parallel.
    The TOTAL equivalent capacity of this combination, in microfarads, is

    A. 2.5   B. 10   C. 14   D. 40

17. The peak voltage of an alternating emf is 141 volts. The EFFECTIVE value of the voltage, in volts, is

    A. 70.5   B. 100   C. 141   D. 200

18. In a step-down transformer, the secondary winding is usually thicker than the primary winding because the secondary has the HIGHER

    A. current
    B. wattage
    C. voltage
    D. resistance

19. A 100-watt lamp is able to generate more light and heat than a 60-watt lamp because the 100-watt lamp

   A. draws less current
   B. is usually operated at a higher voltage
   C. usually uses a different filament material
   D. has less resistance

20. Three ideal components: a resistor, an inductor, and a capacitor, are connected in series to a source of AC. The potential difference across each component is 40 volts. The TOTAL voltage across the three components is

   A. zero B. $40\sqrt{2}V$ C. 40V D. 120V

21. The potential difference across a 6-ohm resistor is 6 volts. The power used by the resistor is, in watts,

   A. 6 B. 12 C. 18 D. 24

22. In a sinusoidal alternating current, the peak value of the current equals

   A. the effective value of the current
   B. 0.707 times the effective value of the current
   C. 1.41 times the effective value of the current
   D. 0.707 times the peak value of the emf divided by the resistance

23. Electrical resistance is equivalent to which one of the following?

   A. Work/charge
   B. Work • time/charge
   C. Work • time/charge^2
   D. Work • time/current

24. At 60 cycles per second, a coil has an inductive reactance of 100 ohms and a certain capacitor has a capacitive reactance of 400 ohms.
   At what frequency, in cy/sec, will the two devices have the SAME reactance?

   A. 30 B. 120 C. 180 D. 240

25. Which one of the following purposes may be served by a diode in a vacuum tube circuit?

   A. Amplifier
   B. Condenser
   C. Resistor
   D. Detector

26. In a series-wound motor, the current present in the armature winding is _____ is applied to the motor.

   A. DC even when AC
   B. DC when DC
   C. AC only when AC
   D. AC even when DC

27. The electromotive force, in volts, of 4 fresh similar dry cells connected in parallel, is usually CLOSEST to which one of the following?

   A. 1.5 B. 3 C. 4.5 D. 6

28. An alternating current generator differs from a direct current generator by having

   A. splip-rings
   B. brushes
   C. a split-ring commutator
   D. an armature

29. The GREATEST number of 100 watt lamps which can be connected in parallel in a 120 volt system without blowing a 10 ampere fuse is

    A. 12 B. 18 C. 24 D. 30

30. The construction of a direct current motor is basically the SAME as that of a(n)

    A. direct current generator
    B. alternating current motor
    C. alternating current generator
    D. ballistic galvanometer

31. A galvanometer may be used as an ammeter by

    A. shunting the galvanometer with a high resistance
    B. connecting a low resistance in parallel with the galvanometer
    C. connecting a low resistance in series
    D. connecting a high resistance in series

32. Resistances of 20 ohms and 60 ohms are connected in parallel to a generator. If the current in the 60 ohm resistance is 1 ampere, the current in the 20 ohm resistance will be _____ ampere(s).

    A. 1 B. 1/3 C. 2/3 D. 3

33. Direct current may be changed to alternating current by the use of a

    A. transformer   B. rectifier
    C. spark coil   D. diode

34. Iron and copper wires of equal lengths and cross-sections are connected in series. During the passage of current through the wires for a period of two minutes, the

    A. voltage drop across the copper will be larger than across the iron
    B. current through the copper will be greater than that through the iron
    C. current through the iron will be greater than that through the copper
    D. heat generated in the iron will be greater than that in the copper

35. If the current flowing through a given resistor is doubled, the amount of heat generated is multiplied by

    A. 1/2 B. 1 C. 2 D. 4

36. In wiring an electrical circuit, the laboratory assistant should make the *live* connection the _____ act in assembling and the _____ act in disassembling.

    A. last; first   B. first; first
    C. last; last   D. first; last

37. The electric current used in the school laboratory should be

    A. alternating and not direct
    B. direct and not alternating
    C. below 20 volts
    D. sent through a limiting load resistance

38. Which one of the following pairs of factors determines the direction of an induced electromotive force?
Direction of

   A. motion and direction of field
   B. motion and rate of rotation
   C. field and rate of rotation
   D. field and number of turns on coil

39. A rectifier is a device used to

   A. change direct current into alternating current
   B. increase the voltage
   C. filter out stray currents
   D. change alternating current to direct current

40. When a small quantity of a gas like mercury vapor is introduced into a diode, its net effect is to do which one of the following?

   A. Reduce plate current flow
   B. Increase the number of negative ions
   C. Increase the number of electrons reaching the plate
   D. Decrease the number of positive ions

41. The capacitive reactance of a circuit is increased by which one of the following?
A(n)

   A. increase in the frequency of the voltage
   B. decrease in the frequency of the voltage
   C. increase in the resistance of the circuit
   D. decrease in the resistance of the circuit

42. In an electrical circuit containing both inductance and capacitance, if the capacitance increases, the natural frequency of the circuit will

   A. increase
   B. decrease
   C. increase to a maximum then decrease
   D. remain constant

43. Of the following, the type of coupling in a radio circuit that is LEAST likely to introduce distortion is

   A. resistance   B. transformer
   C. impedance   D. capacitative

44. The function of the grid in a triode is to

   A. supply electrons
   B. control the plate current
   C. control the temperature of the tube
   D. control the plate voltage

45. The ESSENTIAL difference between an audio and a radio frequency transformer is the absence in the radio transformer of a(n)

    A. capacitor
    B. iron core
    C. quartz crystal
    D. transistor element

46. The PRINCIPAL effect of the space charge in a vacuum tube is to

    A. decrease the plate current
    B. increase the plate current
    C. increase the plate voltage
    D. increase the electron emission from the cathode

47. In the expression for induced emf, $V = \frac{-d\varnothing}{dt}$, the minus sign is a consequence of _____ Law.

    A. Coulomb's
    B. Biot-Savart
    C. Lenz's
    D. Faraday's

48. An oscillating circuit contains an inductance of 10uh, a capacitor of 5uf, and a capacitor of 25uf, all in parallel. The natural frequency of the circuit, in kilocycles/sec, is CLOSEST to which one of the following?

    A. 4.7   B. 9.2   C. 4,700   D. 9,200

49. During normal operation, AC is present in which one of the following?

    A. Armature winding of a DC motor
    B. Field winding of a DC motor
    C. Field winding of a DC generator
    D. Coil of a ballistic galvanometer

50. The emission of electrons from the surface of a heated conductor was FIRST observed by

    A. Fleming   B. Hertz   C. Armstrong   D. Edison

KEY (CORRECT ANSWERS)

1. B	11. A	21. A	31. B	41. B
2. A	12. B	22. C	32. D	42. B
3. B	13. B	23. C	33. C	43. A
4. B	14. D	24. B	34. D	44. B
5. B	15. C	25. D	35. D	45. B
6. C	16. D	26. D	36. A	46. A
7. D	17. B	27. A	37. D	47. C
8. D	18. A	28. A	38. A	48. B
9. C	19. D	29. A	39. D	49. A
10. B	20. C	30. A	40. C	50. D

TEST 2

DIRECTIONS: Each question or incomplete statement is followed by several suggested answers or completions. Select the one that BEST answers the question or completes the statement. *PRINT THE LETTER OF THE CORRECT ANSWER IN THE SPACE AT THE RIGHT.*

1. Lenz's Law states that the

   A. induced current is always equal in magnitude to the impressed current
   B. induced field has a direction opposite to that of the original field if this is decreasing
   C. induced field always has such direction as to aid the motion of a conductor moving in the field
   D. induced field has the same direction as the original if this is decreasing

   1.____

2. A long straight wire is in a magnetic field and, when the wire carries a current of 4 amp, the magnetic field exerts on it a force per unit length equal to K.
   If the current is changed to one amp and the magnetic flux density is doubled, the force per unit length is

   A. K/8   B. K/4   C. K/2   D. K

   2.____

3. In an AC series circuit, the inductive reactance, capacitive reactance, and resistance are 25 ohms each.
   When a 100 volt AC potential difference is applied, the current flow, in amperes, will equal

   A. 1.3   B. 4   C. 13   D. 2500

   3.____

4. The plate current in an electron tube is initially 10 milliamperes under certain conditions. When the plate voltage is increased by 10 volts, the plate current becomes 11 milliamperes. Under the same original conditions, an increase of grid voltage of 1 volt increases the plate current to 11 milliamperes.
   The amplification factor of the tube is then

   A. 0.1   B. 10   C. 100   D. 110

   4.____

5. To obtain the HIGHEST possible transformer efficiency, it would be desirable to have the

   A. turn ratio as high as possible
   B. input current low and output current high
   C. core made of solid copper
   D. hysteresis loop as narrow as possible

   5.____

6. If a capacitor, 10^{-4} farad capacity, and a 1 megohm resistor are connected in series to a 100 volt battery, the time constant, in seconds, for this circuit is

   A. 10^{-2} B. 10^{-1} C. 10^2 D. 10^4

   6.____

7. The impedance Z of an alternating current circuit is ALWAYS given by the formula Z =

   A. $2\pi fL$
   B. $1/2\pi fC$
   C. $2\pi fL - 1/2\pi fC$
   D. $\sqrt{R^2 + (2\pi fL - 1/2\pi fC)^2}$

   7.____

8. The transmission of an electric current through an electrolyte is done by means of

   A. electrons *only*
   B. positive and negative ions
   C. positive ions *only*
   D. positive ions and electrons

9. Of the following, a device which is ALWAYS connected in parallel in a circuit is a(n)

   A. ammeter   B. fuse   C. switch   D. voltmeter

10. A diode may be used as which one of the following?

    A. Amplifier
    B. Oscillator
    C. Rectifier
    D. Transformer

11. In an n-p-n transistor used as an amplifier, which one of the following is a NECESSARY connection?
    _____ side of battery _____.

    A. Negative; A to emitter
    B. Negative; B to collector
    C. Negative; A to base
    D. Positive; B to base

12. When two 4 ohm resistors are joined in series and connected to a power supply which consists of a 7 volt battery whose positive terminal is connected to that of a 9V battery, the current flow in the resistors is, in amperes, the two free terminals being connected to the resistors,

    A. 0.25   B. 1.0   C. 2.0   D. 8.0

13. A wattmeter, when properly connected in the circuit, is connected

    A. only in series
    B. only in parallel
    C. either in series or in parallel
    D. both in series and in parallel

14. When an incandescent lamp rated at 120V, 60W draws a current of 0.5 amp, the number of electrons/sec passing through the wire is

    A. $(0.5)(6.25 \times 10^{18})$
    B. $(0.5)(1.6 \times 10^{-19})$
    C. $(60)(0.5)(1.6 \times 10^{-19})$
    D. $(60)(0.5)(6.25 \times 10^{18})$

15. When a resistor and a capacitor are connected in series to a dry cell, at the instant of closing the circuit, the

    A. voltage across the resistor is zero
    B. voltage across the capacitor is at maximum
    C. charge on the capacitor is at maximum
    D. current in the circuit is at maximum

16. An electron and a proton are accelerated from rest through a potential difference of 1000 volts.
    As a result, the ratio of the kinetic energy of the proton to that of the electron is

    A. 1:1   B. 1840:1   C. 1:1840   D. 1000:1

17. If a uniform wire 10 feet long having a resistance of 1.0 ohm is cut into 10 equal pieces which are then connected in parallel with each other, the resistance of this parallel array, expressed in ohms, is

    A. 0.010   B. 0.10   C. 1.0   D. 10

18. When a 30 volt, 60-cycle AC source is connected to a 90-ohm resistor in series with a 50 uf capacitor and a 60 millihenry inductance, the impedance of the circuit, in ohms, is CLOSEST to which one of the following?

    A. 45   B. 70   C. 95   D. 120

19. When a 10 foot length of copper wire having a resistance of 2 ohms is drawn out, with uniform thickness, to a length of 30 feet, its resistance, in ohms, will be which one of the following?

    A. 2   B. 6   C. 12   D. 18

20. The force of attraction between two opposite electric charges is 24 dynes.
    If the positive charge is doubled, and the negative charge is halved, the force of attraction will be

    A. halved   B. unchanged
    C. doubled   D. quadrupled

21. Wire A has a resistance of 1,000 ohms.
    If wire B, which is of the same material as A and at the same temperature, is twice as long as A and has a cross-sectional area 5 times that of A, the resistance of B, in ohms, will be

    A. 100   B. 400   C. 2,500   D. 10,000

22. If a 1-HP electric motor draws 4 amp when operating from a 220-volt line, the efficiency of the motor, in percent, is CLOSEST to which one of the following?

    A. 65   B. 75   C. 85   D. 95

23. Which one of the following represents, in ohms, the resistance of a 1,000-watt DC electric heater drawing a current of 10 amp?

    A. 10   B. 100   C. 900   D. 10,000

24. If a 30-volt, 60-cycle AC source is connected to a circuit containing in series a 90-ohm resistor, a 50 uf capacitor, and a 60 millihenry inductance, the tangent of the phase angle is CLOSEST to which one of the following?

    A. .17   B. .34   C. .51   D. .68

25. A circuit containing an inductance of 320 uh and a capacitance of 80 uuf will have a resonant frequency, in c/sec, CLOSEST to which one of the following?

   A. 60   B. 1×10^3 C. 1×10^4 D. 1×10^6

26. If an electric iron whose resistance is 24 ohms draws 5 amperes, what heat energy will be produced, in joules, in one hour?

   A. 2.16×10^5 B. 5.18×10^5 C. 2.16×10^6 D. 5.18×10^6

27. A galvanometer having a resistance of 50 ohms reads full scale with a current of 1 milliampere.
   To convert the galvanometer to a 10-volt voltmeter requires a multiplier whose resistance, in ohms, is

   A. 9,500   B. 9,950   C. 10,000   D. 10,050

28. When three capacitors, 8, 10, and 40 uf, respectively, are connected in series to a 300-volt DC source, the combined capacitance in the circuit, in uf, is CLOSEST to which one of the following?

   A. 4   B. 5.14   C. 29   D. 58

29. In order for a 30-volt, 90-watt lamp to work properly when inserted in a 120-volt DC line, it should have in series with it a resistor whose resistance, in ohms, is

   A. 10   B. 20   C. 30   D. 40

30. The combined resistance of two resistors (R_1 and R_2) in parallel is given by which one of the following formulas?
   $R_T =$

   A. $\dfrac{R_1 + R_2}{R_1 R_2}$ B. $\dfrac{R_1 R_2}{R_1 + R_2}$ C. $\dfrac{2R_1}{R_1 + R_2}$ D. $\dfrac{2R_2}{R_1 + R_2}$

31. If an ordinary dry cell delivers 30 amp when shortcircuited, which one of the following is the internal resistance of the cell, in ohms?

   A. 0.033   B. 0.05   C. 0.066   D. 0.2

32. When a 60-watt, 120-volt incandescent lamp is connected in parallel with a 40-watt, 120-volt lamp, the combined resistance of the lamps, in ohms, is CLOSEST to which one of the following?

   A. 24   B. 144   C. 240   D. 360

33. The name plate on a certain motor gives the following information: 5hp, 230V, 18 amp, 1200 rpm.
   The efficiency of the motor should, therefore, be

   A. 80%   B. 85%   C. 90%   D. 95%

34. In an AC series circuit, there is an inductive reactance of 20 ohms, a capacitive reactance of 10 ohms, and a resistance of 5 ohms.
    The impedance to current flow, in ohms, in this circuit will be CLOSEST to which one of the following?

    A. 6 B. 11 C. 15 D. 35

35. When an inductance coil of 2.5 henrys is tuned to resonate at 100 cycles/sec, the capacitor should have a magnitude, in microfarads, CLOSEST to which one of the following?

    A. 0.5 B. 1.0 C. 10.0 D. 100.0

36. When a resistor, a coil, and a capacitor are connected in series to an AC generator, the current through the capacitor must be in phase with the voltage across the

    A. resistor
    B. coil
    C. capacitor
    D. whole circuit

37. If two adjacent parallel conductors free to move are placed within 1 cm of each other, and a 20 ampere direct current is sent through each in the same direction, the tendency of the conductors will be to

    A. move apart
    B. remain stationary
    C. come together
    D. rotate in either a clockwise or counter-clockwise direction

38. An electron beam is moving from left to right in a cathode ray tube.
    When a strong S pole is placed above the beam, the electron beam will be deflected

    A. toward the observer
    B. vertically upward
    C. away from the observer
    D. vertically downward

39. When a pear-shaped metallic shell is charged positively, the potential of the more pointed end is

    A. less than that of the opposite end
    B. greater than that of the opposite end
    C. the same as that of the opposite end
    D. less than that of the adjacent surface

40. When a parallel-plate capacitor is kept connected to a battery of constant emf, and the plates of the capacitor are moved further apart by the use of insulated handles, which one of the following occurs?
    The

    A. capacitance increases
    B. capacitance remains the same
    C. charge on the capacitor remains the same
    D. charge on the capacitor decreases

41. Voltage may be correctly expressed in which one of the following ways?

    A. Coulombs/elementary charge
    B. Coulombs/sec

C. Dynes/cm
D. Joules/elementary charge

42. In the half-wave power supply, the filter capacitor does which one of the following? It

    A. increases input voltage variation
    B. increases maximum voltage output
    C. reduces output voltage variation
    D. limits the input voltage

43. The term *effective current,* as used in sinusoidal AC circuits, means the SAME as the term _____ current.

    A. average
    B. root-mean-square
    C. peak
    D. instantaneous

44. When an AC generator produces its peak voltage of 160V, the instantaneous current flow, in amperes, in a 20 ohm resistance connected to it will be

    A. 4   B. 5.7   C. 8   D. 28.2

45. Of the following, the material with the HIGHEST resistivity is

    A. silver   B. copper   C. aluminum   D. nichrome

46. A 0-10 milliampere meter has a resistance of 20 ohms.
    To convert this meter to an ammeter with a range of 0-1 ampere, we should connect a resistance of

    A. approximately 2000 ohms in series
    B. approximately 2000 ohms in parallel
    C. 200 ohms in series
    D. 1/5 ohm in parallel

47. A 60 watt lamp and a 600 watt toaster are operating in parallel on a 120 volt circuit. The resistance ratio of lamp to toaster is

    A. 1/100   B. 1/10   C. 10/1   D. 100/1

48. When the secondary circuit of a transformer is completed, the current in the primary

    A. decreases
    B. remains the same
    C. increases
    D. increases or decreases, depending on the ratio of turns

49. The phase angle in an alternating current circuit is zero degrees when the circuit

    A. contains resistance *only*
    B. contains inductance *only*
    C. contains capacitance *only*
    D. is not closed

50. When a capacitor of 10 microfarads capacity is connected to a 100 volt current source, 50.____
    the charge acquired by the capacitor will have a magnitude, in coulombs, of

    A. 10^{-6} B. 10^{-4} C. 10^2 D. 10^3

KEY (CORRECT ANSWERS)

1. D	11. A	21. B	31. B	41. D
2. C	12. A	22. C	32. B	42. C
3. B	13. D	23. A	33. C	43. B
4. B	14. A	24. B	34. B	44. C
5. D	15. D	25. D	35. B	45. D
6. C	16. A	26. C	36. A	46. D
7. D	17. A	27. B	37. C	47. C
8. B	18. C	28. A	38. C	48. C
9. D	19. D	29. C	39. C	49. A
10. C	20. B	30. B	40. D	50. B

EXAMINATION SECTION
TEST 1

DIRECTIONS: Each question or incomplete statement is followed by several suggested answers or completions. Select the one that BEST answers the question or completes the statement. *PRINT THE LETTER OF THE CORRECT ANSWER IN THE SPACE AT THE RIGHT.*

1. Linseed oil putty would MOST likely be used to secure glass in _____ windows.   1.____

    A. steel casement B. aluminum jalousie
    C. wood double hung D. aluminum storm

2. Of the following, the one type of glass that should NOT be cut with the ordinary type glass cutter is _____ glass.   2.____

    A. safety B. plate C. wire D. herculite

3. Thermopane is made of two sheets of glass separated by   3.____

    A. a sheet of celluloid B. wire mesh
    C. an air space D. mica

4. Glass is NEVER cut so that it fits snugly inside the frame of a steel casement window. Of the following, the MAIN reason for allowing this space between the glass and the side of the frame is to   4.____

    A. prevent cracking of the glass in cold weather
    B. permit the glass to be lined up properly
    C. allow space for the putty
    D. eliminate the necessity of polishing the edges of the glass

5. Glass is held in steel sash by means of   5.____

    A. points B. clips C. plates D. blocks

6. When nailing felt to a roof, the nails should be driven through a   6.____

    A. tinned disc B. steel washer
    C. brass plate D. plastic bushing

7. An opening in a parapet wall for draining water from a roof is MOST often called a   7.____

    A. leader B. gutter C. downspout D. scupper

8. Roofing nails are usually   8.____

    A. brass B. cement coated
    C. galvanized D. nickel plated

9. A *street ell* is a fitting having   9.____

    A. male threads at both ends
    B. male threads at one end and female threads at the other end
    C. female threads at both ends
    D. male threads at one end and a solder connection at the other end

10. Of the following pieces of equipment, the one on which you would MOST likely find a safety (pop-off) valve is a(n)

    A. hot air furnace
    B. air conditioning compressor
    C. hot water heater
    D. dehumidifier

11. Compression fittings are MOST often used with

    A. cast iron bell and spigot pipe
    B. steel flange pipe
    C. copper tubing
    D. transite

12. Water hammer is BEST eliminated by

    A. increasing the size of all the piping
    B. installing an air chamber
    C. replacing the valve seats with neoprene gaskets
    D. flushing the system to remove corrosion

13. The BEST type of pipe to use in a gas line in a domestic installation is

    A. black iron   B. galvanized iron
    C. cast iron   D. wrought steel

14. If there is a pinhole in the float of a toilet tank, the

    A. water will flush continually
    B. toilet cannot flush
    C. tank cannot be filled with water
    D. valve will not shut off so water will overflow into the overflow tube

15. Condensation of moisture in humid weather occurs MOST often on _____ pipe(s).

    A. sewage   B. gas
    C. hot water   D. cold water

16. A gas appliance should be connected to a gas line by means of a(n)

    A. union   B. right and left coupling
    C. elbow   D. close nipple

17. A PRINCIPAL difference between a pipe thread and a machine thread is that the pipe thread is

    A. tapered   B. finer   C. flat   D. longer

18. When joining galvanized iron pipe, pipe joint compound is placed on

    A. the female threads only
    B. the male threads only
    C. both the male and female threads
    D. either the male or the female threads depending on the type of fitting

19. If moisture is trapped between the layers of a 3-ply roof, the heat of a summer day will   19._____

    A. dry the roof out
    B. cause blisters to be formed in the roofing
    C. rot the felt material
    D. have no effect on the roofing

20. Of the following, the metal MOST often used for leaders and gutters is   20._____

    A. monel   B. brass
    C. steel   D. galvanized iron

21. When drilling a small hole in sheet copper, the BEST practice is to   21._____

    A. make a dent with a center punch first
    B. put some cutting oil at the point you intend to drill
    C. use a slow speed drill to prevent overheating
    D. use an auger type bit

22. The reason for annealing sheet copper is to make it   22._____

    A. soft and easier to work
    B. more resistant to weather
    C. easier to solder
    D. harder and more resistant to blows

23. In draw filing,   23._____

    A. only the edge of the file is used
    B. a triangle file is generally used
    C. the file is pulled toward the mechanic's body in filing
    D. the file must have a safe edge

24. The type of paint that uses water as a thinner is   24._____

    A. enamel   B. latex   C. shellac   D. lacquer

25. The reason for placing a 6" sub-base of cinders under a concrete sidewalk is to   25._____

    A. provide flexibility in the surface
    B. permit drainage of water
    C. prevent chemicals in the soil from damaging the sidewalk
    D. allow room for the concrete to expand

26. The BEST material to use to lubricate a door lock is   26._____

    A. penetrating oil   B. pike oil
    C. graphite   D. light grease

27. Assume that the color of the flame from a gas stove is bright yellow.   27._____
    To correct this, you should

    A. close the air flap
    B. open the air flap
    C. increase the gas pressure
    D. increase the size of the gas opening

28. In a 110-220 volt three-wire circuit, the neutral wire is usually

   A. black   B. red   C. white   D. green

29. Brushes on fractional horsepower universal motors are MOST often made of

   A. flexible copper strands
   B. rigid carbon blocks
   C. thin wire strips
   D. collector rings

30. Leaks from the stem of a faucet can generally be stopped by replacing the

   A. bibb washer   B. seat   C. packing   D. gasket

31. Of the following, the BEST procedure to follow with a frozen water pipe is to

   A. allow the pipe to thaw out by itself as the weather gets warmer
   B. put anti-freeze into the pipe above the section that is frozen
   C. turn on the hot water heater
   D. open the faucet closest to the frozen pipe and warm the pipe with a blow torch, starting at this point

32. The one of the following that is NOT usually changed by a central air conditioning system is the

   A. volume of air in the system
   B. humidity of the air
   C. dust in the air
   D. air pressure of the system

33. The temperature of a domestic hot water system is MOST often controlled by a(n)

   A. relief valve   B. aquastat   C. barometer   D. thermostat

34. Draft in a chimney is MOST often controlled by a(n)

   A. damper
   B. gate
   C. orifice
   D. cross connection

35. Assume that a refrigerator motor operates continuously for excessively long periods of time.
   The FIRST item you should check to locate the defect is the

   A. plug in the outlet
   B. door gasket
   C. direction of rotation of the motor
   D. motor switch

36. Assume that after replacing a defective motor for a large electric fan, you find that the fan is rotating in the wrong direction.
   If the motor is a split phase motor, with the shaft at one end only, the trouble could be CORRECTED by

   A. reversing the fan on its shaft
   B. turning the motor end for end
   C. interchanging the connections on the field terminals of the motor
   D. reversing the plug in the electric outlet

37. In order to properly hang a door, shims are frequently inserted under the hinges. These shims are MOST often made of

   A. cardboard
   B. sheet steel
   C. bakelite
   D. the same materials as the hinges

38. Flooring nails are usually _____ nails.

   A. casing   B. common   C. cut   D. clinch

39. Over a doorway, to support brick, you will usually find

   A. steel angles
   B. hanger bolts
   C. wooden headers
   D. stirrups

40. Insulation of steam pipes is MOST often done with

   A. asbestos   B. celotex   C. alundum   D. sheathing

41. Assume that only the first few coils of a hot water convector used for heating a room are hot.
   To correct this, you should FIRST

   A. increase the water pressure
   B. increase the water temperature
   C. bleed the air out of the convector
   D. clean the convector pipes

42. The MAIN reason for grounding the outer sheel of an electric fixture is to

   A. provide additional support for the fixture
   B. reduce the cost of installation of the fixture
   C. provide a terminal to which the wires can be attached
   D. reduce the chance of electric shock

43. In woodwork, countersinking is MOST often done for

   A. lag screws
   B. carriage bolts
   C. hanger bolts
   D. flat head screws

44. Bridging is MOST often used in connection with

   A. door frames
   B. window openings
   C. floor joists
   D. stud walls

45. A saddle is part of a

   A. doorway
   B. window
   C. stair well
   D. bulkhead

46. To make it easier to drive screws into hard wood, it is BEST to 46.____

   A. use a screwdriver that is longer than that used for soft wood
   B. rub the threads of the screw on a bar of soap
   C. oil the screw threads
   D. use a square shank screwdriver assisted by a wrench

47. In using a doweled joint to make a repair of a wooden door, it is important to remember 47.____
   that the dowel

   A. hole must be smaller in diameter than the dowel so that there is a tight fit
   B. hole must be longer than the dowel to provide a room for excess glue
   C. must be of the same type of wood as the door frame
   D. must be held in place by a small screw while waiting for the glue to set

48. The edges of MOST finished wood flooring are 48.____

   A. tongue and groove   B. mortise and tenon
   C. bevel and miter   D. lap and scarf

49. For the SMOOTHEST finish, sanding of wood should be done 49.____

   A. in a circular direction
   B. diagonally against the grain
   C. across the grain
   D. parallel with the grain

50. To prevent splintering of wood when boring a hole through it, the BEST practice is to 50.____

   A. drill at a slow speed
   B. use a scrap piece to back up the work
   C. use an auger bit
   D. ease up the pressure on the drill when the drill is almost through the wood

---

KEY (CORRECT ANSWERS)

1. C	11. C	21. A	31. D	41. C
2. D	12. B	22. A	32. D	42. D
3. C	13. A	23. C	33. B	43. D
4. A	14. D	24. B	34. A	44. C
5. B	15. D	25. B	35. B	45. A
6. A	16. B	26. C	36. C	46. B
7. D	17. A	27. B	37. A	47. B
8. C	18. B	28. C	38. C	48. A
9. B	19. B	29. B	39. A	49. D
10. C	20. D	30. C	40. A	50. B

TEST 2

DIRECTIONS: Each question or incomplete statement is followed by several suggested answers or completions. Select the one that BEST answers the question or completes the statement. *PRINT THE LETTER OF THE CORRECT ANSWER IN THE SPACE AT THE RIGHT.*

1. A *speed nut* has

    A. no threads
    B. threads that are coarser than a standard nut
    C. threads that are finer than s standard nut
    D. fewer threads than a standard nut

2. The BEST tool to use to remove the burr and sharp edge resulting from cutting tubing with a tube cutter is a

    A. file B. scraper C. reamer D. knife

3. A router is used PRINCIPALLY to

    A. clean pipe
    B. cut grooves in wood
    C. bend electric conduit
    D. sharpen tools

4. The principle of operation of a sabre saw is MOST similar to that of a _____ saw

    A. circular B. radial C. swing D. jig

5. A full thread cutting set would have both taps and

    A. cutters B. bushings C. dies D. plugs

6. The proper flux to use for soldering electric wire connections is

    A. rosin
    B. killed acid
    C. borax
    D. zinc chloride

7. A fusestat differs from an ordinary plug fuse in that a fusestat has

    A. less current carrying capacity
    B. different size threads
    C. an aluminum shell instead of a copper shell
    D. no threads

8. A grounding type 120-volt receptacle differs from an ordinary electric receptacle MAINLY in that a grounding receptacle

    A. is larger than the ordinary receptacle
    B. has openings for a three prong plug
    C. can be used for larger machinery
    D. has a built-in circuit breaker

9. A carbide tip is MOST often found on a bit used for drilling

    A. concrete B. wood C. steel D. brass

10. The MAIN reason for using oil on an oilstone is to

    A. make the surface of the stone smoother
    B. prevent clogging of the pores of the stone
    C. reduce the number of times the stone has to be *dressed*
    D. prevent gouging of the stone's surface

11. The sum of the following numbers, 1 3/4, 3 1/6, 5 1/2, 6 5/8, and 9 1/4, is

    A. 26 1/8   B. 26 1/4   C. 26 1/2   D. 26 3/4

12. If a piece of plywood measures 5' 1 1/4" x 3' 2 1/2", the number of square feet in this board is MOST NEARLY

    A. 15.8   B. 16.1   C. 16.4   D. 16.7

13. Assume that in quantity purchases the city receives a discount of 33 1/3%.
    If a one gallon can of paint retails at $5.33 per gallon, the cost of 375 gallons of this paint is MOST NEARLY

    A. $1,332.50   B. $1,332.75   C. $1,333.00   D. $1,333.25

14. Assume that eight barrels of cement together weigh a total of 3004 lbs. and 12 oz.
    If there are four bags of cement per barrel, then the weight of one bag of cement is MOST NEARLY _____ lbs.

    A. 93.1   B. 93.5   C. 93.9   D. 94.3

15. Assume that one man cuts 50 nameplates per hour, whereas his co-worker cuts 55 nameplates per hour.
    At the end of 7 hours, the first man will have cut fewer nameplates than the second man by

    A. 9.3%   B. 9.5%   C. 9.7%   D. 9.9%

16. Under the same conditions, the one of the following that dries the FASTEST is

    A. shellac   B. varnish   C. enamel   D. lacquer

17. Interior wood trim in a building is MOST often made of

    A. hemlock   B. pine   C. cedar   D. oak

18. Gaskets are seldom made of

    A. rubber   B. lead   C. asbestos   D. vinyl

19. Toggle bolts are MOST frequently used to

    A. fasten shelf supports to a hollow block wall
    B. fasten furniture legs to table tops
    C. anchor machinery to a concrete floor
    D. join two pieces of sheet metal

20. Rubber will deteriorate FASTEST when it is constantly in contact with

    A. air   B. water   C. oil   D. soapsuds

21. Stoppage of water flow is often caused by dirt accumulating in an elbow.
    As used in the above sentence, the word accumulating means MOST NEARLY

    A. clogging   B. collecting   C. rusting   D. confined

22. The surface of the metal was embossed.
    As used in the above sentence, the word embossed means MOST NEARLY

    A. polished   B. rough   C. raised   D. painted

Questions 23-24.

DIRECTIONS: Questions 23 and 24 are to be answered in accordance with the following paragraph.

When fixing an upper sash cord, you must also remove the lower sash. To do this, the parting strip between the sash must be removed. Now remove the cover from the weight box channel, cut off the cord as before, and pull it over the pulleys. Pull your new cord over the pulleys and down into the channel, where it may be fastened to the weight. The cord for an upper sash is cut off 1" or 2" below the pulley with the weight resting on the floor of the pocket and the cord held taut. These measurements allow for slight stretching of the cord. When the cord is cut to length, it can be pulled up over the pulley and tied with a single common knot in the end to fit into the socket in the sash groove. If the knot protrudes beyond the face of the sash, tap it gently to flatten. In this way, it will not become frayed from constant rubbing against the groove.

23. When repairing the upper sash cord, the FIRST thing to do is to

    A. remove the lower sash
    B. cut the existing sash cord
    C. remove the parting strip
    D. measure the length of new cord necessary

24. According to the above paragraph, the rope may become frayed if the

    A. pulley is too small   B. knot sticks out
    C. cord is too long   D. weight is too heavy

25. In the repair of the sash cord mentioned in the paragraph for Questions 23 and 24, the MAIN reason for cutting off the sash cord below the bottom of the pulley is to

    A. prevent the cord from tangling
    B. save on amount of cord used
    C. prevent the sash weight from hitting the bottom of the frame in use
    D. provide room for tying the knot

26. Of the following drawings, the one that would be considered an *elevation* of a building is the

    A. floor plan   B. front view   C. cross section   D. site plan

27. On a plan, the symbol shown at the right USUALLY represents a(n)

    A. duplex receptacle   B. electric switch
    C. ceiling outlet   D. pull box

28. On a plan, the symbol _____ - _____ - USUALLY represents a

    A. center line
    B. hidden outline
    C. long break
    D. dimension line

29. Assume that on a plan you see the following: 1/4" - 20 NC-2. This refers to the

    A. diameter of a hole
    B. size and type of screw thread
    C. taper of a pin
    D. scale at which the plan is drawn

30.

    In reference to the above sketch, the length of the diagonal part of the plate indicated by the question mark is MOST NEARLY

    A. 13"   B. 14"   C. 15"   D. 16"

31. To increase the workability of concrete without changing its strength, the BEST procedure to follow is to increase the percentage of

    A. water
    B. cement and sand
    C. cement and water
    D. water and sand

32. The MAIN reason for covering freshly poured concrete with tar paper is to

    A. prevent evaporation of water
    B. stop people from walking on the concrete
    C. protect the concrete from rain
    D. keep back any earth that may fall on the concrete

33. The MAIN reason for using air-entrained cement in sidewalks is to

    A. protect the concrete from the effects of freezing
    B. color the concrete
    C. speed up the setting time of the concrete
    D. make the concrete more workable

34. Assume that a reinforcing bar used for concrete is badly rusted. Before using this bar,

    A. it is not necessary to remove any rust
    B. only loose rust need be removed
    C. all rust should be removed
    D. all rust should be removed and a coat of red lead paint is applied

35. Assume that freshly poured concrete has been exposed to freezing temperatures for 6 hours.
    In all likelihood, this concrete

    A. has been permanently damaged
    B. will harden properly as soon as the air temperature warms up
    C. will harden properly even though the temperature remains below freezing
    D. will eventually harden properly, but it will take much longer than usual

36. Assume that concrete for a floor in a play yard is to be placed directly on the earth. On checking, you find that, because of a recent rain, the earth is damp.
    You should

    A. wait till the sun dries the earth before placing the concrete
    B. use a waterproofing material between the concrete slab and the earth
    C. use less water in the concrete mix
    D. ignore the damp earth and place the concrete as you normally would

37. The MAJOR disadvantage of *floating* the surface of concrete too much is that the

    A. surface will become too rough
    B. surface will become weak and will wear rapidly
    C. initial set will be disturbed
    D. concrete cannot be cured properly

38. In addition to water and sand, mortar mix for a cinder block wall is usually made of

    A. gravel and lime
    B. plaster and cement
    C. gravel and cement
    D. lime and cement

39. The *nominal* size of a standard cinder block is

    A. 8" x 6" x 16"
    B. 8" x 8" x 16"
    C. 8" x 12" x 12"
    D. 6" x 8" x 12"

40. The *bond* of a brick wall refers to the

    A. arrangement of headers and stretchers
    B. time it takes for the mortar to set
    C. way a brick wall is tied in to an intersecting wall
    D. type of mortar used in the wall

41. The purpose of *tooling* when erecting a brick wall is to

    A. cut the brick to fit into a small space
    B. insure that the brick is laid level
    C. compact the mortar at the joints
    D. hold the brick in place till the mortar sets

42. Mortar is BEST cleaned off the face of a brick wall by using

   A. muriatic acid
   B. lye
   C. oxalic acid
   D. sodium hypochlorite

43. A brick wall is *pointed* to

   A. make sure it is the correct height
   B. repair the mortar joints
   C. set the brick in place
   D. arrange the mortar bed before setting the brick

44. The second coat in a three-coat plaster job is the _____ coat.

   A. scratch
   B. brown
   C. putty
   D. lime

45. To repair fine cracks in a plastered wall, the PROPER material to use is

   A. lime
   B. cement wash
   C. perlite
   D. spackle

46. Gypsum lath for plastering is purchased in

   A. strips 5/16" x 1 1/2" x 4'
   B. rolls 3/8" x 48" x 96"
   C. boards 1/2" x 16" x 48"
   D. sheets 5/16" x 27" x 96"

47. The PRINCIPAL reason for using acoustic tile instead of ordinary tile is that the acoustic tile

   A. deadens sound
   B. is easier to apply
   C. is longer lasting
   D. costs less

48. The MAXIMUM thickness of the finish coat of white plaster is MOST NEARLY

   A. 1/8"
   B. 1/4"
   C. 3/8"
   D. 1/2"

49. When using tape to conceal joints in dry wall construction, the FIRST operation is

   A. channelling the grooves between boards
   B. applying cement to the joints
   C. sanding the edges of the joints
   D. packing the tape into the joints

50. For the FIRST coat of plaster on wire lath, plaster of paris is mixed with

   A. cement
   B. sand
   C. lime
   D. mortar

KEY (CORRECT ANSWERS)

1. A	11. B	21. B	31. C	41. C
2. C	12. C	22. C	32. A	42. A
3. B	13. A	23. C	33. A	43. B
4. D	14. C	24. B	34. B	44. B
5. C	15. D	25. C	35. A	45. D
6. A	16. D	26. B	36. D	46. C
7. B	17. B	27. C	37. B	47. A
8. B	18. D	28. A	38. D	48. A
9. A	19. A	29. B	39. B	49. B
10. B	20. C	30. A	40. A	50. B

EXAMINATION SECTION
TEST 1

DIRECTIONS: Each question or incomplete statement is followed by several suggested answers or completions. Select the one that BEST answers the question or completes the statement. *PRINT THE LETTER OF THE CORRECT ANSWER IN THE SPACE AT THE RIGHT.*

1. When assembling a piece of equipment which has been disassembled, a part which can *usually* be re-used is a   1.____

   A. gasket
   B. flat washer
   C. cotter pin
   D. lock washer

2. An offset screwdriver is MOST useful for turning a wood screw when   2.____

   A. a strong force needs to be applied
   B. the screw head is marred
   C. space is limited
   D. speed is desired

3. The plug of a portable tool should be removed from a receptacle by grasping the plug, and NOT by pulling on the cord, because   3.____

   A. the plug is easier to grip than the cord
   B. pulling on the cord may allow the plug to fall on the floor and break
   C. the plug is generally better insulated than the cord
   D. pulling on the cord may break the wires off the plug

4. Of the following orders for tools or materials used in the building trades, the one which is INCOMPLETE is   4.____

   A. 1 paintbrush, flat, 2 in. wide
   B. 1 drill, twist, straight shank, high speed, 3/8 in.
   C. 1 snake, steel, 3/4 in. wide by 1/8 in. thick
   D. 1 keg of nails, 10 penny, common wire, galvanized

5. The tool that is *generally* used to slightly elongate a round hole in strap-iron is a   5.____

   A. rat-tail file
   B. reamer
   C. drill
   D. rasp

6. If a fellow worker has stopped breathing after an electric shock, the BEST first-aid treatment is   6.____

   A. artificial respiration
   B. to massage his chest
   C. an application of cold compresses
   D. a hot drink

7. Lumber used in certain types of outdoor construction work is treated with creosote before being used. The creosote serves to   7.____

   A. decrease the rusting of the nails used for fastening
   B. prevent the lumber from checking or peeling

C. act as a good undercoat for paint
D. prevent the lumber from rotting

8. Drilling must be done with special care when using any one of the very small sizes of twist drills because the

   A. drill is apt to break
   B. drill is apt to overheat
   C. cut material will clog the drill
   D. drill speed may be too fast

9. The BEST way to locate a point on the floor directly below a given point on the ceiling is by using a

   A. plumber's snake   B. plumb bob
   C. flashlight   D. chalk line

10. When the term "10-24" is used to specify a machine screw, the number 24 refers to the

    A. number of screws per pound
    B. diameter of the screw
    C. length of the screw
    D. number of threads per inch

11. In the run of piping, the dimension marked "X" is
    A. 19"
    B. 11"
    C. 9"
    D. 5"

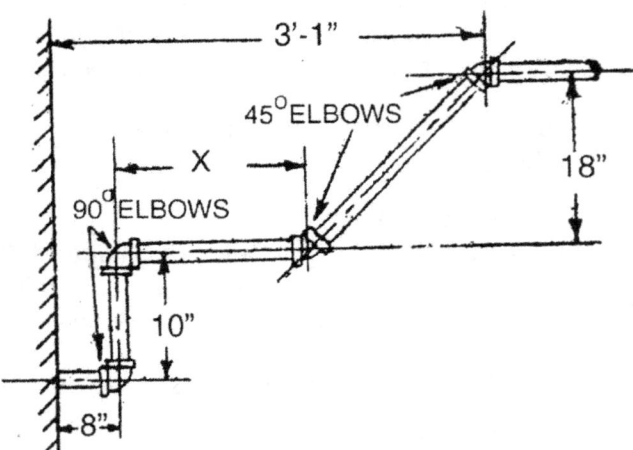

12. The *approximate* dimensions of a common brick are as shown. The volume of the brick (in cubic feet) is
    A. 64
    B. 5 1/3
    C. 4/9
    D. 1/27

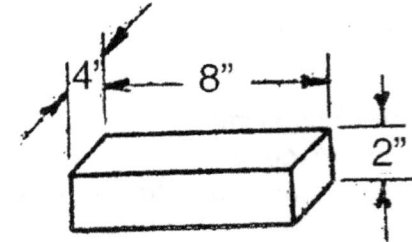

13. If the shaded portion is cut from the plate shown, the area (in square inches) of the remaining portion is
    A. 26
    B. 29
    C. 32
    D. 58

14. A nut is shown with a wrench placed on it in positions 1 and 2. The numbered arrows show the directions of forces applied to the wrench to turn it. In order to tighten the nut, the CORRECT combination of wrench position and direction of applied force is
    A. 1-3
    B. 1-4
    C. 2-5
    D. 2-6

15. Shown is an open-top round tin container. In order to make the container so that the metal used for the bottom area (πR^2) is equal to the metal used for the cylindrical side area ($2\pi Rh$), the radius R must be equal to
    A. 1/2"
    B. 1"
    C. 2"
    D. 4"

16. Tools used in maintenance work should ALWAYS be kept in good condition because
    A. a good job can never be done without perfect tools
    B. tools that are in good condition require no care
    C. defective tools may cause accidents or damage
    D. good tools are less easily lost

17. If you are assigned by your foreman to a job which you do NOT understand, you should
    A. try to do the job because you learn from experience
    B. explain and request further instructions from your foreman
    C. do the job to the best of your ability as that is all that can be expected
    D. ask a more experienced helper how to proceed with the job

18. When wooden forms used in concrete work are taken down, the nails in the lumber which is saved for future use are removed rather than bent over and clinched. The purpose of this procedure is to

A. prevent the old nails from being unbent and used again
B. prevent the possible staining of the concrete by contact with rusty nails
C. avoid damage to the saw if the lumber is cut
D. permit future use of the same nail holes

19. Twist drills ranging in size from 5/16" to 1/2" and having 1/4" shanks are available for use in electric drills. These drills are designed in this manner so that they may be used

   A. in 1/4" electric drills for high speed drilling of steel
   B. in 1/4" electric drills for drilling wood
   C. when it is important that, if the twist drill breaks, it does not do so in the hole being drilled
   D. in 1/2" electric drills in order to increase the peripheral speed of the twist drill

20. The wrench is shown in position to unloosen a tight nut. If the hand is placed on the wrench at A, the force necessary to start the nut as compared to the force necessary if the hand were placed at B would be

   A. 150%
   B. 110%
   C. 85%
   D. 70%

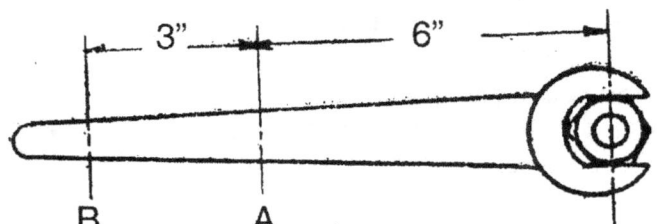

21. With the valve closed, each of the two identical tanks holds water in the amount shown. If the valve is opened, the amount of water (in gallons) in tanks X and Y after flow has stopped will be, respectively,

   A. 6000-5000
   B. 5500-5500
   C. 5000-6000
   D. 3500-7500

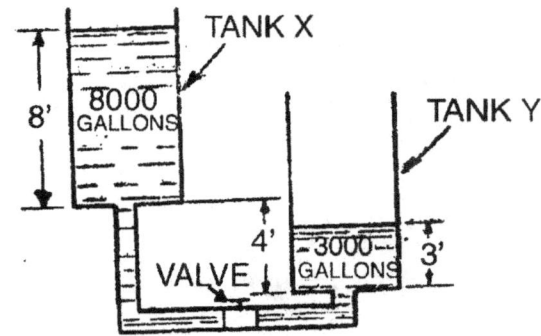

22. If the windlass shown is turned clockwise by means of the crank and handle at a rate of 35 revolutions per minute, the weight will rise at a rate of _____ ft. per minute.

   A. 65
   B. 110
   C. 235
   D. 480

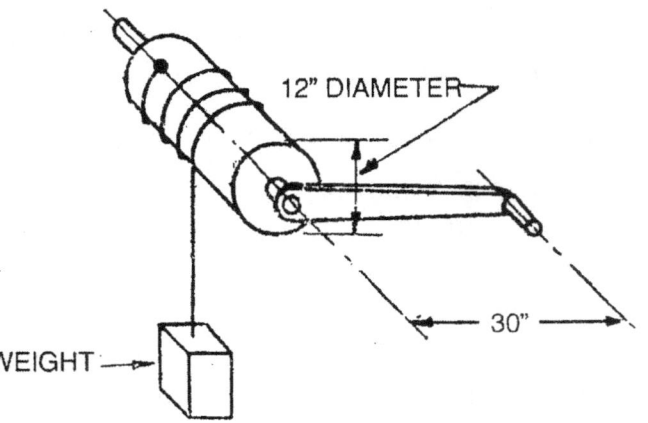

23. In order to have the two stringlines perpendicular to each other, the distance "X" on the tape must be _____ ft.
    A. 21
    B. 16
    C. 15
    D. 14

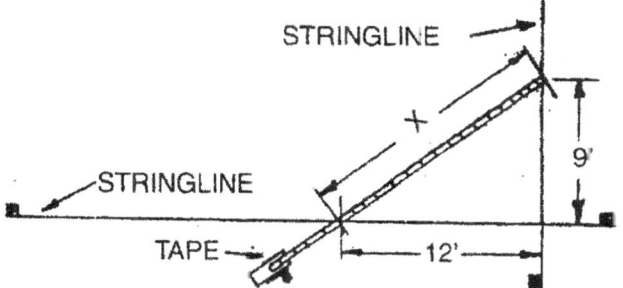

24. The dimension "X" on the plate is
    A. 1 7/8"
    B. 2 1/8"
    C. 2 1/4"
    D. 2 3/8"

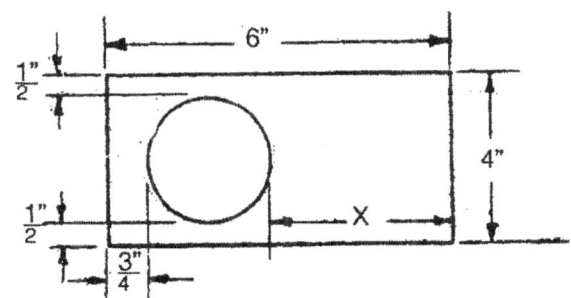

QUESTIONS 25-30.

Questions 25-30 inclusive in Column I are structural materials each of which would be ordered by using one of the quantity-terms listed in Column II. For each material in Column I, select the appropriate quantity-term from Column II. PRINT on your answer sheet, in the correspondingly numbered item space, the letter given beside your selected quantity-term.

	Column I (structural materials)	Column II (quantity-term)
25.	sandpaper	A. cartons
26.	paint	B. feet
27.	cinders	C. pounds
28.	sash cord	D. bags
29.	cement	E. gallons
30.	nails	H. rolls
		J. square feet
		K. cubic yards
		L. sheets

KEY (CORRECT ANSWERS)

1. B
2. C
3. D
4. C
5. A

6. A
7. D
8. A
9. B
10. D

11. B
12. D
13. C
14. D
15. D

16. C
17. B
18. C
19. B
20. A

21. D
22. B
23. C
24. C
25. L

26. E
27. K
28. B
29. D
30. C

TEST 2

DIRECTIONS: Each question or incomplete statement is followed by several suggested answers or completions. Select the one that BEST answers the question or completes the Statement. *PRINT THE LETTER OF THE CORRECT ANSWER IN THE SPACE AT THE RIGHT.*

QUESTIONS 1-10.

Questions 1-10 inclusive in Column I are materials each of which is commonly identified for size by one of the terms listed in Column II. For each material in Column I, select the appropriate size-term from Column II. Print in the correspondingly numbered item space the letter given beside your selected size-term.

<u>Column I</u>
(materials)

<u>Column II</u>
(size terms)

1. strap iron
2. manila rope
3. steel wool
4. carriage bolts
5. steel sheets
6. plywood panels
7. copper tacks
8. wood screws
9. cement blocks
10. pipe reducer

A. 20 gauge
B. 3/4"
C. 1/2" x 6"
D. 8" x 8" x 16"
E. 1/8" x 2 1/2"
H. #8 x 3/4"
J. No. 6
K. 3/4" x 1/2"
L. 4' x 4' x 3/4"
M. #00

1.____
2.____
3.____
4.____
5.____
6.____
7.____
8.____
9.____
10.____

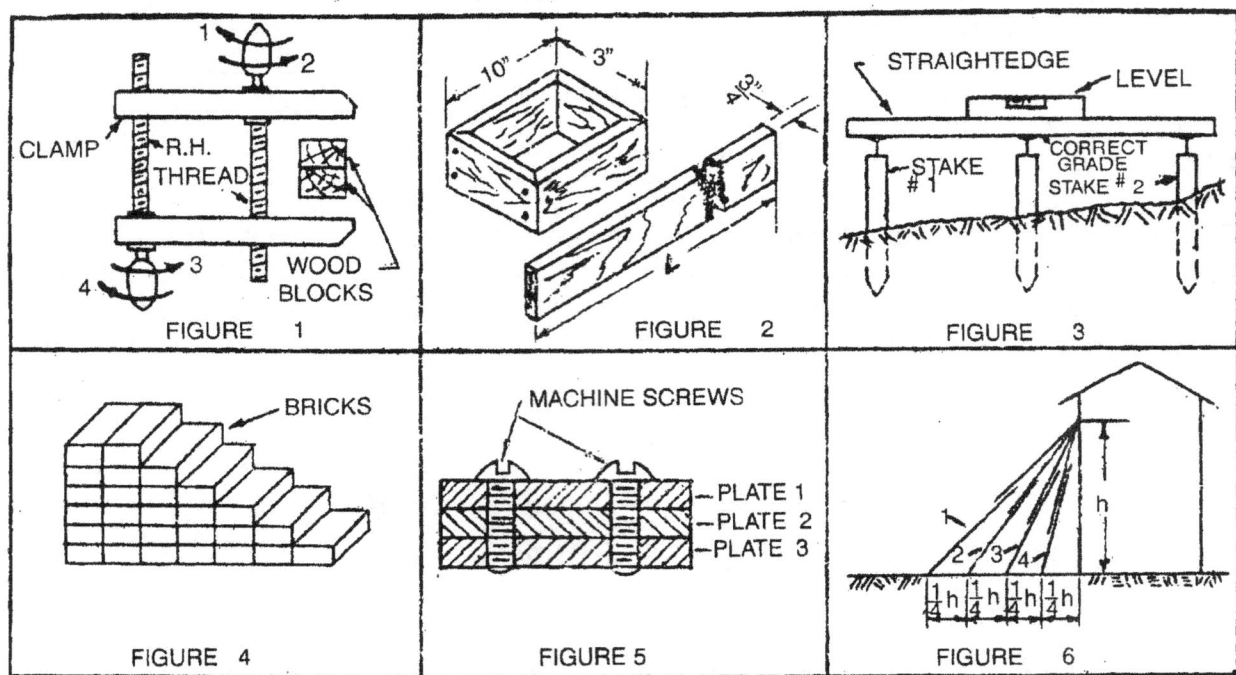

QUESTIONS 11-16.

Questions 11-16 inclusive refer to the figures above.

11. In Figure 1, in order to press together the two wood blocks, the handles of the clamp should be turned in the directions

    A. 1-3 B. 1-4 C. 2-3 D. 2-4

12. In order to make the form shown in Figure 2 from the board also shown, the length "L" of the board (making allowance for 1/8" saw-cuts) should NOT be LESS than

    A. 32 1/2" B. 34 1/2" C. 35 1/2" D. 38 1/2"

13. In Figure 3, in order to obtain the correct grade at stakes #1 and #2, it will be necessary to LOWER the nail in stake

    A. #1
    B. #2
    C. #1 and RAISE the nail in stake #2
    D. #2 and RAISE the nail in stake #1

14. In Figure 4, in order to rearrange the bricks shown into the LEAST number of equal piles, the number of bricks required to be moved is

    A. 11 B. 10 C. 9 D. 8

15. To fasten the three metal plates in Figure 5 together with machine screws as shown, the *proper* method is to tap

    A. all three plates
    B. plate 3 *only*
    C. plates 2 and 3 *only*
    D. plates 1 and 3 *only*

16. In Figure 6, the extension ladder is shown placed in four different positions against the side of a house. The CORRECT position is   16._____

   A. 1   B. 2   C. 3   D. 4

17. The width (in inches) of each of the identical slots in the plate is   17._____
    A. 1/4
    B. 3/16
    C. 1/8
    D. 1/16

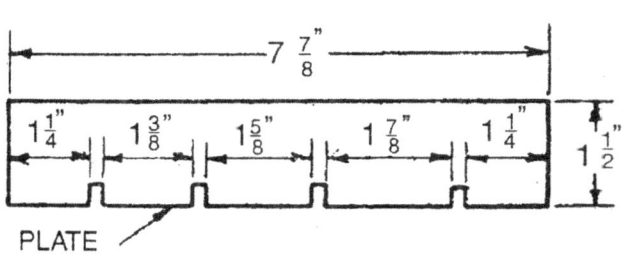

18. The number of feet of wire fencing needed to enclose the area shown is   18._____
    A. 100
    B. 140
    C. 150
    D. 170

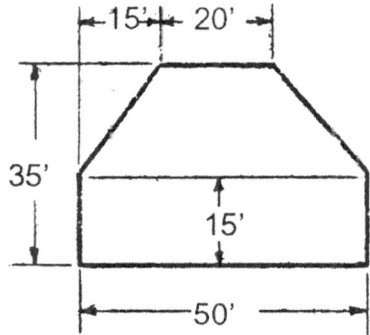

19. To bring the level of the water in the two open-top tanks down to a height of 6 inches, the quantity of water to be removed by opening the valve is _____ gallons.   19._____
    A. 10 1/2
    B. 9
    C. 7 1/2
    D. 6

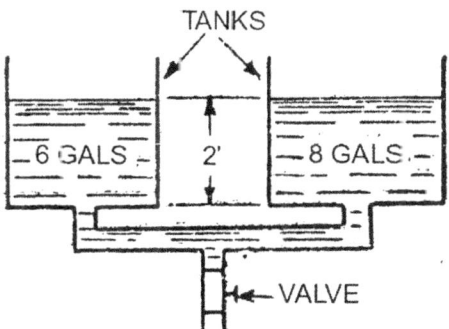

20. If concrete weighs 150 lbs. per cubic foot, the weight of the concrete manhole shown (open top and bottom) is   20._____
    A. between 1/2 ton and 1 ton
    B. exactly 1 ton
    C. between 1 ton and 1 1/2 tons
    D. exactly 2 tons

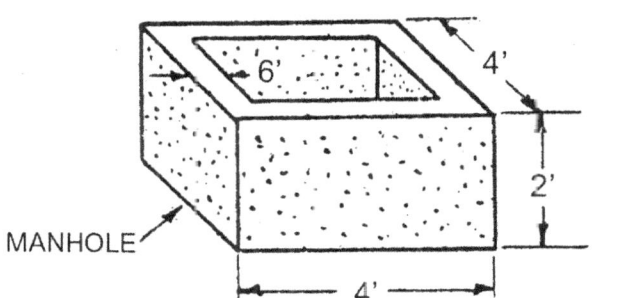

21. The MAXIMUM number of gaskets shown which can be cut from the gasket material as shown is
    A. 19
    B. 60
    C. 135
    D. 270

22. A desirable quality of a concrete foundation wall is a smooth, even surface. To obtain this result, the
    A. faces, of the forms must be oiled before the concrete is placed
    B. concrete must be worked next to the form faces with a spading tool
    C. forms must be made of plywood
    D. concrete placed at the form faces must contain more water than the concrete placed in the center of the forms

23. Galvanized pipe is used on many plumbing installations instead of plain pipe in order to
    A. retard corrosion
    B. reduce sweating of the pipe
    C. add mechanical strength
    D. prevent the pipe from freezing in cold weather

24. Tarred roofing materials are NOT recommended for steep sloping roofs because of the
    A. difficulty of applying the tar
    B. impossibility of keeping the roofing felts lined up until the tar sets
    C. hazardous condition caused by the slippery surface
    D. tendency of the tar to run down in hot weather

25. If a hand saw becomes worn so that the teeth are no longer properly set, the
    A. blade will lose its temper
    B. saw will not cut straight
    C. cut will have jagged edges
    D. blade will tend to bind in the cut

26. Many portable electric power tools, such as electric drills, have a third conductor in the power lead which is used to connect the case of the tool to a grounded part of the electric outlet. The reason for this extra conductor is to
    A. have a spare wire in case one power wire should break
    B. strengthen the power lead so it cannot easily be damaged
    C. prevent the user of the tool from being shocked
    D. enable the tool to be used for long periods of time without overheating

27. When the foot of an extension ladder, placed against a high wall, rests on a sidewalk or another such similar surface, it is advisable to tie a rope between the bottom rung of the ladder and a point on the wall opposite this rung. This is done to prevent
    A. people from walking under the ladder
    B. another worker from removing the ladder

C. the ladder from vibrating when ascending or descending
D. the foot of the ladder from slipping

28. If you were unable to tighten a nut by means of a ratchet wrench because, although the nut turned on with the forward movement of the wrench, it turned off with the backward movement, you should

   A. make the nut hand-tight before using the wrench
   B. reverse the ratchet action
   C. put a few drops of oil on the wrench
   D. use a different socket in the handle

29. If you were installing a long wood screw and found you were unable to drive this screw more than three-quarters of its length by the use of a properly-fitting straight-handled screwdriver, the PROPER subsequent action would be for you to

   A. take out the screw and put soap on it
   B. change to the use of a screwdriver-bit and brace
   C. take out the screw and drill a deeper hole before re-driving
   D. use a pair of pliers on the blade of the screwdriver

30. Good practice requires that the end of a pipe to be installed in a plumbing system be reamed to remove the inside burr after it has been cut to length to

   A. restore the original inside diameter of the pipe at the end
   B. remove loose rust
   C. make the threading of the pipe easier
   D. finish the pipe accurately to length

KEY (CORRECT ANSWERS)

1.	E	16.	D
2.	B	17.	C
3.	M	18.	C
4.	C	19.	A
5.	A	20.	C
6.	L	21.	B
7.	J	22.	B
8.	H	23.	A
9.	D	24.	D
10.	K	25.	D
11.	A	26.	C
12.	B	27.	D
13.	C	28.	A
14.	B	29.	A/C
15.	B	30.	A

TEST 3

DIRECTIONS: Each question or incomplete statement is followed by several suggested answers or completions. Select the one that BEST answers the question or completes the statement. *PRINT THE LETTER OF THE CORRECT ANSWER IN THE SPACE AT THE RIGHT.*

1. When laying tongue and groove flooring, each piece is laid with the tongue to the front and the groove fitted to the tongue of the previously laid piece. In order to make this a tight fit before nailing into place, it is GOOD practice when laying each piece to

    A. temporarily toe-nail through its tongue to draw it up tight
    B. fit a small piece of scrap flooring to it and strike the scrap piece
    C. strike it only on the middle of the tongue
    D. pull it into place using a chisel as a pry bar

    1.____

2. In construction work, *almost all* accidents can be blamed on the

    A. failure of an individual to give close attention to the job assigned to him
    B. use of improper tools
    C. lack of cooperation among the men in a gang
    D. fact that an incompetent man was placed in a key position

    2.____

3. If it is necessary for you to do some work with your hands under a piece of heavy equipment, while a fellow worker lifts up and holds one end of it by means of a pinch bar, one IMPORTANT precaution you should take is to

    A. wear gloves
    B. watch the bar to be ready if it slips
    C. insert a temporary block to support the piece
    D. work as fast as possible

    3.____

4. Protective goggles should NOT be worn when

    A. standing on a ladder drilling a steel beam
    B. descending a ladder after completing a job
    C. chipping concrete near a third rail
    D. sharpening a cold chisel on a grinding stone

    4.____

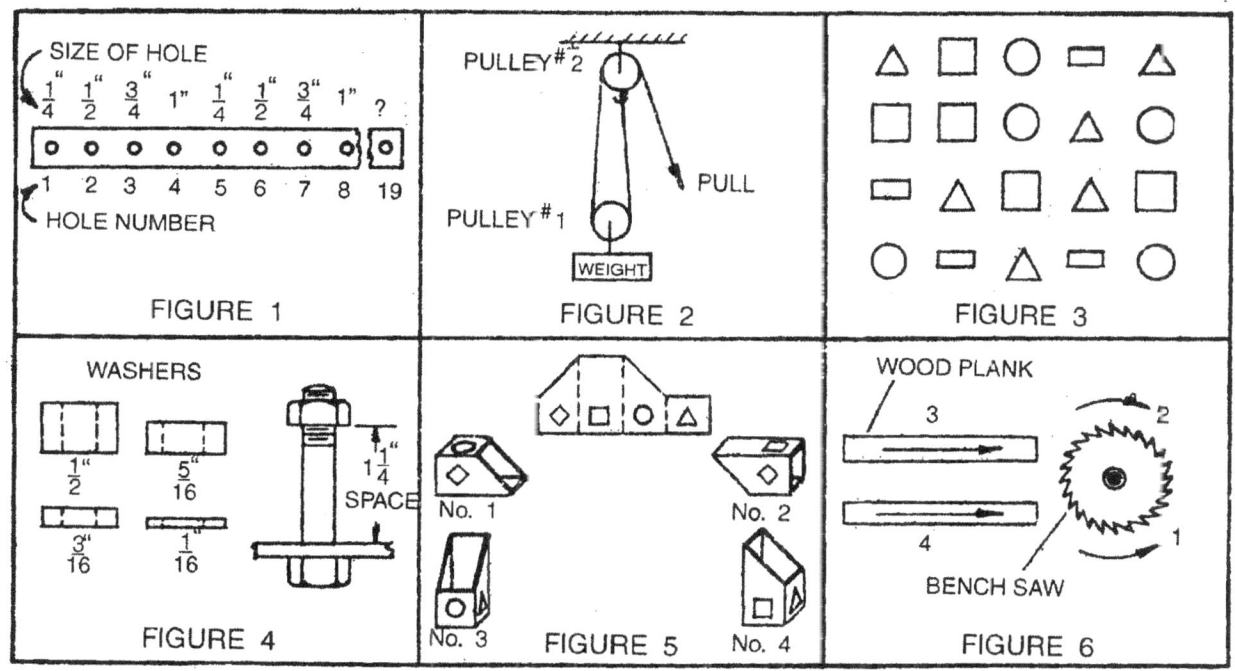

QUESTIONS 5-10.

Questions 5-10 inclusive refer to the figures above.

5. If the holes shown in Figure 1 continue in the same pattern along the entire strip, the 19th hole would be

   A. 1/4" B. 1/2" C. 3/4" D. 1"

6. In Figure 2, the block and tackle shown has two pulleys of equal diameter. While the weight is being raised, pulley #2 will rotate at _____ the speed of pulley #1.

   A. twice B. one time C. one-half D. one-third

7. Figure 3 shows four basic shapes. The shapes appearing the MOST number of times is

   A. A B. B C. C D. D

8. In figure 4, using only the sizes of washers shown, the LEAST number of washers needed to *exactly* fill the 1 1/4" space is

   A. 7 B. 6 C. 4 D. 2

9. The flat cut sheet in Figure 5, with cut-outs as shown, can be bent along the dotted lines to make one of the shapes shown. The resulting shape is No.

   A. 1 B. 2 C. 3 D. 4

10. Figure 6 shows a bench saw with directions of rotation 1 and 2, and a plank ready for cutting in positions 3 and 4. The *proper* combination of rotation and position is

    A. 1 and 3 B. 1 and 4 C. 2 and 3 D. 2 and 4

11. In preparing to raise a steel beam to position during steel erection, the man placing the slings puts only one sling near the center of the beam rather than a sling at each end. This procedure is

   A. *poor* because of the possibility of the beam slipping through the one sling
   B. *good* because it allows the beam to be tilted at the ends for necessary maneuvering
   C. *poor* because the safeguards against sling breakage is cut in half
   D. *good* because the one sling can be placed faster than the two

12. The wrench that would prove LEAST useful in uncoupling several pieces of pipe is a _____ wrench.

   A. socket   B. chain   C. strap   D. stillson

13. Concrete (a mixture of cement, sand and coarse aggregate), if made from 1 part of one material, 3 parts of a second material and 5 parts of the remaining material, is known as 1:3:5 concrete. It would be LOGICAL to conclude that the parts would be

   A. 1 cement, 3 coarse aggregate, 5 sand
   B. 1 coarse aggregate, 3 cement, 5 sand
   C. 1 sand, 3 coarse aggregate, 5 cement
   D. 1 cement, 3 sand, 5 coarse aggregate

14. Gaskets are commonly used between the flanges of large pipe joints to

   A. provide space for assembly
   B. take up expansion and contraction
   C. prevent the flanges from rusting together
   D. make a tight connection

15. If you do NOT understand the operation of some special tool which is used in your work, your BEST procedure would be to

   A. study up on its operation at home
   B. ask a maintainer to explain its operation
   C. ask another helper to explain its operation
   D. bother nobody and expect to pick up a little more knowledge each time you use the tool

16. The number of board feet in a piece of lumber is equal to the cross-sectional area in square inches divided by 12 and multiplied by the length of the piece in feet. Therefore, among four different pieces of lumber of equal length, the GREATEST number of board feet would be in the piece whose other two dimensions are

   A. 1" x 12"   B. 2" x 10"   C. 3" x 8"   D. 4" x 4"

17. When sandpapering wood by hand, the sanding should be done

   A. with the grain   B. across the grain
   C. diagonally to the grain D. with a circular motion

18. A drift pin is used to

   A. line up holes   B. set nails
   C. enlarge holes   D. keep a nut from turning

19. Holes are *usually* countersunk when installing

    A. carriage bolts
    B. lag screws
    C. flat-head screws
    D. square nuts

20. Of the following, the tool that is LEAST easily broken is a

    A. file
    B. pry bar
    C. folding rule
    D. hacksaw blade

21. A hacksaw blade having 32 teeth to the inch is the BEST blade to use when cutting

    A. cold rolled steel shafting
    B. wrought iron pipe
    C. stainless steel plate
    D. copper tubing

22. The joints in long vertical supporting timbers of wooden scaffolds are made with the timbers butted, rather than lapped, *principally* because this results in

    A. better appearance
    B. more resistance to the weather
    C. lighter timbers
    D. less strain on the nails

23. Practically all valves used in plumbing work are made so that the hand wheel is turned clockwise instead of counterclockwise to close the valve. The *probable* reason is that

    A. the hand wheel is less likely to loosen
    B. it is easier to remember since screws and nuts move inward when turned clockwise
    C. greater force can be exerted
    D. most poeple are right handed

24. The transit authority gives some of its maintenance employees instruction in first aid. The MOST likely reason for doing this is to

    A. eliminate the need for calling a doctor in case of accident
    B. reduce the number of accidents
    C. lower the cost of accidents to the transit authority
    D. provide temporary first aid

25. Wooden platforms on elevated stations are built of 2" x 6" planks with a small opening between the planks. The purpose of this construction is to

    A. provide for drainage
    B. create a more attractive design
    C. provide a non-slip surface
    D. use less lumber for a given area

26. In order to determine the exact location of a leak in an air hose from a portable compressor, you should

    A. paint the suspected area with soap suds
    B. test with a lighted match

C. cut fine strips of paper and hold them near the location
D. hold your ear close to the hose

27. After No. 20, the next smaller twist drill size is No.

   A. 18   B. 19   C. 21   D. 22

28. If you had to telephone for an ambulance because of an accident, the MOST important information for you to give the person who answered the telephone would be the

   A. exact time of the accident
   B. place where the ambulance is needed
   C. cause of the accident
   D. names and addresses of those injured

29. Good practice dictates that an adjustable open-end wrench should be used *primarily* when the

   A. nut to be turned is soft and must not be scored
   B. extra leverage is needed
   C. proper size of fixed wrench is not available
   D. location is cramped permitting only a small turning angle

30. The ends of a length of manila rope are "whipped" (wrapped with thin twine) in order to

   A. make the rope more flexible
   B. prevent the strands from unraveling
   C. prevent rotting of the ends
   D. reduce the diameter of the rope at the ends

KEY (CORRECT ANSWERS)

1.	B	16.	C
2.	A	17.	A
3.	C	18.	A
4.	B	19.	C
5.	C	20.	B
6.	A	21.	D
7.	C	22.	D
8.	C	23.	B
9.	B	24.	D
10.	A	25.	A
11.	A/B	26.	A/D
12.	A	27.	C
13.	D	28.	B
14.	D	29.	C
15.	B	30.	B

EXAMINATION SECTION

TEST 1

DIRECTIONS: Each question or incomplete statement is followed by several suggested answers or completions. Select the one that BEST answers the question or completes the statement. *PRINT THE LETTER OF THE CORRECT ANSWER IN THE SPACE AT THE RIGHT.*

Questions 1-17:
Use the following diagrams of tools to answer questions 1 through 17. (Tools are NOT drawn to scale.)

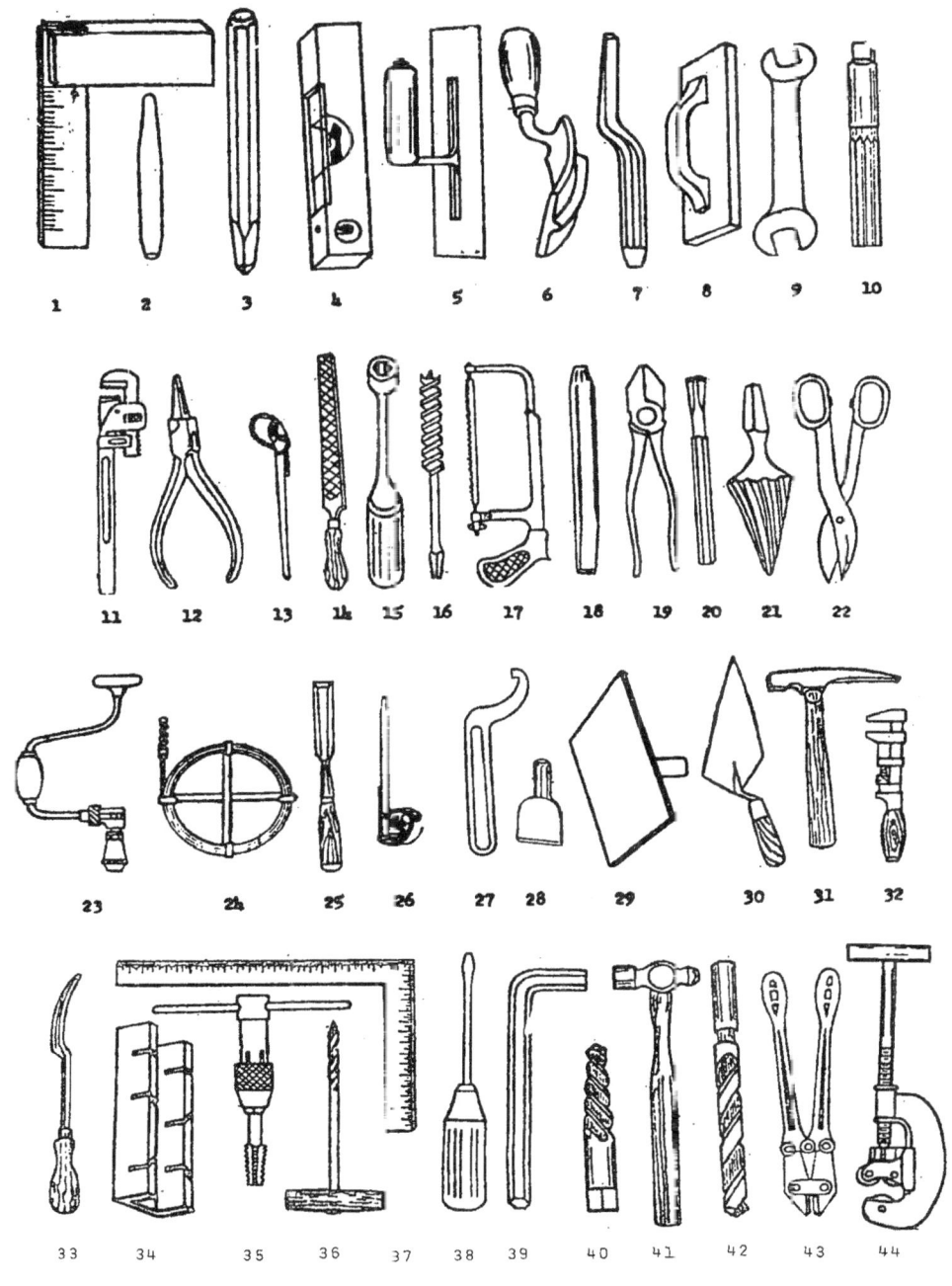

1. To tighten an elbow on a threaded pipe, a mechanic should use tool number
   A. 9   B. 11   C. 26   D. 32

2. To cut grooves in a newly poured cement floor, a mechanic should use tool number
   A. 5   B. 6   C. 28   D. 29

3. To "caulk" a lead joint, a mechanic should use tool number
   A. 7   B. 10   C. 25   D. 33

4. The term "snips" should be applied by a mechanic to tool number
   A. 12   B. 22   C. 36   D. 43

5. To slightly enlarge an existing 17/32" diameter hole in a metal plate, a mechanic should use tool number
   A. 3   B. 10   C. 14   D. 35

6. The term "snake" should be applied by a mechanic to tool number
   A. 21   B. 23   C. 24   D. 40

7. If the threaded portion of a 1/2" brass pipe breaks off inside a gate valve, the piece should be removed with tool number
   A. 15   B. 35   C. 39   D. 40

8. To cut a face brick into a bat, a mechanic should use tool number
   A. 3   B. 18   C. 25   D. 28

9. A mechanic should cut a 3" x 2" x 3/16" angle iron with tool number
   A. 3   B. 17   C. 22   D. 43

10. A mechanic should tighten a chrome-plated water supply pipe by using tool number
    A. 11   B. 19   C. 26   D. 32

11. The term "hawk" should be applied by a mechanic to tool number
    A. 28   B. 29   C. 30   D. 33

12. If your coworker asks you to pass him the "star" drill, you should hand him tool number
    A. 16   B. 20   C. 40   D. 42

13. After threading a 1" diameter piece of pipe, a mechanic should debur the inside by using tool number
    A. 14   B. 21   C. 36   D. 40

14. A mechanic should apply the term "float" to tool number
    A. 4   B. 6   C. 8   D. 28

15. If a mechanic has to cut a dozen 15-inch lengths of 3/4" steel pipe for spacers, he should use tool number
    A. 18   B. 26   C. 43   D. 44

16. If a mechanic is erecting two structural steel plates and needs to line up the bolt holes, he should use tool number
    A. 2   B. 3   C. 33   D. 42

17. To cut reinforcing wire mesh to be used in a concrete floor, you should use tool number
    A. 7   B. 17   C. 18   D. 43

18. The MAIN reason for overhauling a power tool on a regular basis is to
    A. make the men more familiar with the tool
    B. keep the men busy during slack times
    C. insure that the tool is used occasionally
    D. minimize breakdowns

19. A mechanic should NOT press too heavily on a hacksaw while using it to cut through a steel rod because this may
    A. create flying steel particles
    B. bend the frame
    C. break the blade
    D. overheat the rod

20. Creosote is COMMONLY used with wood to
    A. speed up the seasoning
    B. make the wood fireproof
    C. make painting easier
    D. preserve the wood

21. A mitre box should be used to
    A. hold a saw while sharpening it
    B. store expensive tools
    C. hold a saw at a fixed angle
    D. encase steel beams for protection

22. Wood scaffold planks should be inspected
    A. at regular intervals
    B. once a week
    C. before they are stored away
    D. each time before use

23. Continuous sheeting should be used when excavating deep trenches in
    A. rock
    B. stiff clay
    C. firm earth
    D. unstable soil

24. The MAIN reason for requiring that certain special tools be returned to the tool room after a job has been completed is that
    A. missing tools can be replaced
    B. the men will not need to care for the tools
    C. more tools will be available for use
    D. this permits easier inspection and maintenance of tools

24._____

25. The BEST material to use to extinguish an oil fire is
    A. sand   B. water   C. sawdust   D. gravel

25._____

26. A "Lally" column is
    A. fabricated from angles and plates
    B. fabricated by tying two channels together with lattice bars
    C. a steel member that has unequal sections
    D. a pipe fitted with a base plate at each end

26._____

27. The BEST action for you to take if you discover a small puddle of oil on the shop floor is to first
    A. have it cleaned up
    B. find out who spilled it
    C. discover the source of the leak
    D. cover it with newspaper

27._____

28. You should listen to your foreman even when he insists on explaining the procedure for a job you have done many times before because
    A. you can do the job the way you want when he leaves
    B. he may make an error and you can show that you know your job
    C. it is wise to humor him even if he is wrong
    D. you are required to do the job the way the foreman wants it

28._____

Questions 29-34:
Answer questions 29 through 34 by referring to the sketches that follow.

29. The indicated pressure is, MOST NEARLY, _____ psi.   29._____
    A. 132   B. 137   C. 143   D. 148

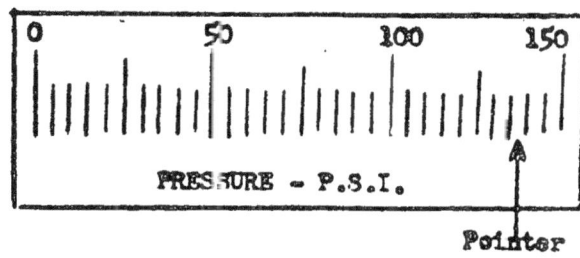

30. The LEAST number of shims, of any combination of thickness, required to   30._____
    exactly fill the 1/4" gap shown is
    A. 7   B. 8   C. 9   D. 10

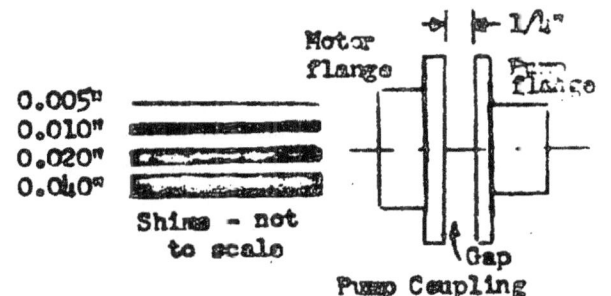

31. The dimension "X" on the keyway shown is   31._____
    A. 3-3/8"   B. 3-9/16"   C. 3-3/4"   D. 4"

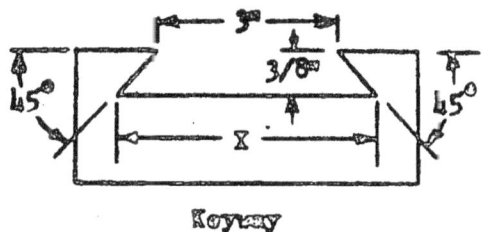

32. If the tank gauge reads 120 psi, then the pipe gauge should read ___ psi.   32._____
    A. 80   B. 120   C. 180   D. 240

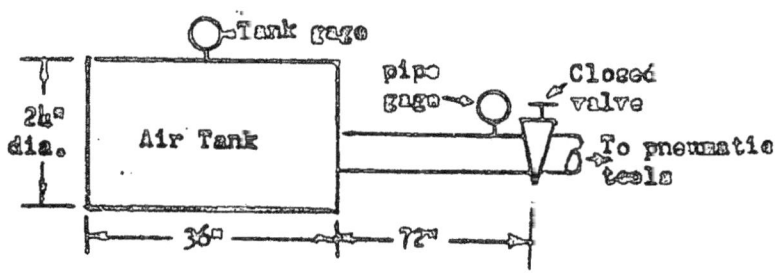

33. The MINIMUM number of feet of chainlink fence needed to completely enclose the storage yard shown is
   A. 278   B. 286   C. 295   D. 304

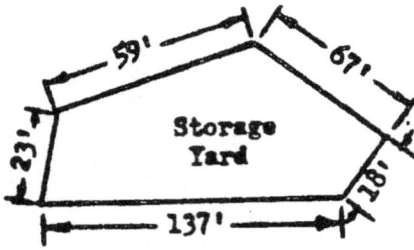

34. The distance "X" between the holes is
   A. 1-7/8"   B. 2-1/16"   C. 2-3/8"   D. 2-9/16"

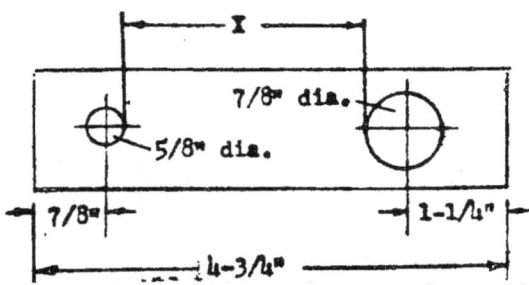

35. A rule requires all employees to report defective equipment to their superiors, even when the maintenance of the particular pieces of equipment is handled by someone else. The MAIN purpose of this rule is to
   A. determine who is doing the job improperly
   B. have repairs made before trouble occurs
   C. encourage all employees to be alert at all times
   D. reduce the cost of equipment

36. Some equipment is fitted with wing nuts. Such nuts are ESPECIALLY useful when
   A. the nut is to be wired closed
   B. space is limited
   C. the equipment is subject to vibration
   D. the nuts must be removed frequently

37. It is considered BAD practice to use water to put out electrical fires MAINLY because the water may
   A. rust the equipment
   B. short circuit the lines
   C. cause a serious shock
   D. damage the electrical insulation

38. The BEST instrument to use to make certain that two points, separated by a vertical distance of nine feet, are in perfect vertical alignment is a
   A. square   B. level   C. plumb bob   D. protractor

39. While you are being trained, you will be assigned to work with an experienced mechanic. It would be BEST for you to
    A. remind the mechanic that he is responsible for your training
    B. tell him frequently how much you know about the work
    C. let him do all the work while you observe closely
    D. be as cooperative and helpful a you can

39._____

40. If a measurement scaled from a drawing is one inch, and the scale of the drawing is 1/8 inch to the foot, then the one-inch measurement would represent an ACTUAL length of
    A. 8 feet   B. 2 feet   C. 1/8 of a foot   D. 8 inches

40._____

KEY (CORRECT ANSWERS)

1. B	11. B	21. C	31. C
2. B	12. B	22. D	32. B
3. A	13. B	23. D	33. D
4. B	14. C	24. D	34. A
5. B	15. D	25. A	35. B
6. C	16. A	26. D	36. D
7. D	17. D	27. A	37. C
8. D	18. D	28. D	38. C
9. B	19. C	29. B	39. D
10. C	20. D	30. A	40. A

TEST 2

DIRECTIONS: Each question or incomplete statement is followed by several suggested answers or completions. Select the one that BEST answers the question or completes the statement. *PRINT THE LETTER OF THE CORRECT ANSWER IN THE SPACE AT THE RIGHT.*

1. Cloth tapes should NOT be used when accurate measurements must be obtained because
    A. the numbers soon become worn and thus difficult to read
    B. there are not enough subdivisions of each inch on the tape
    C. the ink runs when wet, thus making the tape difficult to read
    D. small changes in the pull on the tape will make considerable differences in tape readings

    1._____

2. It is considered GOOD practice to release the pressure from an air hose before uncoupling the hose connection because this avoids
    A. wasting air
    B. possible personal injury
    C. damage to the air tool
    D. damage to the air compressor

    2._____

3. In brick construction, a structural steel member is used to support the wall above door and window openings. This member is called a
    A. purlin   B. sill   C. truss   D. lintel

    3._____

4. The BEST procedure to use to properly ignite an oxyacetylene cutting torch is to
    A. crack the acetylene valve, apply the spark, and open the oxygen valve
    B. crack the acetylene valve, then the oxygen valve, and apply the spark
    C. crack the oxygen valve, then the acetylene valve, and apply the spark
    D. crack the oxygen valve, apply the spark, open the acetylene valve

    4._____

5. The information in an accident report which may be MOST useful in helping to prevent similar-type accidents from happening is the
    A. cause of the accident   B. time of day it happened
    C. type of injuries suffered   D. number of people injured

    5._____

6. The MAIN reason why each coat of paint should be of a different color when two coats of paint are specified is that
    A. cheaper paint can be used as the undercoat
    B. less care need be taken in applying the coats
    C. any missed areas will be easier to spot
    D. the colors do not have to be exact

    6._____

7. To prevent manila hoisting ropes from raveling, the ends are
   A. moused   B. whipped   C. spliced   D. eyed

8. The MAIN advantage of aluminum ladders over wooden ladders is that they are
   A. much stronger
   B. lighter
   C. cheaper
   D. more stable

9. The splices in columns in steel construction are USUALLY made
   A. two feet above floor level
   B. two feet below floor level
   C. at floor level
   D. midway between floors

10. Open-end wrenches with small openings are generally made shorter in overall length than open-end wrenches with larger openings. The MOST important reason for this is to
    A. save material
    B. provide compactness
    C. prevent overstressing the wrench
    D. provide correct leverage

11. Galvanized steel wire is wire that has been coated with
    A. zinc   B. copper   C. tin   D. lead

12. "Camber" in a steel roof truss refers to the
    A. grade of steel used
    B. stress in the steel
    C. finish applied to the steel
    D. upward curve of the lower chord

13. A structural member is marked 8 WF 18. The 18 in this designation is the
    A. depth of the web
    B. width of the flange
    C. length of the member
    D. weight per foot

14. A strictly enforced safety rule in a rigging gang is that only one man gives the signals to the crane operator. However the ONE signal that anyone in the gang is allowed to give is the
    A. hoist-up signal
    B. boom-down signal
    C. swing signal
    D. stop signal

15. "Turnbuckles" are GENERALLY used to
    A. raise heavy loads
    B. splice two cables
    C. tie a cable to a column
    D. tighten a cable

16. If a mechanic opens the strands of a piece of manila rope and finds   16._____
    sawdust-like material inside the rope, it means the rope
    - A. has dried out and must be re-oiled before use
    - B. is relatively new
    - C. has been damaged and should be discarded
    - D. is to be used only for light loads until the sawdust has been cleaned out

Questions 17-21:
Refer to the passage below to answer questions 17 through 21.

REGULATIONS FOR SMALL GROUPS WHO MOVE
FROM POINT TO POINT ON THE TRACKS

Employees who perform duties on the tracks in small groups and who move from point to point along the trainway, must be on the alert at all times and prepared to clear the track when a train approaches without unnecessarily slowing it down. Underground at all times, and out-of-doors between sunset and sunrise, such employees must not enter upon the tracks unless each of them is equipped with an approved light. Flashlights must not be used for protection by such groups. Upon clearing the track to permit a train to pass, each member of the group must give a proceed signal, by hand or light, to the motorman of the train. Whenever such small groups are working in an area protected by caution lights or flags, but are not members of the gang for whom the flagging protection was established, they must not give proceed signals to motormen. The purpose of this rule is to avoid a motorman's confusing such signal with that of the flagman who is protecting a gang. Whenever a small group is engaged in work of an engrossing nature or at any time when the view of approaching trains is limited by reason of curves or otherwise, one man of the group, equipped with a whistle, must be assigned properly to warn and protect the man or men at work and must not perform any other duties while so assigned.

17. If a small group of men are traveling along the tracks toward their work   17._____
    location and a train approaches, they should
    - A. stop the train
    - B. signal the motorman to go slowly
    - C. clear the track
    - D. stop immediately

18. Small groups may enter upon the tracks   18._____
    - A. only between sunset and sunrise
    - B. provided each has an approved light
    - C. provided their foreman has a good flashlight
    - D. provided each man has an approved flashlight

4 (#2)

19. After a small group has cleared the tracks in an area unprotected by caution lights or flags, 19._____
   A. each member must give the proceed signal to the motorman
   B. the foreman signals the motorman to proceed
   C. the motorman can proceed provided he goes slowly
   D. the last member off the tracks gives the signal to the motorman

20. If a small group is working in an area protected by the signals of a track gang, the members of the small group 20._____
   A. need not be concerned with train movement
   B. must give the proceed signal together with the track gang
   C. can delegate one of their members to give the proceed signal
   D. must not give the proceed signal

21. If the view of approaching trains is blocked, the small group should 21._____
   A. move to where they can see the trains
   B. delegate one of the group to warn and protect them
   C. keep their ears alert for approaching trains
   D. refuse to work at such locations

Questions 22-28:
Refer to the sketched below to answer questions 22 through 28.

22. The distance "Y" is 22._____
   A. 5/8"   B. 7/8"   C. 1-1/8"   D. 1-3/8"

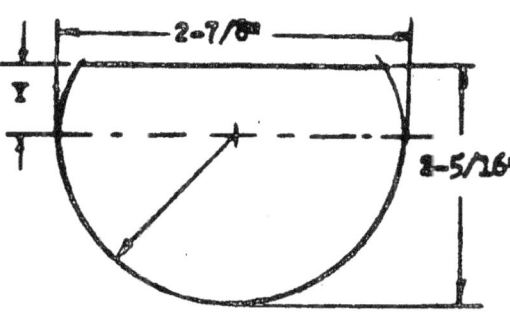

23. The sketch shows the float-operated trippers for operating a sump pump. If you want the pump to start sooner, you should 23._____
   A. lower the upper tripper   B. lower the lower tripper
   C. raise the upper tripper   D. raise the lower tripper

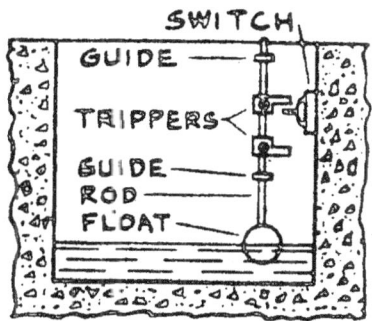

24. The width of the wood stud shown is 24._____
   A. 1-1/8"   B. 1-5/16"   C. 1-5/8"   D. 3-5/8"

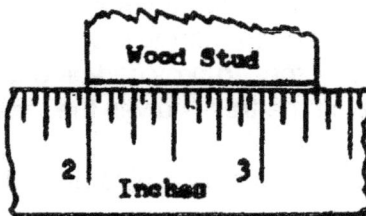

25. The right angle shown has been divided into four unequal parts. The 25._____
    number of degrees in angle "X" is
   A. 31°   B. 33°   C. 38°   D. 45°

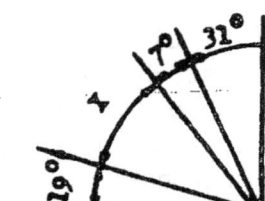

26. The reading on the meter shown is MOST NEARLY 26._____
   A. 0465   B. 0475   C. 0566   D. 1566

27. The length "X" of the slot shown is 27._____
   A. 2-3/8"   B. 2-7/16"   C. 2-1/2"   D. 2-9/16"

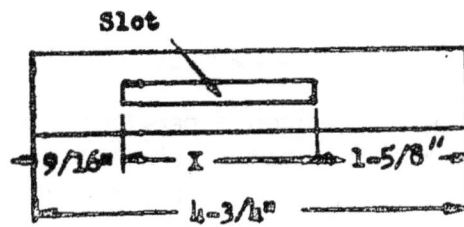

28. The volume of the bar shown is _____ cubic inches. 28._____
   A. 132   B. 356   C. 420   D. 516

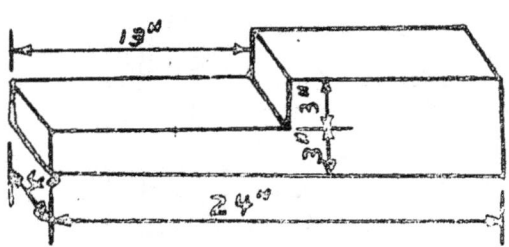

Questions 29-34:
Use the sketch below to answer questions 29 through 34.

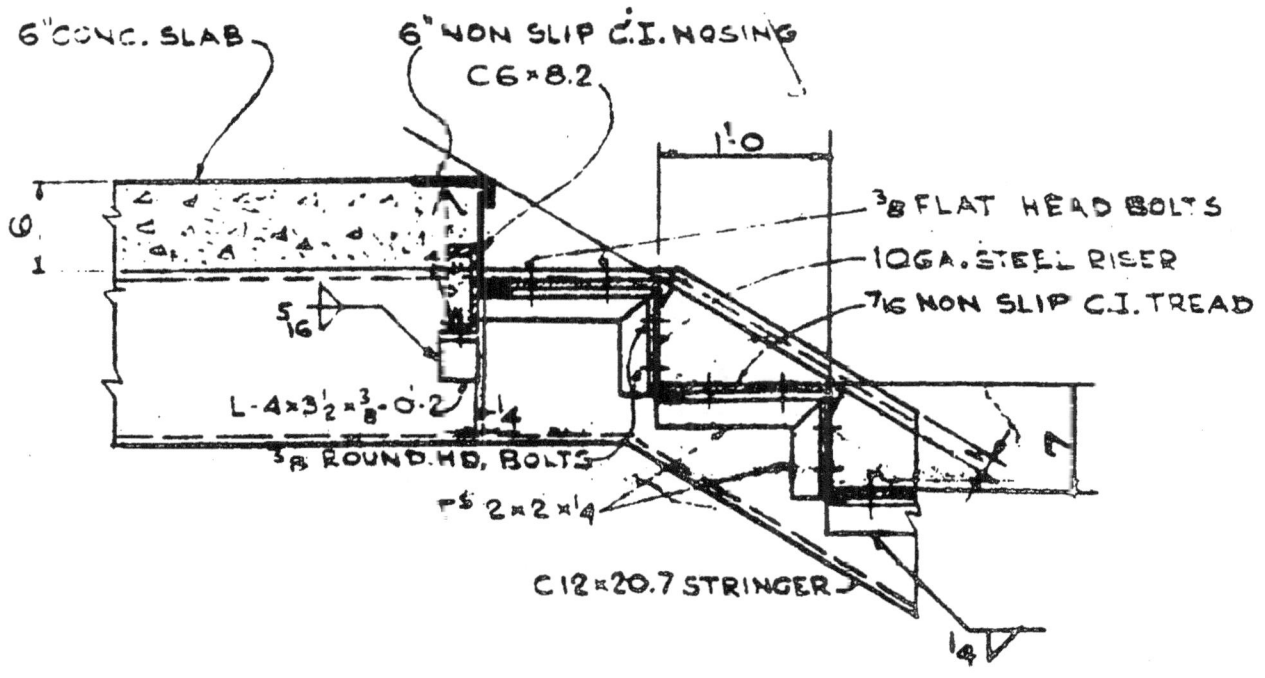

29. The stringer for this stair is a(n)
    A. I-beam   B. angle   C. H-beam   D. channel

    29._____

30. The riser is made of
    A. concrete   B. sheet metal
    C. cast iron   D. wood

    30._____

31. The 2 x 2 x 1/4 angles are secured to the stringer by
    A. 5/16" welds   B. 1/4" welds
    C. 3/8" flat head bolts   D. 3/8" round head bolts

    31._____

32. The treads are made of
    A. concrete   B. sheet metal
    C. cast iron   D. wood

    32._____

33. The height of the riser is
    A. 6"   B. 7"   C. 8"   D. 12"

    33._____

34. The width of the tread is
    A. 6"   B. 7"   C. 8"   D. 12"

    34._____

Questions 35-40:

DIRECTIONS: Questions 35 through 40 show the top view of an object in the first column, the front view of the same object in the second column, and four drawings in the third column, one of which correctly represents the RIGHT side view of the object. Select the CORRECT right side view. As a guide, the first one is an illustrative example, the correct answer of which is C.

KEY (CORRECT ANSWERS)

1. D	11. A	21. B	31. B
2. B	12. D	22. B	32. C
3. D	13. D	23. D	33. B
4. A	14. D	24. B	34. D
5. A	15. D	25. B	35. C
6. C	16. C	26. A	36. A
7. B	17. C	27. D	37. C
8. B	18. B	28. C	38. B
9. A	19. A	29. D	39. B
10. D	20. D	30. B	40. C

MECHANICAL APTITUDE EXAMINATION SECTION
TEST 1

MECHANICAL COMPREHENSION

DIRECTIONS: Questions 1 through 4 test your ability to understand general mechanical devices. Pictures are shown and questions asked about the mechanical devices shown in the picture. Read each question and study the picture. Each question is followed by four choices. For each question, choose the one BEST answer (A, B, C, or D). Then, *PRINT THE LETTER OF THE CORRECT ANSWER IN THE SPACE AT THE RIGHT.*

1.

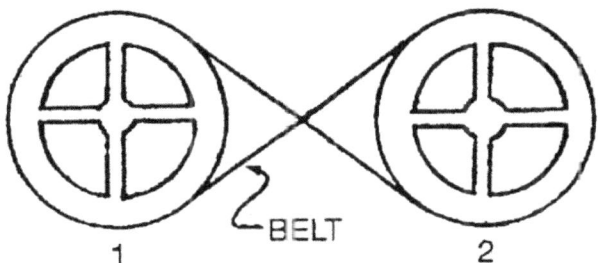

The reason for crossing the belt connecting these wheels is to
 A. make the wheels turn in opposite directions
 B. make wheel 2 turn faster than wheel 1
 C. save wear on the belt
 D. take up slack in the belt

1._____

2.

The purpose of the small gear between the two large gears is to
 A. increase the speed of the larger gears
 B. allow the larger gears to turn in different directions
 C. decrease the speed of the larger gears
 D. make the larger gears turn in the same direction

2._____

3.

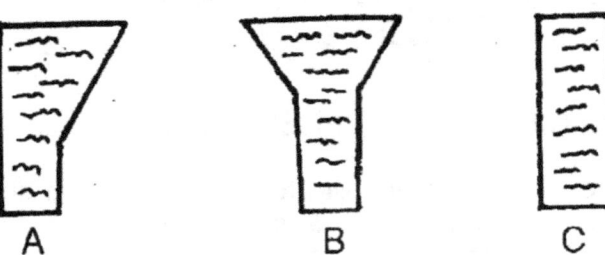

Each of these three-foot-high water cans have a bottom with an area of one square foot.
The pressure on the bottom of the cans is
   A. least in A   B. least in B   C. least in C   D. the same in all

4.

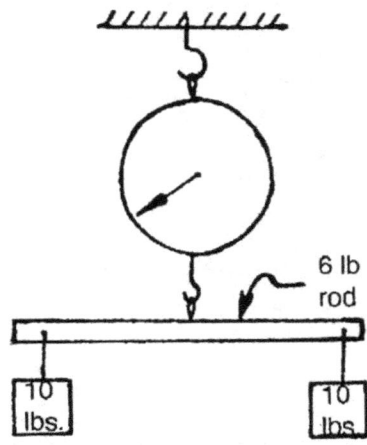

The reading on the scale should be
   A. zero   B. 10 pounds   C. 13 pounds   D. 26 pounds

KEY (CORRECT ANSWERS)

1. A
2. D
3. D
4. D

TEST 2

DIRECTIONS: Questions 1 through 6 test knowledge of tools and how to use them. For each question, decide which one of the four things shown in the boxes labeled A, B, C, or D normally is used with or goes best with the thing in the picture on the left. *PRINT THE LETTER OF THE CORRECT ANSWER IN THE SPACE AT THE RIGHT.*

NOTE: All tools are NOT drawn to the same scale.

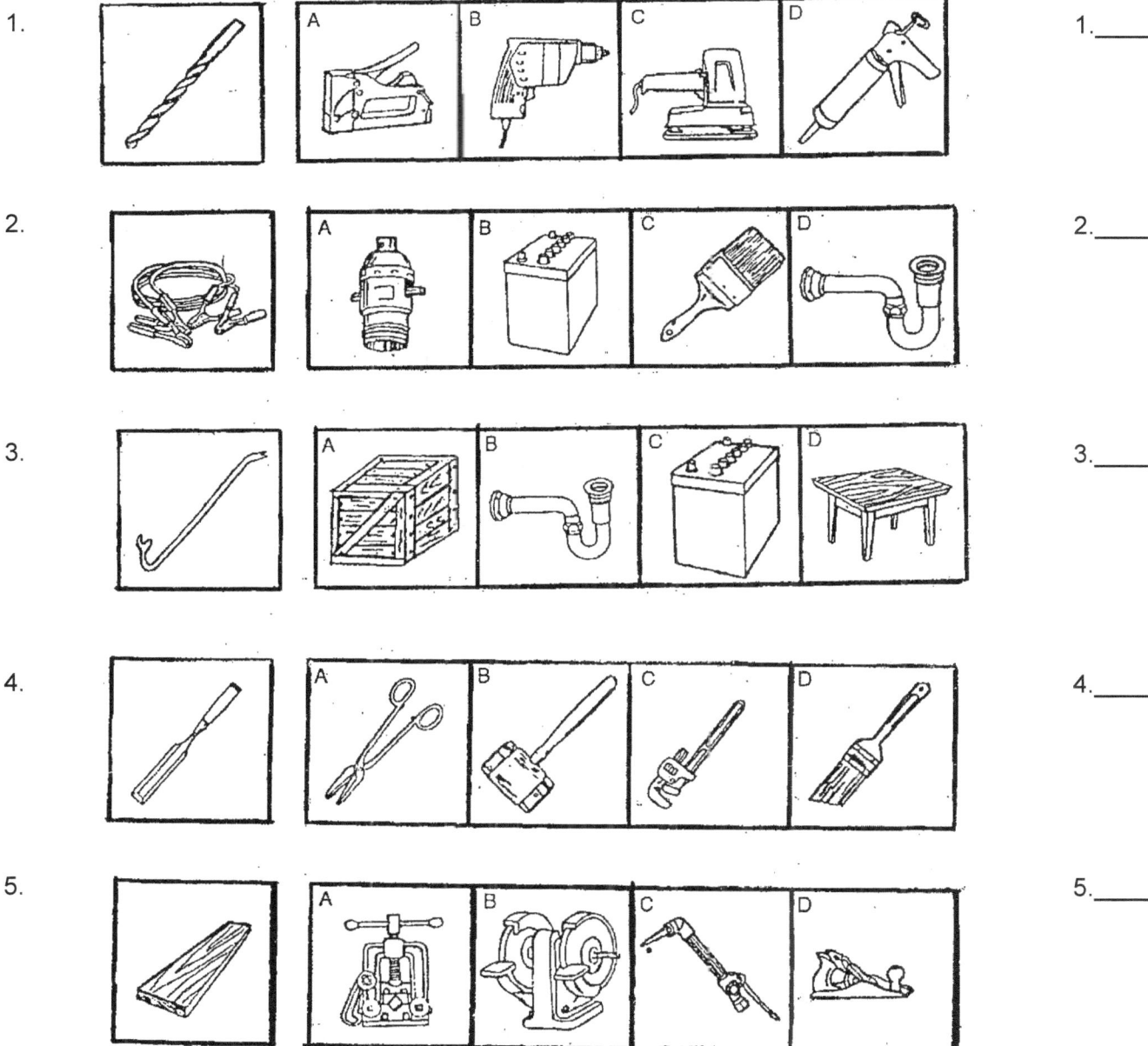

151

2 (#2)

6. 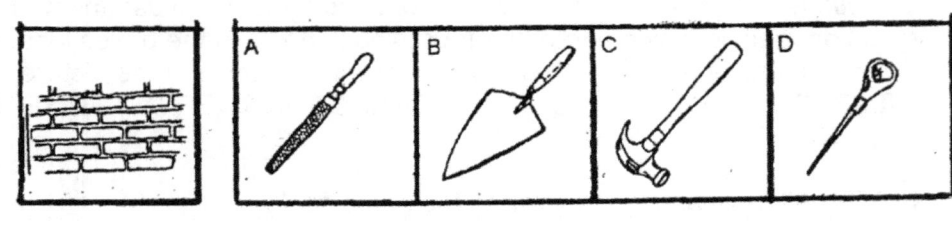 6._____

KEY (CORRECT ANSWERS)

1. B   4. B
2. B   5. D
3. A   6. B

MECHANICAL APTITUDE
MECHANICAL COMPREHENSION
EXAMINATION SECTION
TEST 1

DIRECTIONS: Each question or incomplete statement below is followed by several suggested answers or completions. Select the *one* that *BEST* answers the question or completes the statement. *PRINT THE LETTER OF THE CORRECT ANSWER IN THE SPACE AT THE RIGHT.*

Questions 1-3.

DIRECTIONS: Questions 1 to 3 inclusive are based upon the following paragraph.

The only openings permitted in fire partitions except openings for ventilating ducts shall be those required for doors. There shall be but one such door opening unless the provision of additional openings would not exceed, in total width of all doorways, 25 percent of the length of the wall. The minimum distance between openings shall be three feet. The maximum area for such a door opening shall be 80 square feet, except that such openings for the passage of motor trucks may be a maximum of 140 square feet.

1. According to the above paragraph, openings in fire partitions are permitted *only* for   1.____

   A. doors
   B. doors and windows
   C. doors and ventilation ducts
   D. doors, windows and ventilation ducts

2. In a fire partition, 22 feet long and 10 feet high, the *MAXIMUM* number of doors, 3 feet wide and 7 feet high, is   2.____

   A. 1   B. 2   C. 3   D. 4

3.

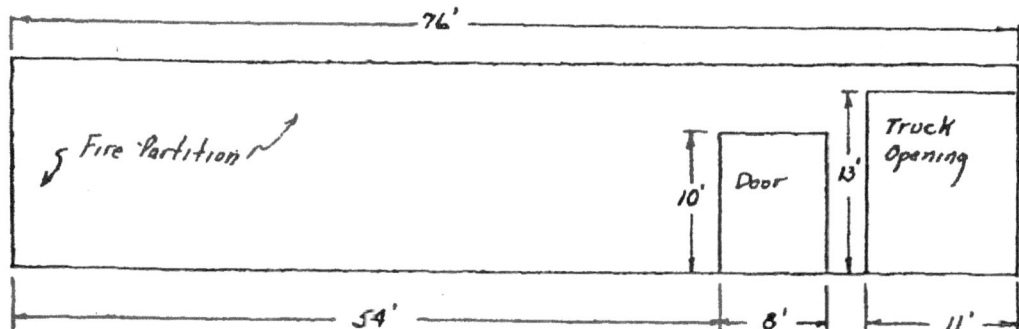

   The one of the following statements about the layout shown above that is *MOST* accurate is that the   3.____

   A. total width of the openings is too large
   B. truck opening is too large
   C. truck and door openings are too close together
   D. layout is acceptable

153

4. At a given temperature, a wet hand will freeze to a bar of metal, but NOT to a piece of wood, because the

   A. metal expands and contracts more than the wood
   B. wood is softer than the metal
   C. wood will burn at a lower temperature than the metal
   D. metal is a better conductor of heat than the wood

5. Of the following items commonly found in a household, the one that uses the MOST electric current is a(n)

   A. 150-watt light bulb
   B. toaster
   C. door buzzer
   D. 8" electric fan

6. Sand and ashes are frequently placed on icy pavements to prevent skidding. The effect of the sand and ashes is to increase

   A. inertia   B. gravity   C. momentum   D. friction

7. The air near the ceiling of a room usually is warmer than the air near the floor because

   A. there is better air circulation at the floor level
   B. warm air is lighter than cold air
   C. windows usually are nearer the floor than the ceiling
   D. heating pipes usually run along the ceiling

8.

   DIA. 1   DIA. 2

   It is safer to use the ladder positioned as shown in diagram 1 than as shown in diagram 2 because, in diagram 1,

   A. less strain is placed upon the center rungs of the ladder
   B. it is easier to grip and stand on the ladder
   C. the ladder reaches a lower height
   D. the ladder is less likely to tip over backwards

9.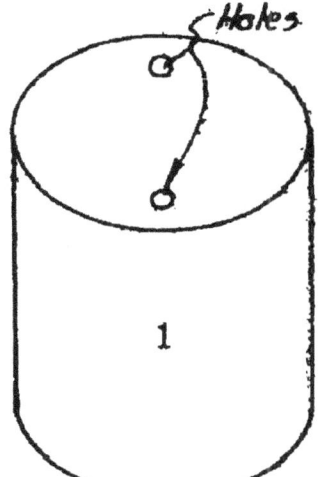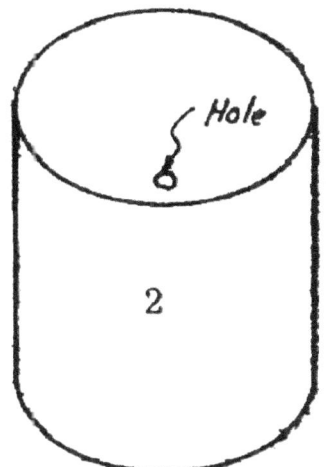

It is *easier* to pour a liquid from:

A. Can 1 because there are two holes from which the liquid can flow
B. Can 1 because air can enter through one hole while the liquid comes out the other hole
C. Can 2 because the liquid comes out under greater pressure
D. Can 2 because it is easier to direct the flow of the liquid when there is only one hole

10. A substance which is subject to "spontaneous combustion" is one that

A. is explosive when heated
B. is capable of catching fire without an external source of heat
C. acts to speed up the burning of material
D. liberates oxygen when heated

11. The sudden shutting down of a nozzle on a hose discharging water under high pressure is a *bad* practice CHIEFLY because the

A. hose is likely to whip about violently
B. hose is likely to burst
C. valve handle is likely to snap
D. valve handle is likely to jam

12. Fire can continue where there are present fuel, oxygen from the air or other source, and a sufficiently high temperature to maintain combustion. The method of extinguishment of fire MOST commonly used is to

A. remove the fuel
B. exclude the oxygen from the burning material
C. reduce the temperature of the burning material
D. smother the flames of the burning material

13.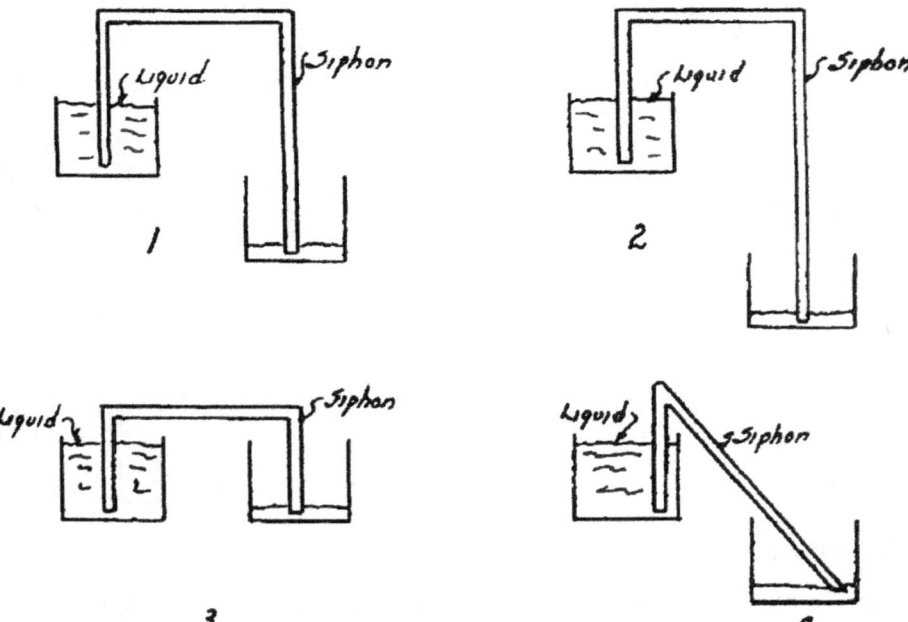

The *one* of the siphon arrangements shown above which would MOST quickly transfer a solution from the container on the left side to the one on the right side is numbered

A. 1   B. 2   C. 3   D. 4

14. Static electricity is a hazard in industry CHIEFLY because it may cause

A. dangerous or painful burns
B. chemical decomposition of toxic elements
C. sparks which can start an explosion
D. overheating of electrical equipment

15.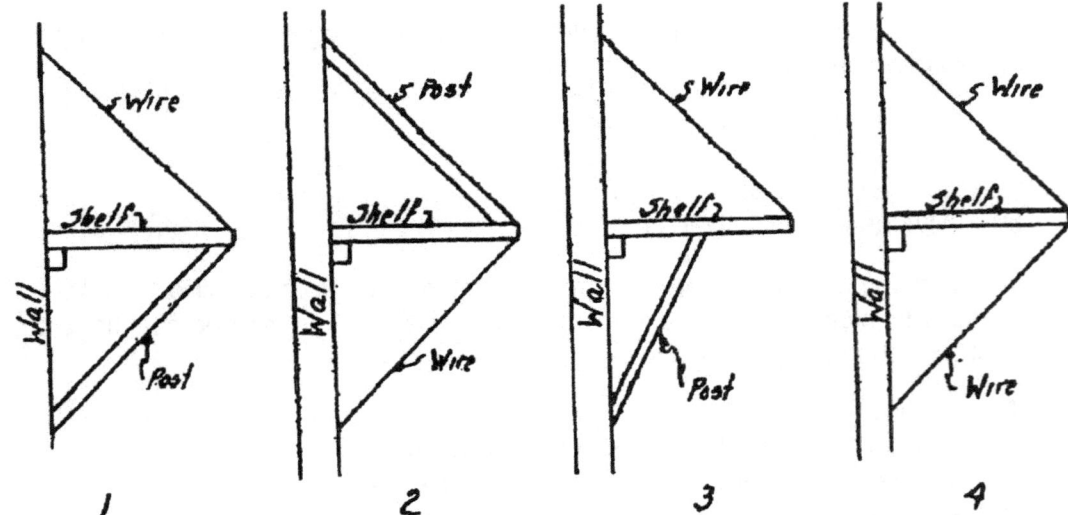

The STRONGEST method of supporting the shelf is shown in diagram

A. 1   B. 2   C. 3   D. 4

16. A row boat will float *deeper* in fresh water than in salt water *because*

    A. in the salt water the salt will occupy part of the space
    B. fresh water is heavier than salt water
    C. salt water is heavier than fresh water
    D. salt water offers less resistance than fresh water

17.

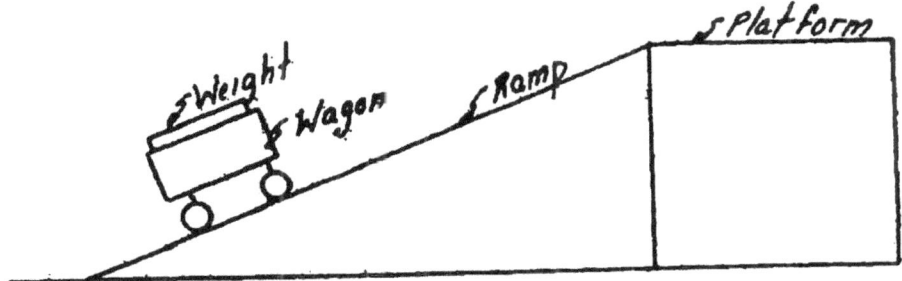

It is easier to get the load onto the platform by using the ramp than it is to lift it directly onto the platform. This is *true* because the effect of the ramp is to

    A. reduce the amount of friction so that less force is required
    B. distribute the weight over a larger area
    C. support part of the load so that less force is needed to move the wagon
    D. increase the effect of the moving weight

18.

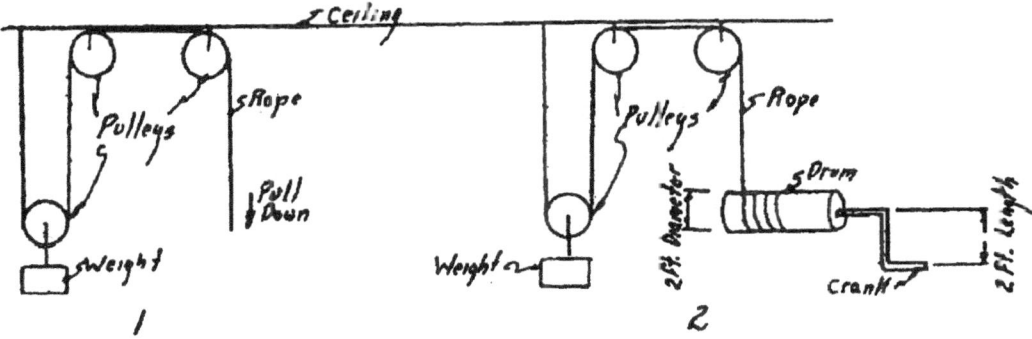

More weight can be lifted by the method shown in diagram 2 than as shown in diagram 1 because

    A. it takes less force to turn a crank than it does to pull in a straight line
    B. the drum will prevent the weight from falling by itself
    C. the length of the crank is larger than the radius of the drum
    D. the drum has more rope on it easing the pull

19.

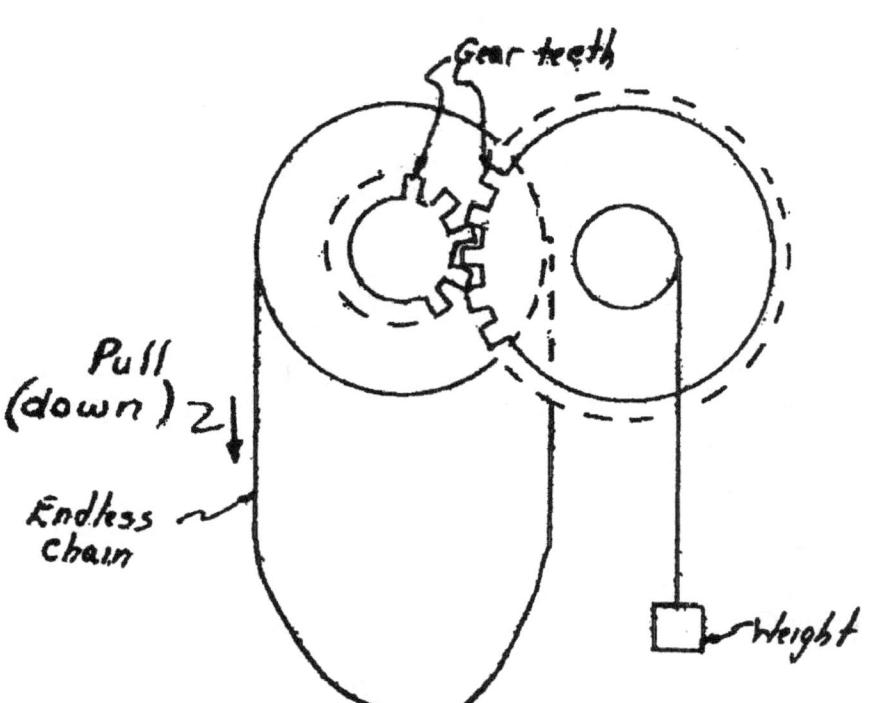

As the endless chain is pulled down in the direction shown, the weight will move

- A. *up* faster than the endless chain is pulled down
- B. *up* slower than the endless chain is pulled down
- C. *down* faster than the endless chain is pulled down
- D. *down* slower than the endless chain is pulled down

20. Two balls of the same size, but different weights, are both dropped from a 10-ft. height. The one of the following statements that is *MOST* accurate is that

- A. both balls will reach the ground at the same time because they are the same size
- B. both balls will reach the ground at the same time because the effect of gravity is the same on both balls
- C. the heavier ball will reach the ground first because it weighs more
- D. the lighter ball will reach the ground first because air resistance is greater on the heavier ball

21. It is considered poor practice to increase the leverage of a wrench by placing a pipe over the handle of the wrench. This is true *PRINCIPALLY* because

- A. the wrench may break
- B. the wrench may slip off the nut
- C. it is harder to place the wrench on the nut
- D. the wrench is more difficult to handle

22.

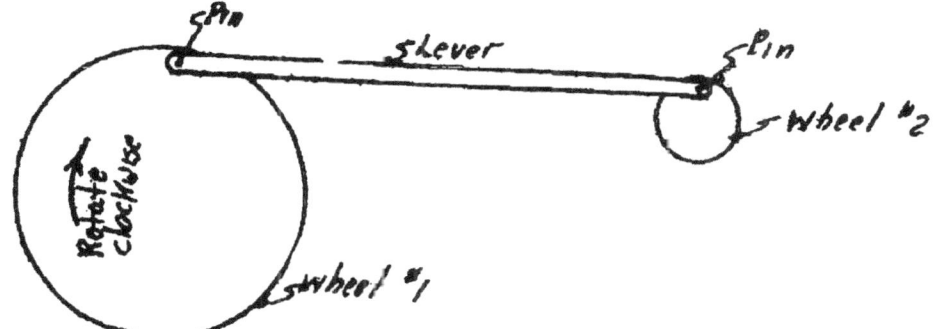

If wheel #1 is turned in the direction shown, wheel #2 will

A. turn continously in a clockwise direction
B. turn continously in a counterclockwise direction
C. move back and fourth
D. became jammed and both wheels will shop

23. ALL SOLID AREAS REPRESENT EQUAL WEIGHTS ATTACHED TO THE FLYWHEEL

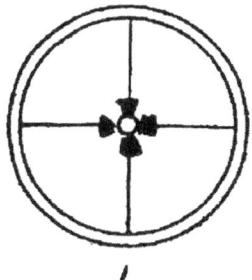 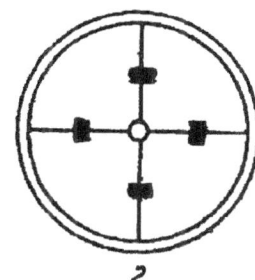 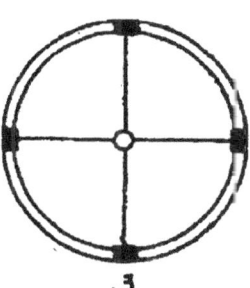

The above diagrams are of flywheels made of the same material with the same dimensions and attached to similar engines. The solid areas represent equal weights attached to the fly wheel. If all three engines are running at the same speed for the same length of time and the power to the engines is shut of simultaneously,

A. wheel 1 will continue turning longest
B. wheel 2 will continue turning longest
C. wheel 3 will continue turning longest
D. all three wheels will continue turning for the same time

24. The one of the following substance which expands when freezing is

A. alcohol   B. ammonia   C. mercury   D. water

25. A piece of copper wire 30 feet long is cut into two pieces, 20 feet and 10 feet. The resistance of the *longer* piece, compared to the shorter, is

A. one-half as much
C. one and one-half as much
B. two-thirds as much
D. twice as much

KEY (CORRECT ANSWERS)

1.	C	11.	B
2.	A	12.	C
3.	B	13.	B
4.	D	14.	C
5.	B	15.	A
6.	D	16.	C
7.	B	17.	C
8.	D	18.	C
9.	B	19.	D
10.	B	20.	B

21. A
22. D
23. C
24. D
25. D

TEST 2

DIRECTIONS: Each question or incomplete statement below is followed by several suggested answers or completions. Select the *one* that *BEST* answers the question or completes the statement. *PRINT THE LETTER OF THE CORRECT ANSWER IN THE SPACE AT THE RIGHT.*

Questions 1-2.

DIRECTIONS: Questions 1 and 2 are to be answered in accordance with the information in the following statement:

The electrical resistance of copper wires varies directly with their lengths and inversely with their cross section areas.

1. A piece of copper wire 30 feet long is cut into two pieces, 20 feet and 10 feet. The resistance of the *longer* piece, compared to the shorter, is

   A. one-half as much
   B. two-thirds as much
   C. one and one-half as much
   D. twice as much

2. Two pieces of copper wire are each 10 feet long but the cross section area of one is 2/3 that of the other. The resistance of the piece with the *larger* cross-section area is

   A. one-half the resistance of the smaller
   B. two-thirds the resistance of the smaller
   C. one and one-half times the resistance of the smaller
   D. twice the resistance of the smaller

3.

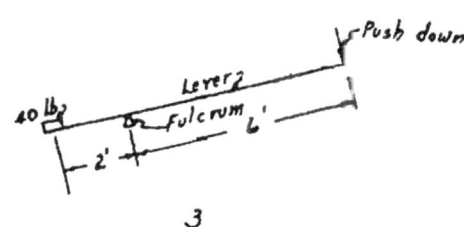

The arrangement of the lever which would require the *LEAST* amount of force to move the weight is shown in the diagram numbered

   A. 1   B. 2   C. 3   D. 4

4. Steel supporting beams in buildings often are surrounded by a thin layer of concrete to keep the beams from becoming hot and collapsing during a fire.
The *one* of the following statements which *BEST* explains how collapse is prevented by this arrangement is that concrete

   A. becomes stronger as its temperature is increased

161

B. acts as an insulating material
C. protects the beam from rust and corrosion
D. reacts chemically with steel at high temperatures

5. If boiling water is poured into a drinking glass, the glass is likely to crack. If, however, a metal spoon first is placed in the glass, it is much less likely to crack. The reason that the glass with the spoon is *less likely* to crack is that the spoon

   A. distributes the water over a larger surface of the glass
   B. quickly absorbs heat from the water
   C. reinforces the glass
   D. reduces the amount of water which can be poured into the glass

6. It takes *more* energy to force water through a *long* pipe than through a *short* pipe of the same diameter. The PRINCIPAL reason for this is

   A. gravity   B. friction   C. inertia   D. cohesion

7. A pump, discharging at 300 lbs.-per-sq.-inch pressure, delivers water through 100 feet of pipe laid horizontally. If the valve at the end of the pipe is shut so that no water can flow, then the pressure at the valve is, for practical purposes,

   A. *greater* than the pressure at the pump
   B. *equal to* the pressure at the pump
   C. *less* than the pressure at the pump
   D. *greater or less* than the pressure at the pump, depending on the type of pump used

8. The explosive force of a gas when stored under various pressures is given in the following table:

Storage Pressure	Explosive Force
10	1
20	8
30	27
40	64
50	125

   The *one* of the following statements which BEST expresses the relationship between the storage pressure and explosive force is that
   A. there is no systematic relationship between an increase in storage pressure and an increase in explosive force
   B. the explosive force varies as the square of the pressure
   C. the explosive force varies as the cube of the pressure
   D. the explosive force varies as the fourth power of the pressure

9.

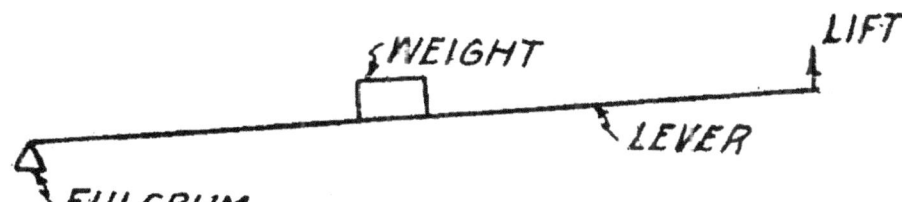

The leverage system in the sketch above is used to raise a weight. In order to *reduce* the amount of force required to raise the weight, it is necessary to

A. decrease the length of the lever
B. place the weight closer to the fulcrum
C. move the weight closer to the person applying the force
D. move the fulcrum further from the weight

10. In the accompanying sketch of a block and fall, if the end of the rope P is pulled so that it moves one foot, the distance the weight will be *raised* is
A. 1/2 ft.
B. 1 ft.
C. 1 1/2 ft.
D. 2 ft.

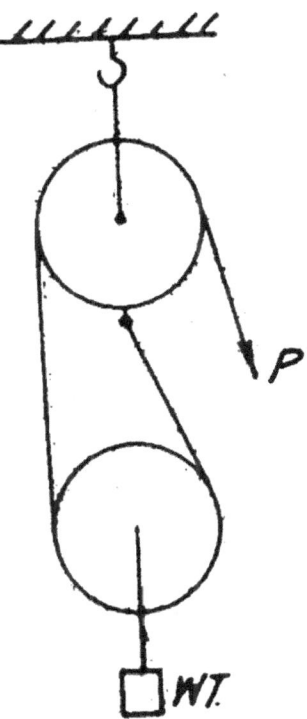

11.

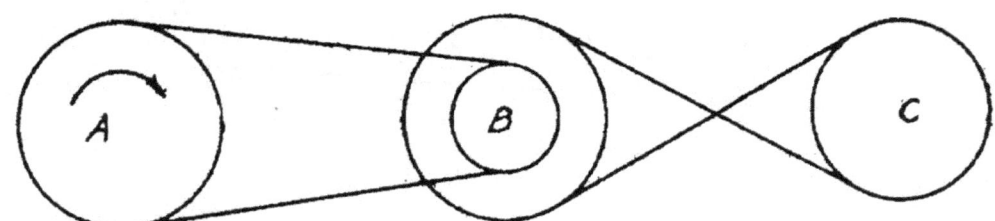

The above sketch diagrammatically shows a pulley and belt system. If pulley A is made to rotate in a clockwise direction, *then* pulley C will rotate

A. faster than pulley A and in a clockwise direction
B. slower than pulley A and in a clockwise direction
C. faster than pulley A and in a counter-clockwise direction
D. slower than pulley A and in a counter-clockwise direction

12.

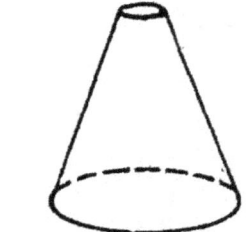 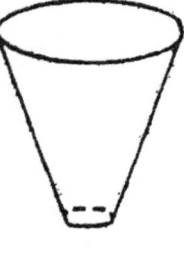 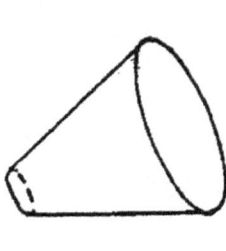 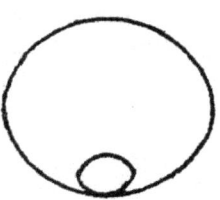

    1   *2*   *3*   *4*

The above diagrams show four positions of the same object. The position in which this object is MOST stable is

A. 1 B. 2 C. 3 D. 4

13. The accompanying sketch diagrammatically shows a system of meshing gears with relative diameters as drawn. If gear 1 is made to rotate in the direction of the arrow, *then* the gear that will turn FASTEST is numbered

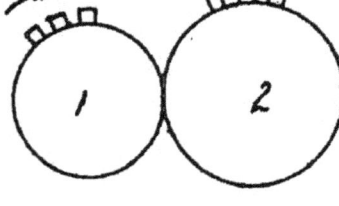

A. 1 B. 2 C. 3 D. 4

14.

The above sketch shows a weight being lifted by means of a crowbar.
The point at which the tendency for the bar to break is GREATEST is

A. 1   B. 2   C. 3   D. 4

15.

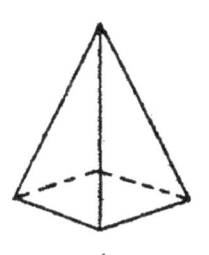 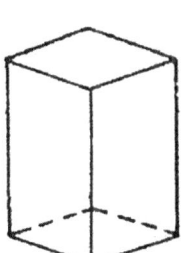 

The above sketches show four objects which weigh the same but have different shapes.
The object which is MOST difficult to tip over is numbered

A. 1   B. 2   C. 3   D. 4

16.

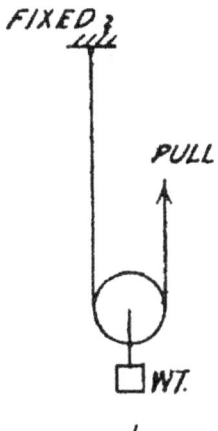  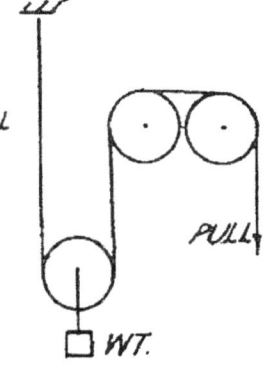

An object is to be lifted by means of a system of lines and pulleys. Of the systems shown above, the one which would require the GREATEST force to be used in lifting the weight is the one numbered

A. 1   B. 2   C. 3   D. 4

17. An intense fire develops in a room in which carbon dioxide cylinders are stored. The PRINCIPAL hazard in this situation is that

    A. the CO_2 may catch fire
    B. toxic fumes may be released
    C. the cylinders may explode
    D. released CO_2 may intensify the fire

18. At a fire involving the roof of a 5-story building, the firemen trained their hose stream on the fire from a vacant lot across the street, aiming the stream at a point about 15 feet above the roof.
    In this situation, water in the stream would be traveling at the GREATEST speed

    A. as it leaves the hose nozzle
    B. at a point midway between the ground and the roof
    C. at the maximum height of the stream
    D. as it drops on the roof

19. A principle of lighting is that the intensity of illumination at a point is inversely proportional to the square of the distance from the source of illumination.
    Assume that a pulley lamp is lowered from a position of 6 feet to one of three feet above a desk. According to the above principle, we would expect that the amount of illumination reaching the desk from the lamp in the lower position, as compared to the higher position, will be

    A. half as much
    B. twice as much
    C. four times as much
    D. nine times as much

20.

    (Four diagrams: 1) circle with diameter 120', 2) square with diagonal 120', 3) circle with diameter 240', 4) square with diagonal 240')

    When standpipes are required in a structure, sufficient risers must be installed so that no point on the floor is more than 120 feet from a riser.
    The one of the above diagrams which gives the MAXIMUM area which can be covered by one riser is

    A. 1   B. 2   C. 3   D. 4

21. Spontaneous combustion may be the reason for a pile of oily rags catching fire.
    In general, spontaneous combustion is the DIRECT result of

    A. application of flame
    B. falling sparks
    C. intense sunlight
    D. chemical action
    E. radioactivity

22. In general, firemen are advised not to direct a solid stream of water on fires burning in electrical equipment. Of the following, the MOST logical reason for this instruction is that

    A. water is a conductor of electricity
    B. water will do more damage to the electrical equipment than the fire
    C. hydrogen in water may explode when it comes in contact with electric current
    D. water will not effectively extinguish fires in electrical equipment
    E. water may spread the fire to other circuits

23. The height at which a fireboat will float in still water is determined CHIEFLY by the

    A. weight of the water displaced by the boat
    B. horsepower of the boat's engines
    C. number of propellers on the boat
    D. curve the bow has above the water line
    E. skill with which the boat is maneuvered

24. When firemen are working at the nozzle of a hose they usually lean forward on the hose. The *most likely* reason for taking this position is that

    A. the surrounding air is cooled, making the firemen more comfortable
    B. a backward force is developed which must be counteracted
    C. the firemen can better see where the stream strikes
    D. the fireman are better protected from injury by falling debris
    E. the stream is projected further

25. In general, the color and odor of smoke will BEST indicate

    A. the cause of the fire
    B. the extent of the fire
    C. how long the fire has been burning
    D. the kind of material on fire
    E. the exact seat of the fire

KEY (CORRECT ANSWERS)

1.	D	11.	C
2.	B	12.	A
3.	A	13.	D
4.	B	14.	C
5.	B	15.	A
6.	B	16.	C
7.	B	17.	C
8.	C	18.	A
9.	B	19.	C
10.	A	20.	C

21. D
22. A
23. A
24. B
25. D

TEST 3

DIRECTIONS: Each question or incomplete statement below is followed by several suggested answers or completions. Select the *one* that BEST answers the question or completes the statement. *PRINT THE LETTER OF THE CORRECT ANSWER IN THE SPACE AT THE RIGHT.*

1. As a demonstration, firemen set up two hose lines identical in every respect except that one was longer than the other. Water was then delivered through these lines from one pump and it was seen that the stream from the longer hose line had a shorter "throw." Of the following, the MOST valid explanation of this difference in "throw" is that the

    A. air resistance to the water stream is proportional to the length of hose
    B. time required for water to travel through the longer hose is greater than for the shorter one
    C. loss due to friction is greater in the longer hose than in the shorter one
    D. rise of temperature is greater in the longer hose than in the shorter one
    E. longer hose line probably developed a leak at one of the coupling joints

2. Of the following toxic gases, the *one* which is MOST dangerous because it cannot be seen and has no odor, is

    A. ether
    B. carbon monoxide
    C. chlorine
    D. ammonia
    E. cooking gas

3. You are visiting with some friends when their young son rushes into the room with his clothes on fire. You immediately wrap him in a rug and roll him on the floor. The MOST important reason for your action is that the

    A. flames are confined within the rug
    B. air supply to the fire is reduced
    C. burns sustained will be third degree, rather than first degree
    D. whirling action will put out the fire
    E. boy will not suffer from shock

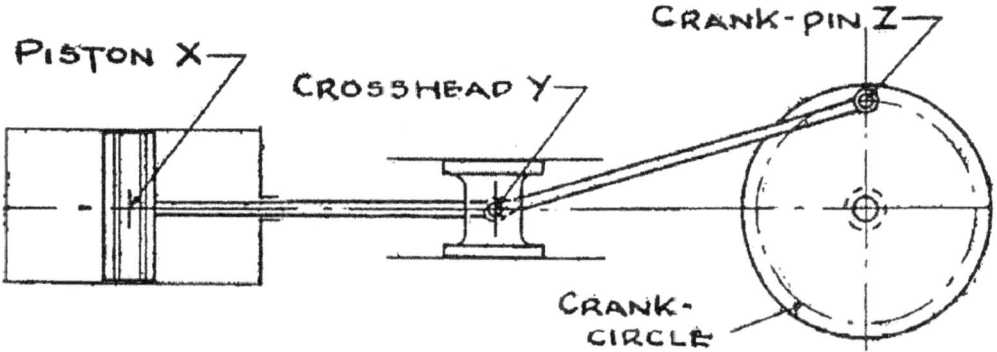

FIGURE I

Questions 4-6,

DIRECTIONS: The device shown in Figure I above represents schematically a mechanism commonly used to change reciprocating (back and forth) motion to rotation (circular) motion.
The following questions, numbered 4 to 6 inclusive, are to be answered with reference to this device.

4. Assume that piston X is placed in its extreme left position so that X, Y and Z are in a horizontal line. If a horizontal force to the right is applied to the piston X, we may then expect that

   A. the crank-pin Z will revolve clockwise
   B. the crosshead Y will move in a direction opposite to that of X
   C. the crank-pin Z will revolve counterclockwise
   D. no movement will take place
   E. the crank-pin Z will oscillate back and forth

5. If we start from the position shown in the above diagram, and move piston X to the right, the result will be that

   A. the crank-pin Z will revolve counterclockwise and cross-head Y will move to the left
   B. the crank-pin Z will revolve clockwise and crosshead Y will move to the left
   C. the crank-pin Z will revolve clockwise and crosshead Y will move to the right
   D. the crank-pin Z will revolve clockwise and crosshead Y will move to the right
   E. crosshead Y will move to the left as piston X moves to the right

6. If crank-pin Z is moved closer to the center of the crank circle, then the length of the

   A. stroke of piston X is increased
   B. stroke of piston X is decreased
   C. stroke of piston X is unchanged
   D. rod between the piston X and crosshead Y is increased
   E. rod between the piston X and crosshead Y is decreased

Questions 7-8.

DIRECTIONS: Figure II represents schematically a block-and-fall tackle. The advantage derived from this machine is that the effect of the applied force is multiplied by the number of lines of rope directly supporting the load. The following two questions, numbered 7 and 8, are to be answered with reference to this figure.

7. Pull P is exerted on line T to raise the load L. The line in which the *LARGEST* strain is finally induced is line

   A. T   B. U   C. V   D. X   E. Y

8. If the largest pull P that two men can apply to line T is 280 lbs., the MAXIMUM load L that they can raise without regard to frictional losses is, most nearly, _____ lbs.
   A. 1960
   B. 1680
   C. 1400
   D. 1260
   E. 1120

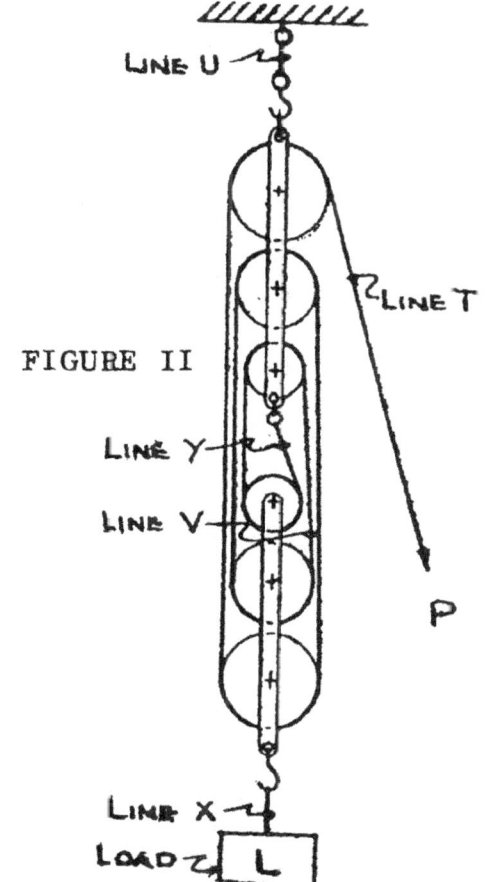

FIGURE II

Questions 9-13.

DIRECTIONS: Answer Questions 9 to 13 on the basis of Figure III. The diagram schematically illustrates part of a water tank. 1 and 5 are outlet and inlet pipes, respectively. 2 is a valve which can be used to open and close the outlet pipe by hand. 3 is a float which is rigidly connected to valve 4 by an iron bar, thus causing that valve to open or shut as the float rises or falls. 4 is a hinged valve which controls the flow of water into the tank.

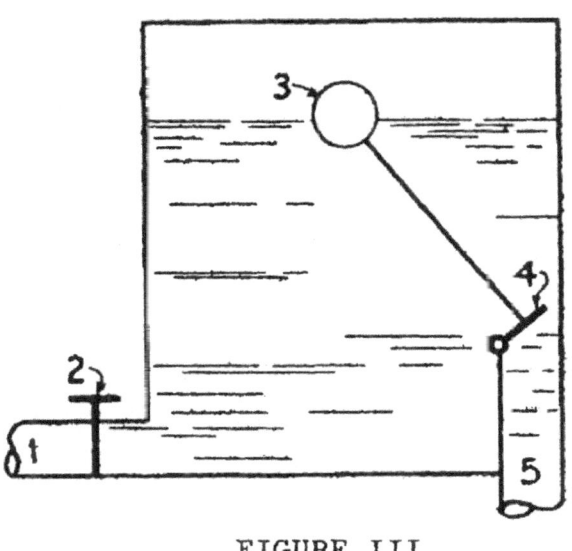

FIGURE III

9. If the tank is half filled and water is going out of pipe 1 more rapidly than it is coming in through pipe 5, *then*

   A. valve 2 is closed
   B. float 3 is rising in the tank
   C. valve 4 is opening wider
   D. valve 4 is closed
   E. float 3 is stationary

10. If the tank is half filled with water and water is coming in through inlet pipe 5 more rapidly than it is going out through outlet pipe 1, *then*

    A. valve 2 is closed
    B. float 3 is rising in the tank
    C. valve 4 is opening wider
    D. valve 4 is closed
    E. float 3 is stationary

11. If the tank is empty, then it can *normally* be expected that

    A. float 3 is at its highest position
    B. float 3 is at its lowest position
    C. valve 2 is closed
    D. valve 4 is closed
    E. water will not come into the tank

12. If float 3 develops a leak, *then*

    A. the tank will tend to empty
    B. water will tend to stop coming into the tank
    C. valve 4 will tend to close
    D. valve 2 will tend to close
    E. valve 4 will tend to remain open

13. Without any other changes being made, if the bar joining the float to valve 4 is removed and a slightly shorter bar substituted, *then*

    A. a smaller quantity of water in the tank will be required before the float closes valve 4
    B. valve 4 will not open
    C. valve 4 will not close
    D. it is not possible to determine what will happen
    E. a greater quantity of water in the tank will be required before the float closes valve 4

Questions 14-18.

DIRECTIONS: Answer Questions 14 to 18 on the basis of Figure IV. A, B, C and D are four meshed gears forming a gear train. Gear A is the driver. Gears A and D each have twice as many teeth as gear B, and gear C has four times as many teeth as gear B. The diagram is schematic: the teeth go all around each gear.

14. *Two* gears which turn in the *same* direction are:

    A. A and B
    B. B and C
    C. C and D
    D. D and A
    E. B and D

15. The *two* gears which revolve at the *same* speed are gears

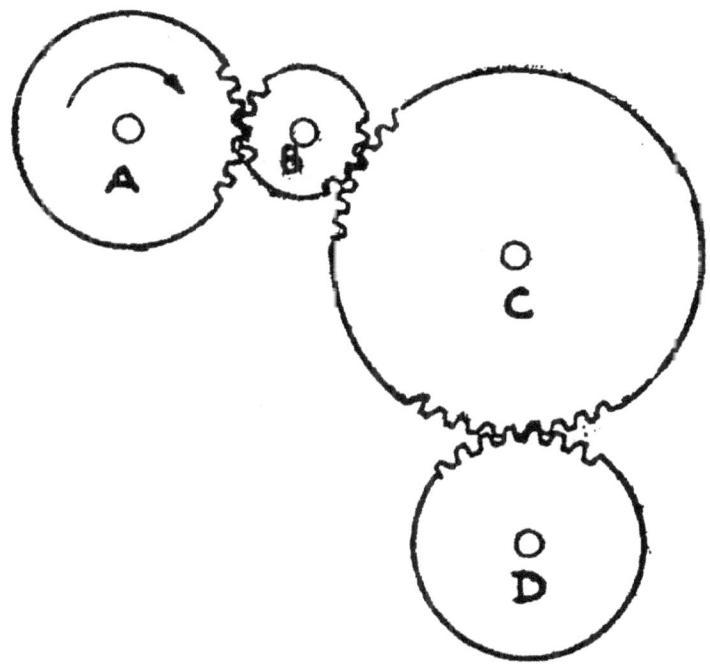

FIGURE IV

   A. A and C   B. A and D   C. B and C
   D. B and D   E. D and C

16. If all the teeth on gear C are stripped without affecting the teeth on gears A, B, and D, then rotation would occur *only* in gear(s)

   A. C   B. D   C. A and B
   D. A, B, and D   E. B and D

17. If gear D is rotating at the rate of 100 RPM, then gear B is rotating at the rate of _____ RPM.

   A. 25   B. 50   C. 100   D. 200   E. 400

18. If gear A turns at the rate of two revolutions per second, then the number of revolutions per second that gear C turns is

   A. 1   B. 2   C. 3   D. 4   E. 8

Questions 19-23.

DIRECTIONS: Answer Questions 19 to 23 on the basis of Figure V. The diagram shows a water pump in cross section: 1 is a check valve, 2 and 3 are the spring and diaphragm, respectively, of the discharge valve, 4 is the pump piston; 5 is the inlet valve, and 6 is the pump cylinder. All valves permit the flow of water in one direction only.

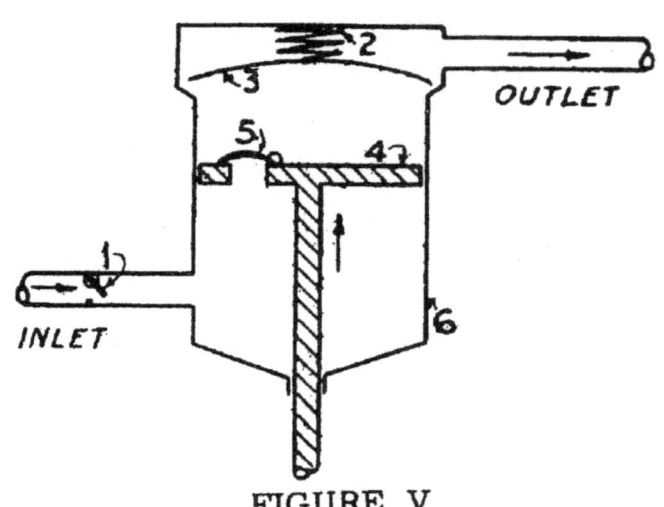

FIGURE V

19. When water is flowing through the outlet pipe,

    A. check valve 1 is closed
    B. diaphragm 3 is closed
    C. valve 5 is closed
    D. spring 2 is fully extended
    E. the piston is on the downstroke

20. If valve 5 does not work properly and stays closed, *then*

    A. the piston cannot move down
    B. the piston cannot move up
    C. diaphragm 3 cannot open
    D. check valve 1 cannot close
    E. the flow of water will be reversed

21. If diaphragm 3 does not work properly and stays in the open position, *then*

    A. check valve 1 will not open
    B. valve 5 will not open
    C. spring 2 will be compressed
    D. spring 2 will be extended
    E. water will not flow through the inlet pipe

22. When valve 5 is open during normal operation of the pump, *then*

    A. spring 2 is fully compressed
    B. the piston is on the upstroke
    C. water is flowing through check valve 1
    D. a vacuum is formed between the piston and the bottom of the cylinder
    E. diaphragm 3 is closed

23. If check valve 1 jams and stays closed, *then*

    A. valve 5 will be open on both the upstroke and down stroke of the piston
    B. a vacuum will tend to form in the inlet pipe between the source of the water supply and check valve 1
    C. pressure on the cylinder side of check valve 1 will increase

D. less force will be required to move the piston down
E. more force will be required to move the piston down

24. The one of the following which *BEST* explains why smoke usually rises from a fire is that 24____

    A. cooler, heavier air displaces lighter, warm air
    B. heat energy of the fire propels the smoke upward
    C. suction from the upper air pulls the smoke upward
    D. burning matter is chemically changed into heat energy

25. The practice of racing a car engine to warm it up in cold weather, generally, is 25____

    A. *good, MAINLY* because repeated stalling of the engine and drain on the battery is avoided
    B. *bad, MAINLY* because too much gas is used to get the engine heated
    C. *good, MAINLY* because the engine becomes operational in the shortest period of time
    D. *bad, MAINLY* because proper lubrication is not established rapidly enough

---

KEY (CORRECT ANSWERS)

1. C	11. B
2. B	12. E
3. B	13. A
4. D	14. E
5. D	15. B
6. B	16. C
7. B	17. D
8. B	18. A
9. C	19. C
10. B	20. A

21. C
22. E
23. D
24. A
25. D

READING COMPREHENSION
UNDERSTANDING WRITTEN MATERIALS

COMMENTARY

The ability to read and understand written materials—texts, publications, newspapers, orders, directions, expositions—is a skill basic to a functioning democracy and to an efficient business or viable government.

That is why almost all examinations—for beginning, middle, and senior levels—test reading comprehension, directly or indirectly.

The reading test measures how well you understand what you read. This is how it is done: You read a passage followed by several statements. From these statements, you choose the one statement, or answer, that is BEST supported by, or BEST matches, what is said in the paragraph. PRINT THE LETTER OF THE CORRECT ANSWER IN THE SPACE AT THE RIGHT.

SAMPLE QUESTIONS

DIRECTIONS: Answer Questions 1 and 2 ONLY according to the information given in the following passage.

1. When a fingerprint technician inks and takes rolled impressions of a subject's fingers, the degree of downward pressure the technician applies is important. The correct pressure may best be determined through experience and observation. It is quite important, however, that the subject be cautioned to relax and not help the fingerprint technician by also applying pressure, as this prevents the fingerprint technician from gaging the amount needed. A method which is helpful in getting the subject to relax his hand is to instruct him to look at some distant object and not to look at his hands.

1. According to this passage, the technician tries to relax the subject's hands by   1.____
   A. instructing him to let his hands hang loosely
   B. telling him that being fingerprinted is painless
   C. asking him to look at this hand instead of some distant object
   D. asking him to look at something other than his hand

2. The subject is asked NOT to press down on his fingers while being fingerprinted   2.____
   because
   A. the impressions taken become rolled
   B. the subject may apply too little downward pressure and spoil the impressions
   C. the technician cannot tell whether he is applying the right degree of pressure
   D. he doesn't have the experience to apply the exact amount of pressure

CORRECT ANSWERS
1. D
2. C

EXAMINATION SECTION

TEST 1

DIRECTIONS: Questions 1 through 3 are to be answered on the basis of the following reading passage. *PRINT THE LETTER OF THE CORRECT ANSWER IN THE SPACE AT THE RIGHT.*

Thermostats should be tested in hot water for proper opening. A bucket should be filled with sufficient water to cover the thermostat and fitted with a thermometer suspended in the water so that the sensitive bulb portion does not rest directly on the bucket. The water is then heated on a stove. As the temperature of the water passes the 160-165° range, the thermostat should start to open and should be completely opened when the temperature has risen to 185-190°. Lifting the thermostat into the air should cause a pronounced closing action and the unit should be closed entirely within a short time.

1. The thermostat described above is a device which opens and closes with changes in the
   A. position   B. pressure   C. temperature   D. surroundings

   1.____

2. According to the above passage, the closing action of the thermostat should be tested by
   A. working the thermostat back and forth
   B. permitting the water to cool gradually
   C. adding cold water to the bucket
   D. removing the thermostat from the bucket

   2.____

3. The bulb of the thermometer should not rest directly on the bucket because
   A. the bucket gets hotter than the water
   B. the thermometer might be damaged in that position
   C. it is difficult to read the thermometer in that position
   D. the thermometer might interfere with operation of the thermostat

   3.____

KEY (CORRECT ANSWERS)

1. C
2. D
3. A

TEST 2

DIRECTIONS: Questions 1 through 3 are to be answered on the basis of the following reading passage. *PRINT THE LETTER OF THE CORRECT ANSWER IN THE SPACE AT THE RIGHT.*

All idle pumps should be turned daily by hand, and should be run under power at least once a week. Whenever repairs are made on a pump, a record should be kept so that it will be possible to judge the success with which the pump is performing its functions. If a pump fails to deliver liquid, there may be an obstruction in the suction line, the pump's parts may be badly worn, or the packing defective.

1. According to the above passage, pumps 1.____
   A. in use should be turned by hand every day
   B. which are not in use should be run under power every day
   C. which are in daily use should be run under power several times a week
   D. which are not in use should be turned by hand every day

2. According to the above passage, the reason for keeping records of repairs made on pumps is to 2.____
   A. make certain that proper maintenance is being performed
   B. discover who is responsible for improper repairs
   C. rate the performance of the pumps
   D. know when to replace worn parts

3. The one of the following causes of pump failure which is NOT mentioned in the above passage is 3.____
   A. excessive suction lift   B. clogged lines
   C. bad packing   D. worn parts

KEY (CORRECT ANSWERS)

1. A
2. C
3. A

TEST 3

DIRECTIONS: Questions 1 through 5 are to be answered on the basis of the following reading passage. *PRINT THE LETTER OF THE CORRECT ANSWER IN THE SPACE AT THE RIGHT.*

Floors in warehouses, storerooms, and shipping rooms must be strong enough to stay level under heavy loads. Unevenness of floors may cause boxes of materials to topple and fall. Safe floor load capacities and maximum heights to which boxes may be stacked should be posted conspicuously so all can notice it. Where material in boxes, containers, or cartons of the same weight is regularly stored, it is good practice to paint a horizontal line on the wall indicating the maximum height to which the material may be piled. A qualified expert should determine floor load capacity from the building plans, the age and condition of the floor supports, the type of floor, and other related information.

Working aisles are those from which material is placed into and removed from storage. Working aisles are of two types: transportation aisles, running the length of the building, and cross aisles, running across the width of the building. Deciding on the number, width, and location of working aisles is important. While aisles are necessary and determine boundaries of storage areas, they reduce the space actually used for storage.

1. According to the above passage, how should safe floor load capacities be made known to employees? They should be
   A. given out to each employee
   B. given to supervisors only
   C. printed in large red letters
   D. posted so that they are easily seen

   1.____

2. According to the above passage, floor load capacities should be determined by
   A. warehouse supervisors   B. the fire department
   C. qualified experts   D. machine operators

   2.____

3. According to the above passage, transportation aisles
   A. run the length of the building
   B. run across the width of the building
   C. are wider than cross aisles
   D. are shorter than cross aisles

   3.____

4. According to the above passage, working aisles tend to
   A. take away space that could be used for storage
   B. add to space that could be used for storage
   C. slow down incoming stock
   D. speed up outgoing stock

   4.____

5. According to the above passage, unevenness of floors may cause
   A. overall warehouse deterioration   B. piles of stock to fall
   C. materials to spoil   D. many worker injuries

   5.____

KEY (CORRECT ANSWERS)

1. D
2. C
3. A
4. A
5. B

TEST 4

DIRECTIONS: Questions 1 through 3 are to be answered on the basis of the following reading passage. *PRINT THE LETTER OF THE CORRECT ANSWER IN THE SPACE AT THE RIGHT.*

In a retail establishment, any overweight means a distinct loss to the merchant, and even an apparently inconsequential overweight on a single package or sale when multiplied by the total number of transactions, could run into large figures. In addition to the use of reliable scales and weights, and their maintenance in proper condition, there must be proper supervision of the selling force. Such supervision is a difficult matter, particularly on the score of carelessness, as the depositing of extra amounts of material on the scale and failure to remove the same when it overbalances the scale may become a habit. In case of underweight, either in the weighing or by the use of fraudulent scales and weights, the seller soon will hear of it, but there is no reason why the amount weighed out should be in excess of what the customer pays for. Checking sales records against invoices and inventories can supply some indication of the tendency of the sales force to become careless in this field.

1. Of the following, the MOST valid implication of the above passage is that
   A. all overweights which occur in retail stores are in small amounts
   B. even-arm and uneven-arm balances and weights which are unreliable lead more often to underweights than to overweights
   C. overweights due to errors of salesclerks necessarily lead to large losses by a retailer
   D. supervision to prevent overweights is more important to a retailer than remedial measures after their occurrence

1.____

2. Of the following, the MOST valid implication of the above passage is that
   A. depositing of insufficient amounts of commodities on scales and failure to add to them may become a habit with salesclerks
   B. salesclerks should be trained in understanding and maintenance of scale mechanisms
   C. supervision of salesclerks to prevent careless habits in weighing must depend upon personal observation

2.____

3. According to the above passage, the MOST accurate of the following statements is:
   A. For the most part, the ideas expressed in the passage do not apply to wholesale establishments.
   B. Inventories of commodities prepacked in the store are the only ones which can be used in checking losses due to overweight.
   C. Invoices which give the value and weight of merchandise received are useful in checking losses due to overweights.
   D. The principal value of inventories is to indicate losses due to overweights.

3.____

KEY (CORRECT ANSWERS)

1. D
2. C
3. C

TEST 5

DIRECTIONS: Questions 1 through 5 are to be answered on the basis of the following reading passage. *PRINT THE LETTER OF THE CORRECT ANSWER IN THE SPACE AT THE RIGHT.*

TITANIC AIR COMPRESSOR

Valves: The compressors are equipped with Titanic plate valves which are automatic in operation. Valves are so constructed that an entire valve assembly can readily be removed from the head. The valves provide large port areas with short lift and are accurately guided to insure positive seating.

Starting Unloader: Each compressor (or air end) is equipped with a centrifugal governor which is bolted directly to the compressor crank shaft. The governor actuates cylinder relief valves so as to relieve pressure from the cylinders during starting and stopping. The motor is never required to start the compressor tinder load.

Air Strainer: Each cylinder air inlet connection is fitted with a suitable combination air strainer and muffler.

Pistons: Pistons are lightweight castings, ribbed internally to secure strength, and are accurately turned and ground. Each piston is fitted with four (4) rings, two of which are oil control rings. Piston pins are hardened and tempered steel of the full floating type. Bronze bushings are used between piston pin and piston

Connecting Rods: Connecting rods are of solid bronze designed for maximum strength, rigidity, and wear. Crank pins are fitted with renewable steel bushings. Connecting rods are of the one-piece type, there being no bolts, nuts, or cotter pins which can come loose. With this type of construction, wear is reduced to a negligible amount, and adjustment of wrist pin and crank pin bearings is unnecessary.

Main Bearings: Main bearings are of the ball type and are securely held in position by spacers. This type of bearing entirely eliminates the necessity of frequent adjustment or attention. The crank shaft is always in perfect alignment.

Crank Shaft: The crank shaft is a one-piece heat-treated forging of best quality open-hearth steel, of rugged design and of sufficient size to transmit the motor power and any additional stresses which may occur in service. Each crank shaft is counter-balanced (dynamically balanced to reduce vibration to a minimum, and is accurately machined to properly receive the ball-bearing races, crank pin bushing, flexible coupling, and centrifugal governor. Suitable provision is made to insure proper lubrication of all crank shaft bearings and bushings with the minimum amount of attention.

Coupling: Compressor and motor shafts are connected through a Morse Chain Company all-metal enclosed flexible coupling. This coupling consists of two sprockets, one mounted on, and keyed to, each shaft; the sprockets are wrapped by a single Morse Chain, the entire assembly being enclosed in a split aluminum grease-packed cover.

1. The crank pin of the connecting rod is fitted with a renewable bushing made of   1._____
   A. solid bronze   B. steel
   C. a lightweight casting D. ball bearings

2. When the connecting rod is of the one-piece type,
   A. the wrist pins require frequent adjustment
   B. the crank pins require frequent adjustment
   C. the cotter pins frequently will come loose
   D. wear is reduced to a negligible amount

3. The centrifugal governor is bolted directly to the
   A. compressor crank shaft   B. main bearing
   C. piston pin   D. muffler

4. The number of oil control rings required for each piston is
   A. one   B. two   C. three   D. four

5. The compressor and motor shafts are connected through a flexible coupling. These couplings are _____ to the shafts.
   A. keyed   B. brazed   C. soldered   D. press-fit

KEY (CORRECT ANSWERS)

1. B
2. D
3. A
4. B
5. A

TEST 6

DIRECTIONS: Questions 1 through 6 are to be answered on the basis of the following reading passage. *PRINT THE LETTER OF THE CORRECT ANSWER IN THE SPACE AT THE RIGHT.*

Perhaps the strongest argument the mass transit backer has is the advantage in efficiency that mass transit has over the automobile in the urban traffic picture. It has been estimated that given comparable location and construction conditions, the subway can carry four times as many passengers per hour and cost half as much to build as urban highways. Yet public apathy regarding the mass transportation movement in the 1960's resulted in the building of more roads. Planned to provide 42,000 miles of highways in the period from 1956-72, including 7,500 miles within cities, the Federal Highway System project is now about two-thirds completed. The Highway Trust Fund supplies 90 percent of the cost of the system, with state and local sources putting up the rest of the money. By contrast, a municipality has had to put up the bulk of the cost of a rapid transit system. Although the system and its Trust Fund have come under attack in the past few years from environmentalists and groups opposed to the continued building of urban freeways—considered to be the most expensive, destructive, and inefficient segments of the system—a move by them to get the Trust Fund transformed into a general transportation fund at the expiration of the present program in 1972 seems to be headed nowhere.

1. Given similar building conditions and locations, a city that builds a subway instead of a highway can expect to receive for each dollar spent _____ as much transport value.
   A. half   B. twice   C. four times   D. eight times

   1.____

2. The general attitude of the public in the past ten years toward the mass transportation movement has been
   A. favorable   B. indifferent   C. enthusiastic   D. unfriendly

   2.____

3. The number of miles of highways still to be completed in the Federal Highway System project is MOST NEARLY
   A. 2,500   B. 5,000   C. 14,000   D. 28,000

   3.____

4. What do certain groups who object to some features of the Federal Highway System program want to do with the Highway Trust Fund after 1972?
   A. Extend it in order to complete the project
   B. Change it so that the money can be used for all types of transportation
   C. End it even if the project is not completed
   D. Change it so that the money will be used only for urban freeways

   4.____

5. Which one of the following statements is a VALID conclusion based on the facts in the above passage?
   A. The advantage of greater efficiency is the only argument that supporters of the mass transportation movement can offer.
   B. It was easier for cities to build roads rather than mass transit systems in the last 15 years because of the large financial contribution made by the Federal Government.

   5.____

C. Mass transit systems cause as much congestion and air pollution in cities as automobiles.
D. In 1972, the Highway Trust Fund becomes a general transportation fund.

6. The MAIN idea or theme of the above passage is that the 6.____
A. cost of the Federal Highway System is shared by the federal, state, and local governments
B. public is against spending money for building mass transportation facilities in the cities
C. cities would benefit more from expansion and improvement of their mass transit systems than from the building of more highways
D. building of mass transportation facilities has been slowed by the Highway Trust Fund

KEY (CORRECT ANSWERS)

1. D
2. B
3. C
4. B
5. B
6. C

TEST 7

DIRECTIONS: Questions 1 through 5 are to be answered on the basis of the following reading passage. *PRINT THE LETTER OF THE CORRECT ANSWER IN THE SPACE AT THE RIGHT.*

The use of role-playing as a training technique was developed during the past decade by social scientists, particularly psychologists, who have been active in training experiments. Originally, this technique was applied by clinical psychologists who discovered that a patient appears to gain understanding of an emotionally disturbing situation when encouraged to act out roles in that situation. As applied in government and business organizations, the purpose of role-playing is to aid employees to understand certain work problems involving interpersonal relations and to enable observers to evaluate various reactions to them. Thus, for example, on the problem of handling grievances, two individuals from the group might be selected to act out extemporaneously the parts of subordinate and supervisor. When this situation is enacted by various pairs among the class and the techniques and results are discussed, the members of the group are presumed to reach conclusions about the most effective means of handling similar situations. Often the use or role reversal, where participants take parts different from their actual work roles, assists individuals to gain more insight into other people's problems and viewpoints. Although role-playing can be a rewarding training device, the trainer must be aware of his responsibilities. If this technique is to be successful, thorough briefing of both actors and observers as to the situation in question, the participants' roles, and what to look for, is essential.

1. The role-playing technique was FIRST used for the purpose of 1.____
   A. measuring the effectiveness of training programs
   B. training supervisors in business organizations
   C. treating emotionally disturbed patients
   D. handling employee grievances

2. When role-playing is used in private business as a training device, the CHIEF 2.____
   aim is to
   A. develop better relations between supervisor and subordinate in the handling of grievances
   B. come up with a solution to a specific problem that has arisen
   C. determine the training needs of the group
   D. increase employee understanding of the human-relation factors in work situations

3. From the above passage, it is MOST reasonable to conclude that when role- 3.____
   playing is used, it is preferable to have the roles acted out by
   A. only one set of actors
   B. no more than two sets of actors
   C. several different sets of actors
   D. the trainer or trainers of the group

4. It can be inferred from the above passage that a limitation of role-playing as a training method is that
    A. many work situations do not lend themselves to role-play
    B. employees are not experienced enough as actors to play the roles realistically
    C. only trainers who have psychological training can use it successfully
    D. participants who are observing and not acting do not benefit from it

5. To obtain *good* results from the use of role-play in training, a trainer should give participants
    A. a minimum of information about the situation so that they can act spontaneously
    B. scripts which illustrate the best method for handling the situation
    C. a complete explanation of the problem and the roles to be acted out
    D. a summary of work problems which involve interpersonal relations

KEY (CORRECT ANSWERS)

1. C
2. D
3. C
4. A
5. C

WORD MEANING

EXAMINATION SECTION
TEST 1

DIRECTIONS: Each question or incomplete statement is followed by several suggested answers or completions. Select the one that BEST answers the question or completes the statement. *PRINT THE LETTER OF THE CORRECT ANSWER IN THE SPACE AT HE IGHT.*

1. He received a large reward.
   In this sentence, the word *reward* means

   A. capture   B. recompense   C. key   D. praise

2. The aide was asked to transmit a message. In this sentence, the word *transmit* means

   A. change   B. send   C. take   D. type

3. The pest control aide requested the tenant to call the Health Department.
   In this sentence, the word *requested* means the pest control aide

   A. asked   B. helped   C. informed   D. warned

4. The driver had to return the department's truck. In this sentence, the word *return* means

   A. borrow   B. fix   C. give back   D. load up

5. The aide discussed the purpose of the visit. In this sentence, the word *purpose* means

   A. date   B. hour   C. need   D. reason

6. The tenant suspected the aide who knocked at her door. In this sentence, the word *suspected* means

   A. answered   B. called   C. distrusted   D. welcomed

7. The aide was positive that the child hit her. In this sentence, the word *positive* means

   A. annoyed   B. certain   C. sorry   D. surprised

8. The tenant declined to call the Health Department. In this sentence, the word *declined* means

   A. agreed   B. decided   C. refused   D. wanted

9. The porter cleaned the vacant room.
   In this sentence, the word *vacant* means NEARLY the same as

   A. empty   B. large   C. main   D. crowded

10. The supervisor gave a brief report to his men.
    In this sentence, the word *brief* means NEARLY the same as

    A. long   B. safety   C. complete   D. short

11. The supervisor told him to connect the two pieces.
    In this sentence, the word *connect* means NEARLY the same as

    A. join   B. paint   C. return   D. weigh

12. Standing on the top of a ladder is risky.
    In this sentence, the word *risky* means NEARLY the same as

    A. dangerous   B. sensible   C. safe   D. foolish

13. He raised the cover of the machine.
    In this sentence, the word *raised* means NEARLY the same as

    A. broke   B. lifted   C. lost   D. found

14. The form used for reporting the finished work was revised. In this sentence, the word *revised* means NEARLY the same as

    A. printed   B. ordered   C. dropped   D. changed

15. He did his work rapidly.
    In this sentence, the word *rapidly* means NEARLY the same a

    A. carefully   B. quickly   C. slowly   D. quietly

16. The worker was occasionally late.
    In this sentence, the word *occasionally* means NEARLY the same as

    A. sometimes   B. often   C. never   D. always

17. He selected the best tool for the job.
    In this sentence, the word *selected* means NEARLY the same as

    A. bought   B. picked   C. lost   D. broke

18. He needed assistance to lift the package.
    In this sentence, the word *assistance* means NEARLY the same as

    A. strength   B. time   C. help   D. instructions

19. The tools were issued by the supervisor.
    In this sentence, the word *issued* means NEARLY the same as

    A. collected   B. cleaned up   C. given out   D. examined

20. A permit for a tap for unmetered water will be issued only on prepayment of all charges for water to be used. In this sentence, the word *prepayment* means

    A. promise of payment   B. payment in advance
    C. payment as water is used   D. monthly payment

21. Upon application, the department will endeavor to locate a service pipe by means of an electrical indicator.
    In this sentence, the word *endeavor* means

    A. try　　　B. help　　　C. assist　　　D. explore

22. It shall be unlawful for any person to operate certain equipment without previous permission from the department. In this sentence, the word *previous* means

    A. written　　　B. oral　　　C. prior　　　D. provisional

23. All persons must comply with the rules and regulations. In this sentence, the word *comply* means

    A. agree　　　　　　B. coincide
    C. work carefully　　D. act in accord

24. No unauthorized person shall tamper with a water supply valve.
    In this sentence, the words *tamper with* means

    A. open　　　B. operate　　　C. alter　　　D. shut

25. The use of water is permitted subject to such conditions as the department may consider reasonable.
    In this sentence, the word *reasonable* means

    A. necessary　　　B. inexpensive　　　C. fair　　　D. desirable

26. An owner must engage a licensed plumber. In this sentence, the word *engage* means

    A. hire　　　B. pay　　　C. contact　　　D. inform

27. The charges for a machine part are usually for the furnishing, delivering, and installing of the part. In this sentence, the word *furnishing* means

    A. preparing　　　B. manufacturing　　　C. finishing　　　D. supplying

28. The investigator attempted to ascertain the facts.
    As used in this sentence, the word *ascertain* means MOST NEARLY to

    A. disprove　　　B. find out　　　C. go beyond　　　D. explain

29. The speaker commenced the lecture with an anecdote.
    As used in this sentence, the word *commenced* means MOST NEARLY

    A. concluded　　　B. illustrated　　　C. enlivered　　　D. started

30. The use of a hydrant may be authorized for construction purposes.
    As used in this sentence, the word *authorized* means

    A. possible　　　B. permitted　　　C. intended　　　D. stopped

31. Conservation of the water supply is a major goal of the department.
    As used in this sentence, the word *conservation* means MOST NEARLY

    A. estimating
    B. increasing
    C. preserving
    D. purifying

32. Consumers should inspect their faucets frequently to guard against leaks.
    As used in this sentence, the word *consumers* means MOST NEARLY

    A. citizens
    B. owners
    C. producers
    D. users

33. The wire was connected to the adjacent terminal.
    As used in this sentence, the word *adjacent* means MOST NEARLY

    A. out of order
    B. metallic
    C. nearby
    D. negative

34. Some of the equipment supplied to the inspector was defective.
    As used in this sentence, the word *defective* means MOSTNEARLY

    A. expensive
    B. faulty
    C. old
    D. unnecessary

35. The inspector was told to use discretion in dealing with the public.
    As used in this sentence, the word *discretion* means MOST NEARLY

    A. courtesy
    B. firmness
    C. judgment
    D. persuasion

36. It is unlawful to demolish any building without first obtaining a permit.
    As used in this sentence, the word *demolish* means MOST NEARLY

    A. build
    B. make alterations in
    C. occupy
    D. tear down

37. The clerk rendered an account of the cash received.
    As used in this sentence, the word *rendered* means MOST NEARLY

    A. concealed
    B. corrected
    C. forged
    D. gave

38. The permit was revoked by the department.
    As used in this sentence, the word *revoked* means MOST NEARLY

    A. approved
    B. cancelled
    C. renewed
    D. reviewed

39. The incident received much attention in the newspapers. As used in this sentence, the word *incident* means MOST NEARLY

    A. campaign
    B. crime
    C. event
    D. merger

40. The modification of the procedure was approved by the supervisor.
    As used in this sentence, the word *modification* means MOST NEARLY

    A. change B. interpretation
    C. repeal D. termination

41. The workers combined the contents of the two boxes. The word *combined* means

    A. sifted through B. put together
    C. tore apart D. forgot about

42. Don't touch the lever on the left side. The word *lever* means

    A. button B. rope C. handle D. gun

43. All litter should be taken away. The word *litter* means

    A. paint B. bowls C. rubbish D. evidence

44. The inspection of the street was complete. The word *inspection* means

    A. cleaning B. examination
    C. repair D. painting

45. The route must be followed exactly.
    The word *route* means

    A. foreman B. truck C. way D. recipe

46. Don't injure your back.
    The word *injure* means

    A. bend B. use C. hurt D. exercise

47. John repaired the machine.
    The word *repaired* means

    A. fixed B. broke C. ran D. oiled

48. Put the lid on the box.
    The word *lid* means

    A. cover B. ribbon C. rope D. wrapping

49. The rear of the truck should be washed.
    The word *rear* means

    A. hood B. front C. back D. roof

50. Coworkers must assist each other while at work. The word *assist* means

    A. help B. outdo C. like D. hurt

KEY (CORRECT ANSWERS)

1. B	11. A	21. A	31. C	41. B
2. B	12. A	22. C	32. D	42. C
3. A	13. B	23. D	33. C	43. C
4. C	14. D	24. C	34. B	44. B
5. D	15. B	25. C	35. C	45. C
6. C	16. A	26. A	36. D	46. C
7. B	17. B	27. D	37. D	47. A
8. C	18. C	28. B	38. B	48. A
9. A	19. C	29. D	39. C	49. C
10. D	20. B	30. B	40. A	50. A

TEST 2

DIRECTIONS: Each question or incomplete statement is followed by several suggested answers or completions. Select the one that BEST answers the question or completes the statement. *PRINT THE LETTER OF THE CORRECT ANSWER IN THE SPACE AT THE RIGHT.*

1. It is possible to construct a leak-proof home.
   The OPPOSITE of *construct* is   1.____

   A. build   B. erect   C. plant   D. wreck

2. The driver had to repair the flat tire.
   The OPPOSITE of the word *repair* is   2.____

   A. destroy   B. fix   C. mend   D. patch

3. The student tried to shout the answer.
   The OPPOSITE of the word *shout* is   3.____

   A. scream   B. shriek   C. whisper   D. yell

4. Daily visits are the best.
   The OPPOSITE of the word *visits* is   4.____

   A. absences   B. exercises   C. lessons   D. trials

5. It is important to arrive early in the morning.
   The OPPOSITE of the word *arrive* is   5.____

   A. climb   B. descend   C. enter   D. leave

6. Mike is a group leader.
   The OPPOSITE of the word *leader* is   6.____

   A. boss   B. chief   C. follower   D. overseer

7. The exterior of the house needs painting.
   The OPPOSITE of the word *exterior* is   7.____

   A. inside   B. outdoors   C. outside   D. surface

8. He conceded the victory.
   The OPPOSITE of the word *conceded* is   8.____

   A. admitted   B. denied   C. granted   D. reported

9. He watched the team begin.
   The OPPOSITE of the word *begin* is   9.____

   A. end   B. fail   C. gather   D. win

10. Your handwriting is illegible.
    The OPPOSITE of the word *illegible* is   10.____

    A. clear   B. confused   C. jumbled   D. unclear

11. The one of the following words that has the OPPOSITE meaning of *partition* is
    A. division   B. connection   C. barrier   D. compartment

12. The one of the following words that has the OPPOSITE meaning of *obvious* is
    A. concealed   B. known   C. clear   D. apparent

13. The one of the following words that has the OPPOSITE meaning of *assist* is
    A. hinder   B. offer   C. demand   D. aid

14. The one of the following words that has the OPPOSITE meaning of *obsolete* is
    A. neglected   B. traditional   C. rare   D. new

15. The one of the following words that has the OPPOSITE meaning of *stagnant* is
    A. murky   B. active   C. calm   D. dirty

16. The number of applicants exceeded the anticipated figure. As used in this sentence, the word *anticipated* means MOST NEARLY
    A. expected   B. required   C. revised   D. necessary

17. The clerk was told to collate the pages of the report. As used in this sentence, the word *collate* means MOST NEARLY
    A. destroy   B. edit   C. correct   D. assemble

18. Mr. Wells is not authorized to release the information. As used in this sentence, the word *authorized* means MOST NEARLY
    A. inclined   B. pleased   C. permitted   D. trained

19. The secretary chose an appropriate office for the meeting. As used in this sentence, the word *appropriate* means MOST NEARLY
    A. empty   B. decorated   C. nearby   D. suitable

20. The employee performs a complex set of tasks each day. As used in this sentence, the word *complex* means MOST NEARLY
    A. difficult   B. important   C. pleasant   D. large

21. In talking with a homeowner, an inspector should always be polite. As used in this sentence, the word *polite* means
    A. cold   B. courteous   C. aggressive   D. modest

22. In talking with a client, a worker should not discuss trivial matters. As used in this sentence, the word *trivial* means
    A. related   B. essential   C. significant   D. unimportant

23. The one of the following words that is SIMILAR in meaning to *revise* is

    A. edit B. confuse C. complicate D. dismiss

24. The one of the following words that is SIMILAR in meaning to *abandon* is

    A. quit B. use C. remain D. discourage

25. The one of the following words that is SIMILAR in meaning to *adjacent* is

    A. far B. detached C. bordering D. distant

26. The one of the following words that is SIMILAR in meaning to *coarse* is

    A. fine B. smooth C. rough D. slick

27. The one of the following words that is SIMILAR in meaning to *orifice* is

    A. chamber B. enclosure C. opening D. device

28. The aide arrived on time.
    In this sentence, the word *arrived* means

    A. awoke B. came C. left D. delayed

29. The salesman had to deliver books to each person he visited.
    In this sentence, the word *deliver* means

    A. give B. lend C. mail D. sell

30. When estimating materials for interior plaster, consideration must be given to the number of coats.
    As used in this sentence, the word *estimating* means

    A. calculating approximately B. purchasing
    C. mixing together D. finishing

31. As used in the sentence in Question 30 above, the word *consideration* means

    A. extra weight B. careful thought
    C. firmness D. additions

32. When computing quantities of plaster for the scratch coat, no allowance may be made for the space occupied by the metal lath.
    As used in this sentence, the word *computing* means

    A. figuring B. preparing C. slaking D. packing

33. As used in the sentence in Question 32 above, the word *allowance* means

    A. deduction B. addition C. leeway D. closing

34. The supervisor made a ridiculous statement.
    As used in this sentence, the word *ridiculous* means MOST NEARLY

    A. incorrect B. evil C. unfriendly D. foolish

35. That worker is engaged in a hazardous job.
    As used in this sentence, the word *hazardous* means MOST NEARLY

    A. inconvenient   B. dangerous   C. difficult   D. demanding

36. Breaks in water distribution mains are front page news for the very reason that they occur infrequently.
    As used in this sentence, the word *infrequently* means MOST NEARLY

    A. at regular intervals   B. often
    C. rarely   D. unexpectedly

37. Several kinds of self-caulking substitutes for lead have been developed.
    As used in this sentence, the word *substitutes* means MOST NEARLY

    A. additives   B. replacements   C. hardeners   D. softeners

38. Cast iron is essentially an alloy of iron and carbon. As used in this sentence, the word *essentially* means MOST NEARLY

    A. never   B. basically   C. barely   D. sometimes

39. When water moves through pipe, friction is developed between the water and the inside surface of the pipe. As used in this sentence, the word *friction* means MOST NEARLY

    A. resistance   B. heat   C. slippage   D. pressure

40. A person who is confident he can complete a task is said to be

    A. courageous   B. sure   C. bright   D. successful

41. If a child sleeping peacefully is awakened by a sudden cry, he is likely to be

    A. ill   B. uncomfortable   C. startled   D. hungry

42. He could not get his truck on the highway. A *highway* is a type of

    A. lot   B. road   C. scale   D. sidewalk

43. The large vehicle was being repaired.
    Which of the following is a *vehicle*?

    A. Truck   B. Building   C. Boiler   D. Table

44. The fence needs to be painted.
    The one of the following which is MOST like a *fence* is a

    A. door   B. crane   C. wall   D. building

45. Furniture is not taken with the regular garbage collection.
    Which of the following is *furniture*?

    A. Sofas and chairs   B. Cars and trucks
    C. Brooms and mops   D. Bags and boxes

46. The group was assigned to do special work. Which of the following is a *group*? 46._____

    A. Truck B. Boat C. Team D. Foreman

47. Sanitation men often use tools in their work. 47._____
    The one of the following which is MOST often considered a *tool* is a

    A. tire B. shovel C. glove D. basket

48. The man claimed that he could not lift the box. The word *lift* means MOST NEARLY 48._____

    A. bury B. pick up C. refill D. clean

49. Place all the boxes below the second shelf. The word *below* means 49._____

    A. under B. into C. beside D. over

50. This street should be clean when the sanitation men finish. 50._____
    The word *clean* means free of

    A. obstacles B. pedestrians C. traffic D. dirt

KEY (CORRECT ANSWERS)

1. D	11. B	21. B	31. B	41. C
2. A	12. A	22. D	32. A	42. B
3. C	13. A	23. A	33. A	43. A
4. A	14. D	24. A	34. D	44. C
5. D	15. B	25. C	35. B	45. A
6. C	16. A	26. C	36. C	46. C
7. A	17. D	27. C	37. B	47. B
8. B	18. C	28. B	38. B	48. B
9. A	19. D	29. A	39. A	49. A
10. A	20. A	30. A	40. B	50. D

TEST 3

DIRECTIONS: Each question or incomplete statement is followed by several suggested answers or completions. Select the one that BEST answers the question or completes the statement. *PRINT THE LETTER OF THE CORRECT ANSWER IN THE SPACE AT THE RIGHT.*

Questions 1-6.

DIRECTIONS: In the paragraph below, some of the underlined words have been purposely changed and spoil the meaning that the rest of the paragraph is meant to give. Read the paragraph carefully. Then, answer Questions 1 through 6.

The motor vehicle supervisor who is <u>responsible</u> for training drivers in the operation of <u>special</u> equipment cannot expect a man to carry out all of his duties <u>poorly</u> <u>immediately</u> after receiving instruction. The employee may be overwhelmed by all of the details he must master, <u>happy</u> because he is <u>associated</u> with new fellow workers, or fearful that he may not <u>succeed</u> on the job. It is the supervisor's <u>job</u> to make the <u>operator</u> feel at ease and <u>discourage</u> his self-confidence. The supervisor must also vary the speed of the <u>driving</u> according to the operator's <u>capacity</u> to <u>absorb</u> the instruction without undue pressure or confusion. All learners <u>progress</u> through <u>several</u> stages of <u>development</u> <u>unless</u> they become expert in their duties. As the operator's skills <u>increase,</u> he will require <u>more</u> instruction but the supervisor should be available to correct <u>mistakes</u> promptly to prevent wrong <u>habits</u> being formed.

1. Of the following words underlined in the above paragraph, the one that does NOT give the real meaning that the rest of the paragraph is meant to give is

   A. responsible   B. special   C. happy   D. immediately

2. Of the following words underlined in the above paragraph, the one that does NOT give the real meaning that the rest of the paragraph is meant to give is

   A. overwhelmed   B. happy   C. associated   D. succeed

3. Of the following words underlined in the above paragraph, the one that does NOT give the real meaning that the rest of the paragraph is meant to give is

   A. job   B. operator   C. discourage   D. self-confidence

4. Of the following words underlined in the above paragraph, the one that does NOT give the real meaning that the rest of the paragraph is meant to give is

   A. driving   B. capacity   C. absorb   D. pressure

5. Of the following words underlined in the above paragraph, the one that does NOT give the real meaning that the rest of the paragraph is meant to give is

   A. progress   B. several   C. development   D. unless

6. Of the following words underlined in the above paragraph, the one that does NOT give the real meaning that the rest of the paragraph is meant to give is

   A. increase   B. more   C. mistakes   D. habits

Questions 7-13.

DIRECTIONS: Each of Questions 7 through 13 consists of a capitalized word followed by four suggested meanings of the word. Select the word or phrase which means MOST NEARLY the same as the capitalized word.

7. ACCELERATE 7.____
   A. adjust   B. press   C. quicken   D. strip

8. ALIGN 8.____
   A. bring into line   B. carry out
   C. happen by chance   D. join together

9. CONTRACTION 9.____
   A. agreement   B. denial
   C. presentation   D. shrinkage

10. INTERVAL 10.____
    A. ending   B. mixing together of
    C. space of time D. weaken

11. LUBRICATE 11.____
    A. bend back   B. make slippery
    C. rub out   D. soften

12. OBSOLETE 12.____
    A. broken-down   B. hard to find
    C. high-priced   D. out of date

13. RETARD 13.____
    A. delay   B. flatten   C. rest   D. tally

14. Any major components of a fire communication system should be meticulously maintained. 14.____
    In the preceding sentence, the word *meticulously* means MOST NEARLY
    A. indifferently   B. perfunctorily
    C. painstakingly   D. languidly

Questions 15-17.

DIRECTIONS: Questions 15 through 17 are to be answered in accordance with the following statement.

In order to facilitate prompt assembly of designated members, the officer in charge, Bureau of Fire Communications, shall maintain accurate current data on all such matters.

15. The word *facilitate,* as used in the above statement, means MOST NEARLY   15.___

   A. authorize   B. expedite   C. command   D. hinder

16. The word *designated,* as used in the above statement, means MOST NEARLY   16.___

   A. required   B. versatile   C. skillful   D. selected

17. The word *data,* as used in the above statement, means MOST NEARLY   17.___

   A. calculations   B. information   C. forecasts   D. surveillance

Questions 18-19.

   DIRECTIONS: Questions 18 and 19 are to be answered in accordance with the following statement.

   In the event of severe <u>disruption</u> of circuits....members of this squad may be.... <u>detailed</u> to Bureau of Fire Communications for duration of such emergency.

18. The word *disruption,* as used in the above sentence, means MOST NEARLY   18.___

   A. overloading   B. breakdown   C. disuse   D. concurrence

19. The word *detailed,* as used in the above statement, means MOST NEARLY   19.___

   A. assigned   B. reported   C. demoted   D. promoted

20. The officer in command, after verification that the alarm was false, shall transmit by radio the signal 9-2 followed by box number.   20.___
   The word *verification,* as used in the above sentence, means MOST NEARLY

   A. confirmation   B. consideration   C. notification   D. confutation

Questions 21-23.

   DIRECTIONS: Questions 21 through 23 are to be answered on the basis of the following statement.

   The manual of Fire Communications was planned to serve the Fire Department as guide and reference in effective use of its vast, <u>versatile</u> communications network.... Complete understanding of its phases and <u>precepts,</u> together with prompt <u>compliance</u> with all requirements and actions set in motion by its coded signals and radio transmissions, are essential.

21. The word *versatile,* as used in the above statement, means MOST NEARLY   21.___

   A. steady   B. many-sided   C. constant   D. wavering

22. The word *precepts,* as used in the above statement, means MOST NEARLY   22.___

   A. forerunners   B. paragraphs   C. rules   D. sections

23. The word *compliance,* as used in the above statement, means MOST NEARLY   23.____

    A. variance   B. dissension   C. divergence   D. conformance

24. A person who is influenced in making a decision by preconceived opinions is said to be   24.____

    A. subjective   B. obstinate   C. hateful   D. ignorant

25. No time was set for the conference.   25.____
    The word below that BEST describes this fact is

    A. indefinite   B. decisive   C. ignored   D. powerful

26. The truck could not go under the bridge because the bridge was too low.   26.____
    The reason the truck could not go under the bridge was that the bridge was not _____ enough.

    A. high   B. long   C. strong   D. wide

Questions 27-29.

DIRECTIONS: Questions 27 through 29 are to be answered on the basis of the following statement.

In structures exceeding 150 ft. in height, adequate means shall be provided for taking care of the expansion and contraction of all vertical lines of pipe. In addition, adequate means shall be provided to properly support all vertical lines of pipe.

27. The word *adequate,* as used above, means MOST NEARLY   27.____

    A. liquid devices
    B. properly designed and sufficient
    C. strong and thick walled
    D. in very great numbers

28. The word *expansion,* as used above, means MOST NEARLY a(n)   28.____

    A. bulbous swelling
    B. transverse projection
    C. large increase in diameter
    D. an increase in length

29. The word *contraction,* as used above, means MOST NEARLY   29.____

    A. contract to install the vertical line
    B. reduction in length
    C. to group all vertical lines together
    D. to decrease the equivalent length

30. A common mistake is to assume that the strength of equipment is the most important factor.   30.____
    As used in the above sentence, the word *assume* means MOST NEARLY

    A. determine   B. take for granted
    C. figure   D. make sure

KEY (CORRECT ANSWERS)

1. C	11. B	21. B
2. B	12. D	22. C
3. C	13. A	23. D
4. A	14. C	24. A
5. D	15. B	25. A
6. B	16. D	26. A
7. C	17. B	27. B
8. A	18. B	28. D
9. D	19. A	29. B
10. C	20. A	30. B

ARITHMETIC
EXAMINATION SECTION
TEST 1

DIRECTIONS: Each question or incomplete statement is followed by several suggested answers or completions. Select the one that BEST answers the question or completes the statement. PRINT THE LETTER OF THE CORRECT ANSWER IN THE SPACE AT THE RIGHT.

1. Add $4.34, $34.50, $6.00, $101.76, $90.67. From the result, subtract $60.54 and $10.56.   1._____
   A. $76.17   B. $156.37   C. $166.17   D. $300.37

2. Add 2,200, 2,600, 252 and 47.96. From the result, subtract 202.70, 1,200, 2,150 and 434.43.   2._____
   A. 1,112.83   B. 1,213.46   C. 1,341.51   D. 1,348.91

3. Multiply 1850 by .05 and multiply 3300 by .08 and, then, add both results.   3._____
   A. 242.50   B. 264.00   C. 333.25   D. 356.50

4. Multiply 312.77 by .04. Round off the result to the nearest hundredth.   4._____
   A. 12.52   B. 12.511   C. 12.518   D. 12.51

5. Add 362.05, 91.13, 347.81 and 17.46 and then divide the result by 6. The answer, rounded off to the nearest hundredth, is: 5._____
   A. 138.409   B. 137.409   C. 136.41   D. 136.40

6. Add 66.25 and 15.06 and, then, multiply the result by 2 1/6. The answer is, most nearly,   6._____
   A. 176.18   B. 176.17   C. 162.66   D. 162.62

7. Each of the following items contains three decimals. In which case do *all* three decimals have the SAME value?   7._____
   A. .3; .30; .03
   B. .25; .250; .2500
   C. 1.9; 1.90; 1.09
   D. .35; .350; .035

8. Add 1/2 the sum of (539.84 and 479.26) to 1/3 the sum of (1461.93 and 927.27). Round off the result to the nearest whole number.   8._____
   A. 3408   B. 2899   C. 1816   D. 1306

9. Multiply $5,906.09 by 15% and, then, divide the result by 3 and round off to the nearest cent.   9._____
   A. $295.30   B. $885.91   C. $2,657.74   D. $29,530.45

10. Multiply 630 by 517.   10._____
    A. 325,710   B. 345,720   C. 362,425   D. 385,660

11. Multiply 35 by 846.

    A. 4050   B. 9450   C. 18740   D. 29610

12. Multiply 823 by 0.05.

    A. 0.4115   B. 4.115   C. 41.15   D. 411.50

13. Multiply 1690 by 0.10.

    A. 0.169   B. .1.69   C. 16.90   D. 169.0

14. Divide 2765 by 35.

    A. 71   B. 79   C. 87   D. 93

15. From $18.55 subtract $6.80.

    A. $9.75   B. $10.95   C. $11.75   D. $25.35

16. The sum of 2.75 + 4.50 + 3.60 is:

    A. 9.75   B. 10.85   C. 11.15   D. 11.95

17. The sum of 9.63 + 11.21 + 17.25 is:

    A. 36.09   B. 38.09   C. 39.92   D. 41.22

18. The sum of 112.0 + 16.9 + 3.84 is:

    A. 129.3   B. 132.74   C. 136.48   D. 167.3

19. When 65 is added to the result of 14 multiplied by 13, the answer is:

    A. 92   B. 182   C. 247   D. 16055

20. From $391.55 subtract $273.45.

    A. $118.10   B. $128.20   C. $178.10   D. $218.20

KEY (CORRECT ANSWERS)

1.	C	11.	D
2.	A	12.	C
3.	D	13.	D
4.	D	14.	B
5.	C	15.	C
6.	B	16.	B
7.	B	17.	B
8.	D	18.	B
9.	C	19.	C
10.	A	20.	A

SOLUTIONS TO PROBLEMS

1. ($4.34 + $34.50 + $6.00 + $101.76 + $90.67) - ($60.54 + $10.56) = $237.27 - $71.10 = $166.17.

2. (2200 + 2600 + 252 + 47.96) - (202.70 + 1200 + 2150 + 434.43) = 5099.96 - 3987.13 = 1112.83

3. (1850)(.05) + (3300)(.08) = 92.5 + 264 = 356.50

4. (312.77)(.04) = 12.5108 = 12.51 to nearest hundredth

5. $(362.05+91.13+347.81+17.46) \div 6 = 136.40\overline{83} = 136.41$ to nearest hundredth

6. $(66.25+15.06)(2\frac{1}{6}) = 176.171\overline{6} \approx 176.17$

7. .25 = .250 = .2500

8. $(\frac{1}{2})(539.84+479.26) + \frac{1}{3}(1461.93+927.27) = 509.55 + 796.4 = 1305.95 = 1306$ nearest whole number

9. ($5906.09)(.15) ÷ 3 = ($885.9135)/3 = 295.3045 = $295.30 to nearest cent

10. (630)(517) = 325,710

11. (35)(846) = 29,610

12. (823)(.05) = 41.15

13. (1690)(10) = 169.0

14. 2765 ÷ 3.5 = 79

15. $18.55 - $6.80 = $11.75

16. 2.75 + 4.50 + 3.60 = 10.85

17. 9.63 + 11.21 + 17.25 = 38.09

18. 112.0 + 16.9 + 3.84 = 132.74

19. 65 + (14)(13) = 65 + 182 = 247

20. $391.55 - $273.45 = $118.10

TEST 2

DIRECTIONS   Each question or incomplete statement is followed by several suggested answers or completions. Select the one that *BEST* answers the question or completes the statement. *PRINT THE LETTER OF TEE CORRECT ANSWER IN THE SPACE AT THE RIGHT.*

1. The sum of $29.61 + $101.53 + $943.64 is: 1.____
   A. $983.88   B. $1074.78   C. $1174.98   D. $1341.42

2. The sum of $132.25 + $85.63 + $7056,44 is: 2.____
   A. $1694.19   B. $7274.32   C. $8464.57   D. $9346.22

3. The sum of 4010 + 1271 + 838 + 23 is: 3.____
   A. 6142   B. 6162   C. 6242   D. 6362

4. The sum of 53632 + 27403 + 98765 + 75424 is: 4.____
   A. 19214   B. 215214   C. 235224   D. 255224

5. The sum of 76342 + 49050 + 21206 + 59989 is: 5.____
   A. 196586   B. 206087   C. 206587   D. 234487

6. The sum of $452.13 + $963.45 + $621.25 is: 6.____
   A. $1936.83   B. $2036.83   C. $2095.73   D. $2135.73

7. The sum of 36392 + 42156 + 98765 is: 7.____
   A. 167214   B. 177203   C. 177313   D. 178213

8. The sum of 40125 + 87123 + 24689 is: 8.____
   A. 141827   B. 151827   C. 151937   D. 161947

9. The sum of 2379 + 4015 + 6521 + 9986 is: 9.____
   A. 22901   B. 22819   C. 21801   D. 21791

10. From 50962 subtract 36197.   10.____
    A. 14675   B. 14765   C. 14865   D. 24765

11. From 90000 subtract 31928.   11.____
    A. 58072   B. 59062   C. 68172   D. 69182

12. From 63764 subtract 21548.   12.____
    A. 42216   B. 43122   C. 45126   D. 85312

13. From $9605.13 subtract $2715.96.   13.____
    A. $12,321.09   B. $8,690.16   C. $6,990.07   D. $6,889.17

14. From 76421 subtract 73101. 14._____
    A. 3642   B. 3540   C. 3320   D. 3242

15. From $8.25 subtract $6.50. 15._____
    A. $1.25   B. $1.50   C. $1.75   D. $2.25

16. Multiply 583 by 0.50. 16._____
    A. $291.50   B. 28.15   C. 2.815   D. 0.2815

17. Multiply 0.35 by 1045. 17._____
    A. 0.36575   B. 3.6575   C. 36.575   D. 365.75

18. Multiply 25 by 2513. 18._____
    A. 62825   B. 62725   C. 60825   D. 52825

19. Multiply 423 by 0.01. 19._____
    A. 0.0423   B. 0.423   C. 4.23   D. 42.3

20. Multiply 6.70 by 3.2. 20._____
    A. 2.1440   B. 21.440   C. 214.40   D. 2144.0

KEY (CORRECT ANSWERS)

1. B   11. A
2. B   12. A
3. A   13. D
4. D   14. C
5. C   15. C

6. B   16. A
7. C   17. D
8. C   18. A
9. A   19. C
10. B   20. B

3 (#2)

SOLUTIONS TO PROBLEMS

1. $29.61 + $101.53 + $943.64 = $1074.78

2. $132.25 + $85.63 + $7056.44 = $7274.32

3. 4010 + 1271 + 838 + 23 = 6142

4. 53,632 + 27,403 + 98,765 + 75,424 = 255,224

5. 76,342 + 49,050 + 21,206 + 59,989 = 206,587

6. $452.13 + $963.45 + $621.25 = $2036.83

7. 36,392 + 42,156 + 98,765 = 177,313

8. 40,125 + 87,123 + 24,689 = 151,937

9. 2379 + 4015 + 6521 + 9986 = 22,901

10. 50962 - 36197 = 14,765

11. 90,000 - 31,928 = 58,072

12. 63,764 - 21,548 = 42,216

13. $9605.13 - $2715.96 = $6889.17

14. 76,421 - 73,101 = 3320

15. $8.25 - $6.50 = $1.75

16. (583)(.50) = 291.50

17. (.35)(1045) = 365.75

18. (25)(2513) = 62,825

19. (423)(.01) = 4.23

20. (6.70)(3.2) = 21.44

TEST 3

DIRECTIONS: Each question or incomplete statement is followed by several suggested answers or completions. Select the one that *BEST* answers the question or completes the statement. *PRINT THE LETTER OF TEE CORRECT ANSWER IN THE SPACE AT THE RIGHT.*

Questions 1-4.

DIRECTIONS: For each of Questions 1-4, perform the indicated arithmetic and choose the correct answer from among the four choices given.

1. 12.485
   + 347
   A. 12,038   B. 12,128   C. 12,782   D. 12,832

2. 74,137
   + 711
   A. 74,326   B. 74,848   C. 78,028   D. .D. 78,926

3. 3,749
   - 671
   A. 3,078   B. 3,168   C. 4,028   D. 4,420

4. 19,805
   -18904
   A. 109   B. 901   C. 1,109   D. 1,901

5. When 119 is subtracted from the sum of 2016 + 1634, the remainder is:
   A. 2460   B. 3531   C. 3650   D. 3769

6. Multiply 35 X 65 X 15.
   A. 2275   B. 24265   C. 31145   D. 34125

7. 90% expressed as a decimal is:
   A. .009   B. .09   C. .9   D. 9.0

8. Seven-tenths of a foot expressed in inches is:
   A. 5.5   B. 6.5   C. 7   D. 8.4

9. If 95 men were divided into crews of five men each, the *number* of crews that will be formed is:
   A. 16   B. 17   C. 18   D. 19

213

10. If a man earns $19.50 an hour, the *number* of working hours it will take him to earn $4,875 is, most nearly,

   A. 225   B. 250   C. 275   D. 300

11. If 5 1/2 loads of gravel cost $55.00, then 6 1/2 loads will cost:

   A. $60.   B. $62.50   C. $65.   D. $66.00

12. At $2.50 a yard, 27 yards of concrete will cost:

   A. $36.   B. $41.80   C. $54.   D. $67.50

13. A distance is measured and found to be 52.23 feet. In feet and inches, this distance is, most nearly, 52 feet *and*

   A. 2 3/4"   B. 3 1/4"   C. 3 3/4"   D. 4 1/4"

14. If a maintainer gets $5.20 per hour and time and one-half for working over 40 hours, his *gross* salary for a week in which he worked 43 hours would be

   A. $208.00   B. $223.60   C. $231.40   D. $335.40

15. The circumference of a circle is given by the formula $C = \Pi D$, where C is the circumference, D is the diameter, and Π is about 3 1/7.
   If a coil is 15 turns of steel cable has an average diameter of 20 inches, the *total* length of cable on the coil is *nearest to*

   A. 5 feet   B. 78 feet   C. 550 feet   D. 943 feet

16. The measurements of a poured concrete foundation show that 54 cubic feet of concrete have been placed.
   If payment for this concrete is to be on the basis of cubic yards, the 54 cubic feet must be

   A. multiplied by 27   B. multiplied by 3
   C. divided by 27   D. divided by 3

17. If the cost of 4 1/2 tons of structural steel is $1,800, then the cost of 12 tons is, most nearly,

   A. $4,800   B. $5,400   C. $7,200   D. $216,000

18. An hourly-paid employee working 12:00 midnight to 8:00 a.m. is directed to report to the medical staff for a physical examination at 11:00 a.m. of the same day.
   The pay allowed him for reporting will be an extra

   A. 1 hour   B. 2 hours   C. 3 hours   D. 4 hours

19. The *total* length of four pieces of 2" pipe, whose lengths are 7' 3 1/2", 4' 2 3/16", 5' 7 5/16", and 8' 5 7/8", respectively, is:

   A. 24' 6 3/4"   B. 24' 7 15/16"
   C. 25' 5 13/16"   D. 25' 6 7/8"

20. As a senior mortuary caretaker, you are preparing a monthly report, using the following figures:

    No. of bodies received   983
    No. of bodies claimed   720
    No. of bodies sent to city cemetery   14
    No. of bodies sent to medical schools   9

How many bodies remained at the end of the monthly reporting period?

   A. 230   B. 240   C. 250   D. 260

KEY (CORRECT ANSWERS)

1.	D	11.	C
2.	B	12.	D
3.	A	13.	A
4.	B	14.	C
5.	B	15.	B
6.	D	16.	C
7.	C	17.	A
8.	D	18.	C
9.	D	19.	D
10.	B	20.	B

SOLUTIONS TO PROBLEMS

1. $12,485 + 347 = 12,832$

2. $74,137 + 711 = 74,848$

3. $3749 - 671 = 3078$

4. $19,805 - 18,904 = 901$

5. $(2016 + 1634) - 119 = 3650 - 119 = 3531$

6. $(35)(65)(15) = 34,125$

7. $90\% = .90$ or $.9$

8. $(\frac{7}{10})(12) = 8.4$ inches

9. $95 \div 5 = 19$ crews

10. $\$4875 \div \$19.50 = 250$ days

11. Let x = cost. Then, $\dfrac{5\frac{1}{2}}{6\frac{1}{2}} = \dfrac{\$55.00}{x}$. $5\frac{1}{2} = 357.50$. Solving, x = $65

12. $(\$2.50)(27) = \$67.50$

13. .23-ft. = 2.76 in., so 52.23 ft ≈ 52 ft. $2\frac{3}{4}$ in. $(.76 \approx \frac{3}{4})$

14. Salary = $(\$5.20)(40) + (\$7.80)(3) = \$231.40$

15. Length $\approx (15)(3\frac{1}{7})(20) \approx 943$ in. ≈ 78 ft.

16. There are 27 cu.ft. in 1 cu.yd. To change from 54 cu.ft. to cu.yds., divide by 27.

17. $\$1800 \div 4\frac{1}{2} = = \$400$ per ton. Then, 12 tons cost $(\$400)(12) = \$4800$

18. Instead of working 12 to 8, he will be staying until 11 AM, an extra 3 hours.

19. $7'3\frac{1}{2}" + 4'2\frac{3}{16}" + 5'7\frac{5}{16}" + 8'5\frac{7}{8}" = 24'17\frac{30}{16}" = 24'18\frac{7}{8}"$

20. $983 - 720 - 14 - 9 = 240$ bodies left.

ARITHMETICAL REASONING
EXAMINATION SECTION
TEST 1

DIRECTIONS: Each question or incomplete statement is followed by several suggested answers or completions. Select the one that BEST answers the question or completes the statement. *PRINT THE LETTER OF THE CORRECT ANSWER IN THE SPACE AT THE RIGHT.*

1. A supplier quotes a list price of $172.00 less 15 and 10 percent for twelve tools. The actual cost for these twelve tools is MOST NEARLY

    A. $146   B. $132   C. $129   D. $112

2. If the diameter of a circular piece of sheet metal is 1 1/2 feet, the area, in square inches, is MOST NEARLY

    A. 1.77   B. 2.36   C. 254   D. 324

3. The sum of 5'6", 7'3", 9'3 1/2", and 6'7 1/4" is

    A. 19'8 1/2"   B. 22' 1/2"   C. 25'7 3/4"   D. 28'8 3/4"

4. If the floor area of one shop is 15' by 21'3" and the size of an adjacent shop is 18' by 30'6", then the TOTAL floor area of these two shops is _____ square feet.

    A. 1127.75   B. 867.75   C. 549.0   D. 318.75

5. The fraction which is equal to 0.875 is

    A. 7/16   B. 5/8   C. 3/4   D. 7/8

6. The sum of 1/2, 2 1/32, 4 3/16, and 1 7/8 is MOST NEARLY

    A. 9.593   B. 9.625   C. 9.687   D. 10.593

7. If the base of a right triangle is 9" and the altitude is 12", the length of the third side will be

    A. 13"   B. 14"   C. 15"   D. 16"

8. If a steel bar 1" in diameter and 12' long weighs 32 lbs., then the weight of a piece of this bar 5'9" long is MOST NEARLY _____ lbs.

    A. 15.33   B. 15.26   C. 16.33   D. 15.06

9. The diameter of a circle whose circumference is 12" is MOST NEARLY

    A. 3.82"   B. 3.72"   C. 3.62"   D. 3.52"

10. A dimension of 39/64 inches converted to decimals is MOST NEARLY

    A. .600"   B. .609"   C. .607"   D. .611"

11. A farm worker was paid a weekly wage of $415.20 for a 44-hour work week. As a result of a new labor contract, he is paid $431.40 a week for a 40-hour work week with time and one-half pay for time worked in excess of 40 hours in any work week.
    If he continues to work 44 hours weekly under the new contract, the amount by which his average hourly rate for a 44-hour work week under the new contract exceeds the hourly rate previously paid him lies between _____ and _____, inclusive.

    A. 80¢; $1.00   B. $1.00; $1.20
    C. $1.25; $1.45   D. $1.50; $1.70

12. The sum of 4 feet 3 1/4 inches, 7 feet 2 1/2 inches, and 11 feet 1/4 inch is _____ feet _____ inches.

    A. 21; 6 1/4   B. 22; 6   C. 23; 5   D. 24; 5 3/4

13. The number 0.038 is read as

    A. 38 tenths   B. 38 hundredths
    C. 38 thousandths   D. 38 ten-thousandths

14. Assume that an employee is paid at the rate of $10.86 per hour with time and a half for overtime past 40 hours in a week.
    If he works 43 hours in a week, his gross weekly pay is

    A. $434.40   B. $438.40   C. $459.18   D. $483.27

15. The sum of the following dimensions: 3'2 1/4", 8 7/8", 2'6 3/8", 2'9 3/4", and 1'0" is

    A. 16'7 1/4"   B. 10'7 1/4"   C. 10'3 1/4"   D. 9'3 1/4"

16. Two gears are meshed together and have a gear ratio of 6 to 1.
    If the small gear rotates 120 revolutions per minute, the large gear rotates at

    A. 20   B. 40   C. 60   D. 720

17. The vacuum side of a compound gage reads 14 inches of vacuum. The barometer reading is 29.76 inches of mercury. The equivalent absolute pressure of the compound gage reading, in inches of mercury, is MOST likely

    A. 15.06   B. 15.76   C. 43.06   D. 43.76

18. The fraction 5/8 expressed as a decimal is

    A. 0.125   B. 0.412   C. 0.625   D. 0.875

19. If 300 feet of a certain size pipe weighs 450 pounds, the number of pounds that 100 feet will weigh is

    A. 1,350   B. 150   C. 300   D. 250

20. As an oiler, you work for a facility that has automobiles that use, on the average, 600 quarts of one grade of lubricating oil every month.
    The number of one-gallon cans of the above oil that should be ordered each month to meet this requirement is

    A. 100   B. 125   C. 140   D. 150

21. The inside dimensions of a rectangular oil gravity tank are: height 15", width 9", length 10".
    The amount of oil in the tank, in gallons, (231 cu.in. = 1 gallon), when the oil level is 9" high, is MOST NEARLY

    A. 2.3 B. 3.5 C. 5.2 D. 5.8

22. If 30 gallons of oil cost $76.80, 45 gallons of oil at the same rate will cost

    A. $91.20 B. $115.20 C. $123.20 D. $131.20

23. If an oiler earns $18,000 in the first six months of a year and receives a 10% raise in salary for the next six months of the same year, his TOTAL earnings for the year will be

    A. $36,000 B. $37,500 C. $37,800 D. $39,600

24. If the cost of lubricating oil increases 15%, then a gallon of oil which used to cost $10.00 will now cost MOST NEARLY

    A. $10.50 B. $11.00 C. $11.50 D. $12.00

25. The sum of 7/8", 3/4", 1/2", and 3/8" is

    A. 2 1/8" B. 2 1/4" C. 2 3/8" D. 2 1/2"

KEY (CORRECT ANSWERS)

1. B		11. A	
2. C		12. B	
3. C		13. C	
4. B		14. D	
5. D		15. C	
6. A		16. A	
7. C		17. B	
8. A		18. C	
9. A		19. B	
10. B		20. D	

21. B
22. B
23. C
24. C
25. D

SOLUTIONS TO PROBLEMS

1. Actual cost = ($172)(.85)(.90) = $131.58 ≈ $132

2. Radius = .75', then area = (3.14)(.75)^2 ≈ 1.77 sq.ft.
   Since 1 sq.ft. = 144 sq.in., the area ≈ 254 sq.in.

3. 5'6" + 7'3" + 9'3 1/2" + 3'7 1/4" = 24'19 3/4" = 25'7 3/4"

4. Total area = (15)(21.25) + (18)(30.5) = 867.75 sq.ft.

5. .875 = 875/1000 = 7/8

6. 1 1/2 + 2 1/32 + 4 3/16 + 1 7/8 = 8 51/32 = 9 19/32 = 9.593

7. Third side = $\sqrt{9^2+12^2} = \sqrt{225} = 15"$

8. Let x = weight. Then, 12/32 = 5.75/x . Solving, x ≈ 15.33 lbs.

9. 12" = (3.14)(diameter), so diameter ≈ 3.82"

10. $\frac{39}{64}" = .609375" ≈ .609"$

11. Under his new contract, the weekly wage for 44 hours can be found by first determining his hourly rate for the first 40 hours = $431.40 ÷ 40 ≈ $10.80. Now, his time and one-half pay will = ($10.80)(1.5) = $16.20. His weekly wage for the new contract = $431.40 + (4)($16.20) = $496.20. His new hourly rate for 44 hours = $496.20 ÷ 44 ≈ $10.34. Under the old contract, his hourly rate for 44 hours was $415.20 ÷ 44 = $9.44. His hourly rate increase = $10.34 - $9.44 = $0.90. (Answer key: between $0.80 and $1.00)

12. 4'3 1/4" + 7'2 1/2" + 11' 1/4" = 22'6"

13. .038 = 38 thousandths

14. ($10.86)(40) + ($16.29)(3) = $483.27

15. 3'2 1/4" + 8 7/8" + 2'6 3/8" + 2'9 3/4" + 1'0" = 8'25 18/8" = 10'3 1/4"

16. The gear ratio is inversely proportional to the gear size. Let x = large gear's rpm. Then, 6/1 = 120/x . Solving, x = 20

17. Subtract 14 from 29.76

18. 5/8 = .625

19. Let x = number of pounds. Then, 300/450 = 100/x . Solving, x = 150

5 (#1)

20. 600 quarts = 150 gallons, since 4 quarts = 1 gallon

21. (9")(9")(10") = 810 cu.in. Then, 810 ÷ 231 ≈ 3.5

22. Let x = unknown cost. Then, 30/$76.80 = 45/x. Solving, x = $115.20

23. $18,000 + ($18,000)(1.10) = $37,800

24. ($10.00)(1.15) = $11.50

25. 7/8" + 3/4" + 1/2" + 3/8" = 20/8" = 2 1/2"

TEST 2

DIRECTIONS: Each question or incomplete statement is followed by several suggested answers or completions. Select the one that BEST answers the question or completes the statement. *PRINT THE LETTER OF THE CORRECT ANSWER IN THE SPACE AT THE RIGHT.*

1. A sheet metal plate has been cut in the form of a right triangle with sides of 5, 12, and 13 inches.
   The area of this plate, in square inches, is

   A. 30 B. 32 1/2 C. 60 D. 78

   1.____

2. If steel weighs 480 lbs. per cubic foot, the weight of an 18" x 18" x 2" steel base plate is _____ lbs.

   A. 180 B. 216 C. 427 D. 648

   2.____

3. By trial, it is found that by using 2 cubic feet of sand, a 5 cubic foot batch of concrete is produced.
   Using the same proportions, the amount of sand, in cubic feet, required to produce 2 cubic yards of concrete is MOST NEARLY

   A. 7 B. 22 C. 27 D. 45

   3.____

4. The total number of cubic yards of earth to be removed to make a trench 3'9" wide, 25'0" long, and 4'3" deep is MOST NEARLY

   A. 53.1 B. 35.4 C. 26.6 D. 14.8

   4.____

5. A large number of 2 x 4 studs, some 10'5" long and some 6'5 1/2" long, are required for a job.
   To minimize waste, it would be PREFERABLE to order lengths of _____ feet.

   A. 16 B. 17 C. 18 D. 19

   5.____

6. A 6" pipe is connected to a 4" pipe through a reducer. If 100 cubic feet of water is flowing through the 6" pipe per minute, the flow, in cubic feet, per minute through the 4" pipe is

   A. 225 B. 100 C. 66.6 D. 44.4

   6.____

7. If steel weighs 0.28 pounds per cubic inch, then the weight, in pounds, of a 2" square steel bar 120" long is MOST NEARLY

   A. 115 B. 125 C. 135 D. 155

   7.____

8. A three-inch diameter steel bar two feet long weighs MOST NEARLY (assume steel weighs 480 lbs./cu.ft.) _____ lbs.

   A. 48 B. 58 C. 68 D. 78

   8.____

9. The area of a circular plate will be reduced by 5% if a sector removed from it has an angle of _____ degrees.

   A. 18 B. 24 C. 32 D. 60

   9.____

10. If a 4 1/16 inch shaft wears six thousandths of an inch, the NEW diameter will be _____ inches.

    A. 4.0031   B. 4.0565   C. 4.0578   D. 4.0605

11. A set of mechanical plan drawings is drawn to a scale of 1/8" = 1 foot.
    If a length of pipe measures 15 7/16" on the drawing, the ACTUAL length of the pipe is _____ feet.

    A. 121.5   B. 122.5   C. 123.5   D. 124.5

12. An electrical drawing is drawn to a scale of 1/4" = 1'. If a length of conduit on the drawing measures 7 3/8", the actual length of the conduit, in feet, is

    A. 7.5   B. 15.5   C. 22.5   D. 29.5

13. Assume that you have assigned 6 mechanics to do a job that must be finished in 4 days. At the end of 3 days, your men have completed only two-thirds of the job. In order to complete the job on time and because the job is such that it cannot be speeded up, you should assign a MINIMUM of _____ extra men.

    A. 3   B. 4   C. 5   D. 6

14. Assume that a trench is 42" wide, 5' deep, and 100' long. If the unit price of excavating the trench is $105 per cubic yard, the cost of excavating the trench is MOST NEARLY

    A. $6,805   B. $15,330   C. $21,000   D. $63,000

15. If the scale on a shop drawing is 1/4 inch to the foot, then the length of a part which measures 2 3/8 inches long on the drawing is ACTUALLY _____ feet.

    A. 9 1/2   B. 8 1/2   C. 7 1/4   D. 4 1/4

16. It is necessary to pour a new concrete floor for a shop. If the dimensions of the concrete slab for the floor are to be 27' x 18' x 6", then the number of cubic yards of concrete that must be poured is

    A. 9   B. 16   C. 54   D. 243

17. The jaws of a vise move 1/4" for each complete turn of the handle.
    The number of complete turns necessary to open the jaws 2 3/4" is

    A. 9   B. 10   C. 11   D. 12

18. Assume that a jobbing shop is to submit a price for a contract involving 300 pieces of work. Assume that material costs 50 cents per piece, labor costs $7.50 an hour, and a lathe operator can complete 5 pieces in an hour.
    If overhead is 40% of material and labor costs and the profit is 10% of all costs, the submitted price for the entire job will be

    A. $630.24   B. $872.80   C. $900.00   D. $924.00

19. The following formula is used in connection with the three-wire method of measuring pitch diameters of screw threads: $G = \frac{0.57735}{N}$, where G = wire size and N = number of threads per inch.
According to this formula, the proper size of wire for a 1"-8NC thread is MOST NEARLY

   A. .0722"   B. .7217"   C. .0072"   D. .0074"

20. A millimeter is 1/25.4 of an inch and there are 10 millimeters to a centimeter.
If a piece of stock measures 127 centimeters long, the length of the stock, in feet and inches, would be MOST NEARLY

   A. 2'1"   B. 4'2"   C. 8'4"   D. 41'8"

21. For a certain job, you will need 25 steel bars 1 inch in diameter and 4"6" long.
If these bars weigh 3 pounds per foot of length, then the TOTAL weight for all 25 bars is _____ pounds.

   A. 13.5   B. 75.0   C. 112.5   D. 337.5

22. If steel weighs 0.30 pounds per cubic inch, then the weight of a 2 inch square steel bar 90 inches long is _____ pounds.

   A. 27   B. 54   C. 108   D. 360

23. A concrete wall is 36' long, 9' high, and 1 1/2' thick. The number of cubic yards of concrete that were needed to make this wall is

   A. 14   B. 18   C. 27   D. 36

24. If the scale on a shop drawing is 1/2 inch to the foot, then the length of a part which measures 4 1/4 inches long on the drawing has a length of APPROXIMATELY _____ feet.

   A. 2 1/8   B. 4 1/4   C. 8 1/2   D. 10 3/4

25. If the allowable load on a wooden scaffold is 60 pounds per square foot and the scaffold surface area is 3 feet by 12 feet, then the MAXIMUM total distributed load that is permitted on the scaffold is _____ pounds.

   A. 720   B. 1,800   C. 2,160   D. 2,400

KEY (CORRECT ANSWERS)

1. A
2. A
3. B
4. D
5. B

6. B
7. C
8. A
9. A
10. B

11. C
12. D
13. A
14. A
15. A

16. A
17. C
18. D
19. A
20. B

21. D
22. C
23. B
24. C
25. C

SOLUTIONS TO PROBLEMS

1. Area = (1/2)(base)(height) = (1/2)(5")(12") = 30 sq.in.

2. Volume = (18") (18") (2") = 648 cu.in. = 648/1720 cu.ft.
   Then, (480)(648/1720) = $\approx$ 180 lbs.

3. 2 cu.yds. = 54 cu.ft. Let x = required cubic feet of sand. Then, 2/5 = x/54. Solving, x = 21.6 (or about 22)

4. (3.75')(25')(4.25') = 398.4375 cu.ft. $\approx$ 14.8 cu.yds.

5. 10'5" + 6'5 1/2" = 16'10 1/2", so lengths of 17 feet are needed

6. The amount of water flowing through each pipe must be equal.

7. (2")(2")(120") = 480 cu. in. Then, (480)(.28) $\approx$ 135 lbs.

8. Volume = (π) (.125 ')^2 (2) $\approx$ .1 cu.ft. Then, (.1)(480) = 48 lbs.

9. (360°)(.05) - 18°

10. 4 1/16 - .006 = 4.0625 - .006 = 4.0565

11. 15 7/16" ÷ 1/8" = 247/16 . 8/1 = 123.5. Then, (123.5)(1 ft.) = 123.5 ft.

12. 7 3/8" ÷ 1/4" = 59/8 . 4/1 = 29.5   Then, (29.5)(1 ft.) = 29.5 ft.

13. (6)(4) = 24 man-days normally required. Since after 3 days only the equivalent of (2/3)(24) = 16 man-days of work has been 1 done, 8 man-days of work is still left. 16 ÷ 3 = 5 1/3, which means the crew is equivalent to only 5 1/3 men. To do the 8 man-days of work, it will require at least 8 - 5 1/3 = 2 2/3 = 3 additional men.

14. (3.5')(5')(100') = 1750 cu.ft. $\approx$ 64.8 cu.yds. Then, (64.8)($105) $\approx$ $6805

15. 2 3/8" ÷ 1/4" = 19/8 . 4/1 = 9 1/2 Then, (9 1/2)(1 ft.) = 9 1/2 feet

16. (27')(18')(1/2') = 243 cu.ft. = 9 cu.yds. (1 cu.yd. = 27 cu.ft.)

17. 2 3/4" ÷ 1/4" = 11/4 . 4/1 = 11

18. Material cost = (300)($.50) = $150. Labor cost = ($7.50)(300/5) = $450. Overhead = (.40)($150+$450) = $240. Profit = .10($150+$450+$240) = $84. Submitted price = $150 + $450 + $240 + $84 = $924

19. 6 = .57735" ÷ 8 = .0722"

20. 127 cm = 1270 mm = 1270/25.4" ≈ 50" = 4.2"

21. (25)(4.5') = 112.5' Then, (112.5X3) = 337.5 lbs.

22. (2")(2")(90") = 360 cu.in. Then, (360)(30) = 108 lbs.

23. (36')(9')(1 1/2') = 486 cu.ft. = 18 cu.yds. (1 cu.yd. = 27 cu.ft.)

24. 4 1/4" ÷ 1/2" = 17/4 . 2/1 = 8 1/2. Then, (8 1/2)(1 ft.) = 8 1/2 ft.

25. (12')(3') = 36 sq.ft. Then, (36)(60) = 2160 lbs.

TEST 3

DIRECTIONS: Each question or incomplete statement is followed by several suggested answers or completions. Select the one that BEST answers the question or completes the statement. *PRINT THE LETTER OF THE CORRECT ANSWER IN THE SPACE AT THE RIGHT.*

1. A right triangular metal sheet for a roofing job has sides of 36 inches and 4 feet. The length of the remaining side is

    A. 7 feet
    B. 6 feet
    C. 60 inches
    D. 90 inches

2. A U.S. Standard Gauge thickness is given as 0.15625. This thickness, in fractions of an inch, is MOST NEARLY _____ inches.

    A. 1/8   B. 4/32   C. 5/32   D. 3/64

3. The weight per 100 of sheet metal fasteners is given as 2/3 pound. The APPROXIMATE number of fasteners in a 2-pound package is

    A. 166   B. 200   C. 300   D. 266

4. The decimal equivalent of 27/32 is MOST NEARLY

    A. 0.813   B. 0.828   C. 0.844   D. 0.859

5. If a scaled measurement of 1'3" on the drawing of a sheet metal layout represents an actual length of 10"0", then the drawing has been made to a scale of _____ inch to the foot.

    A. 3/4   B. 1 1/4   C. 1 1/2   D. 1 3/4

6. Two and two-thirds tees can be made from one sheet of steel. If 24 tees must be made, then the number of sheets required is

    A. 6   B. 7   C. 8   D. 9

7. A main duct 20 inches in diameter discharges into two branch ducts. The sum of the areas of the branches is to be equal to the area of the main duct. One branch is 12 inches in diameter.
The diameter of the other branch is _____ inches.

    A. 16   B. 12   C. 10   D. 8

8. If steel weighs 480 lbs. per cubic foot, the weight of 10 sheets, each 6 feet by 3 feet by 1/32 inch, is _____ lbs.

    A. 2,700   B. 1,237   C. 270   D. 225

9. The area, in square inches, of a right triangle that has sides of 12 1/2, 10, and 7 1/2 inches is

    A. 18 1/4   B. 37 1/2   C. 75   D. 60

10. In making a container to hold 1 gallon (231 cu.in.) and to be 6 inches in diameter at the top and 8 inches in diameter at the bottom, the height must be, in inches,

    A. 10.0 B. 8.2 C. 4.6 D. 6

11. A sheet metal worker is given a job to make a transition piece from a 8 1/2" diameter duct to an 11 1/4" diameter duct. If the length of the transition piece is 5 1/2" for each inch change in diameter, then the length of the transition piece is

    A. 14 7/8" B. 15" C. 15 1/8" D. 15 1/4"

12. A duct layout is drawn to a scale of 3/8" to a foot. If the length of a run shown on the drawing scales 7 1/2", then the ACTUAL length of the run is

    A. 19'6" B. 19'9" C. 20'0" D. 20'3"

13. An 18" x 24" duct is to be connected to a 24" x 24" duct by means of an eccentric transition piece (3 sides flush). If the taper is to be 1" in 4", then the length of the transition piece is

    A. 6" B. 12" C. 18" D. 24"

14. Twenty-seven pairs of 3/8" diameter rods each 3'3 1/2" long are needed to support a duct.
    If the available rods are ten feet long, then the MINIMUM number of rods that will be needed to make the twenty-seven sets is

    A. 9 B. 12 C. 15 D. 18

15. A rectangular sheet metal air duct with open ends is 12 feet long and 15" x 20" in cross-section. If one square foot of the sheet metal weighs 1/2 pound, then the TOTAL weight of the duct is _____ lbs.

    A. 10 B. 17 1/2 C. 35 D. 150

16. The sum of 1/12 and 1/4 is

    A. 1/3 B. 5/12 C. 7/12 D. 3/8

17. The product of 12 and 2 1/3 is

    A. 27 B. 28 C. 29 D. 30

18. If 4 1/2 is subtracted from 7 1/5, the remainder is

    A. 3 7/10 B. 2 7/10 C. 3 3/10 D. 2 3/10

19. The number of cubic yards in 47 cubic feet is MOST NEARLY

    A. 1.70 B. 1.74 C. 1.78 D. 1.82

20. A wall 8'0" high by 12'6" long has a window opening 4'0" high by 3'6" wide. The net area of the wall (allowing for the window opening) is, in square feet,

    A. 86 B. 87 C. 88 D. 89

21. A worker's hourly rate is $11.36. 21.____
    If he works 11 1/2 hours, he should receive

    A. $129.84   B. $130.64   C. $131.48   D. $132.24

22. The number of cubic feet in 3 cubic yards is 22.____

    A. 81   B. 82   C. 83   D. 84

23. At an annual rate of $.40 per $100, what is the fire insurance premium for one year on a 23.____
    house that is insured for $80,000?

    A. $120   B. $160   C. $240   D. $320

24. A meter equals approximately 1.09 yards. 24.____
    How much longer, in yards, is a 100-meter dash than a 100-yard dash?

    A. 6   B. 8   C. 9   D. 12

25. A train leaves New York City at 8:10 A.M. and arrives in Buffalo at 4:45 P.M. on the same 25.____
    day. How long, in hours and minutes, does it take the train to make the trip?
    _____ hours, _____ minutes.

    A. 6; 22   B. 7; 16   C. 7; 28   D. 8; 35

KEY (CORRECT ANSWERS)

1. C		11. C	
2. C		12. C	
3. C		13. D	
4. C		14. D	
5. C		15. C	
6. D		16. A	
7. A		17. B	
8. D		18. B	
9. B		19. B	
10. D		20. A	

21. B
22. A
23. D
24. C
25. D

SOLUTIONS TO PROBLEMS

1. Let x = remaining side. Converting to inches, $x^2 = 36^2 + 48^2$ So, $x^2 = 3600$. Solving, x = 60 inches.

2. $.15625 = \dfrac{15,625}{100,000} = \dfrac{5}{32}$

3. 2 ÷ 2/3 = 3. Then, (3)(100) = 300 fasteners

4. 27/32 = .84375 ≈ .844

5. 1'3" ÷ 10 = 15" ÷ 10 = 1 1/2"

6. 24 ÷ 2 2/3 = 24/1.3/8 = 9

7. Area of main duct = $(\pi)(10^2) = 100\pi$. One of the branches has an area of $(\pi)(6^2) = 36\pi$. Thus, the area of the 2nd branch = $100\pi - 36\pi = 64\pi$. The 2nd branch's radius must be 8" and its diameter must be 16".

8. Volume = (1/384')(6')(3') = .046875 cu.ft. Then, 10 sheets have a volume of .46875 cu.ft. Now, (.46875)(480) = 225 lbs.

9. Note that $(7\ 1/2)^2 + (10)^2 = (12\ 1/2)^2$, so that this is a right triangle. Area = (1/2)(10")(7 1/2") = 37 1/2 sq.in.

10. $231 = \dfrac{h}{3}[(\pi)(3)^2 + (\pi)(4)^2 + \sqrt{(9\pi)(16\pi)}]$, where h = required height. Then,

    $231 = \dfrac{h}{3}(9\pi + 16\pi + 12\pi)$. Simplifying, $231 = 37\pi h/3$.
    Solving, h ~ 5.96" or 6"

11. 11 1/4 - 8 1/2 = 2 3/4. Then, (2 3/4)(5 1/2) = 11/4 . 11/2 = 15 1/8

12. 7 1/2" ÷ 3/8" = 15/2 . 8/3 = 20 Then, (20)(1 ft.) = 20 feet

13. 24" - 18" = 6" Then, (6")(4) = 24"

14. 3'3 1/2" = 39.5". Now, (27)(2)(39.5") = 2133". 10 ft. = 120".
    Finally, 2133 ÷ 120 = 17.775, so 18 rods are needed.

15. Surface area = (2)(12')(1 1/4') + (2)(12')(1 2/3') = 70 sq.ft.
    Then, (70)(1/2 lb.) - 35 lbs.

16. 1/12 + 1/4 = 4/12 = 1/3

5 (#3)

17. (12)(2 1/3) = 12/1 . 7/3 = 28

18. 7 1/5 - 4 1/2 = 7 2/10 - 4 5/10 = 6 12/10 - 4 5/10 = 2 7/10

19. 47 cu.ft. = 47/27 cu.yds. = 1.74 cu.yds.

20. (8')(12.5') - (4')(3.5') = 86 sq.ft.

21. ($11.36)(11.5) = $130.64

22. 1 cu.yd. = 27 cu.ft., so 3 cu.yds. = 81 cu.ft.

23. $80,000 ÷ $100 = 800. Then, (800)($.40) = $320

24. 100 meters = 109 yds. Then, 109 - 100 = 9 yds.

25. 4:45 P.M. - 8:10 AM. = 8 hrs. 35 min.

ABSTRACT REASONING

EXAMINATION SECTION
COMMENTARY

Since intelligence exists in many forms or phases and the theory of differential aptitudes is now firmly established in testing, other manifestations and measurements of intelligence than verbal or purely arithmetical must be identified and measured.

Classification inventory, or figure classification, involves the aptitude of form perception, i.e., the ability to perceive pertinent detail in objects or in pictorial or graphic material. It involves making visual comparisons and discriminations and discerning slight differences in shapes and shading figures and widths and lengths of lines.

Leading examples of presentation are the figure analogy and the figure classification. The Section that follows presents progressive and varied samplings of this type of question.

SAMPLE QUESTIONS

DIRECTIONS: In each of these sample questions, look at the symbols in the first two boxes. Something about the three symbols in the first box makes them alike; something about the two symbols in the other box with the question mark makes them alike. Look for some characteristic that is common to all symbols in the same box, yet makes them different from the symbols in the other box. Among the five answer choices, find the symbol that can BEST be substituted for the question mark, because it is *like* the symbols in the second box, and, *for the same reason,* different from those in the first box.

1.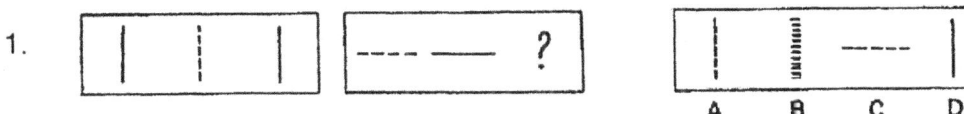

1.____

In sample question 1, all the symbols in the first box are vertical lines. The second box has two lines, one broken and one solid. Their *likeness* to each other consists in their being horizontal; and their being horizontal makes them *different* from the vertical lines in the other box. The answer must be the only one of the five lettered choices that is a horizontal line, either broken or solid. Therefore, the CORRECT answer is C.

2.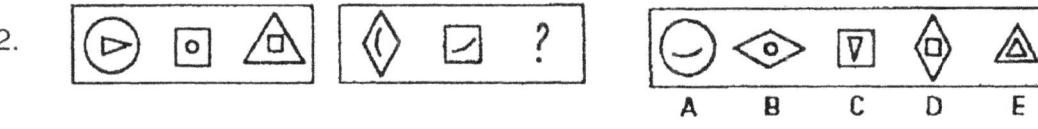

2.____

The CORRECT answer is A.

233

EXAMINATION SECTION
TEST 1

DIRECTIONS: In each of these question, look at the symbols in the first two boxes. Something about the three symbols in the first box makes them alike; something about the two symbols in the other box with the question mark makes them alike. Look for some characteristic that is common to all symbols in the same box, yet makes them different from the symbols in the other box. Among the five answer choices, find the symbol that can BEST be substituted for the question mark, because it is *like* the symbols in the second box, and, *for the same reason,* different from those in the first box.

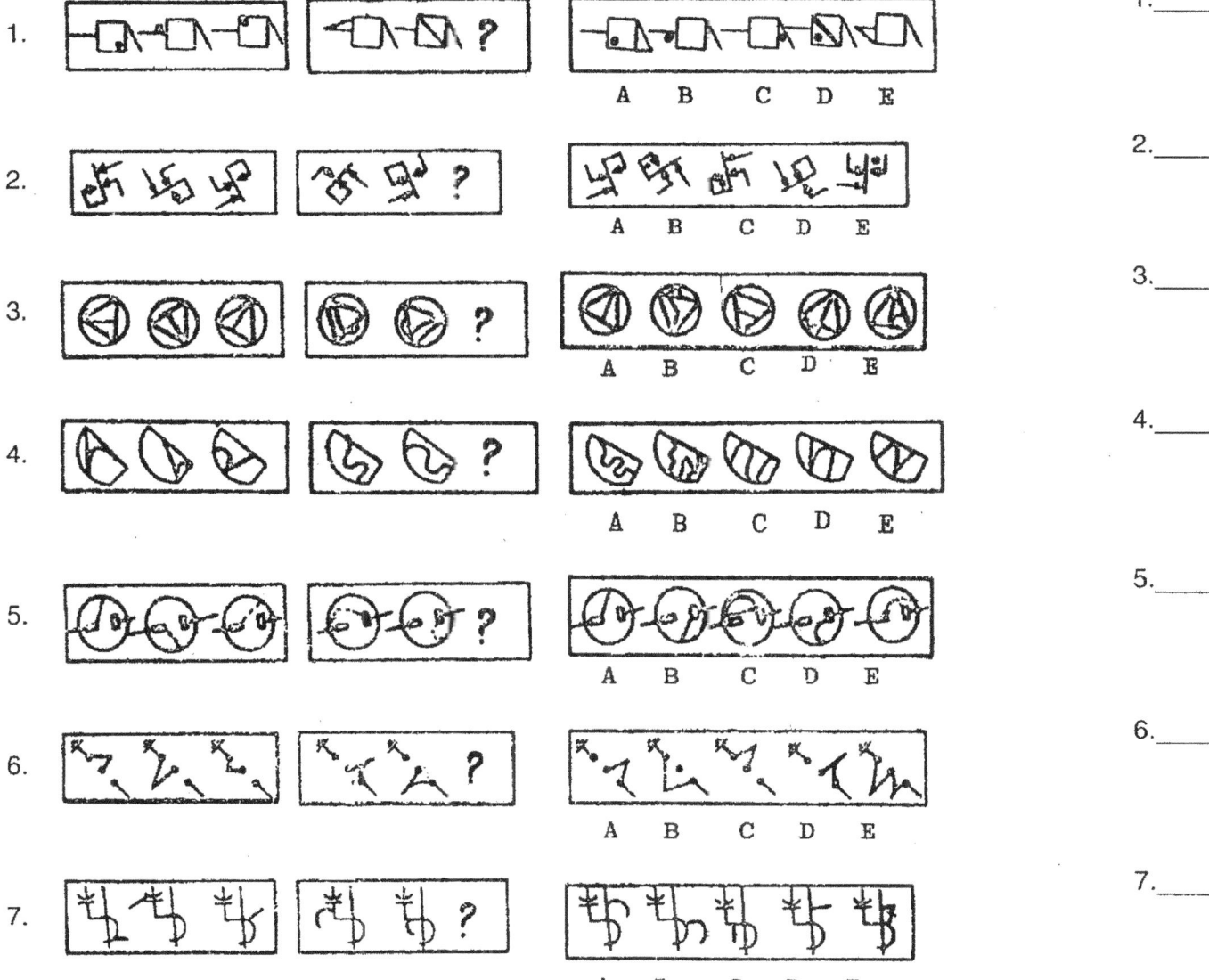

2 (#1)

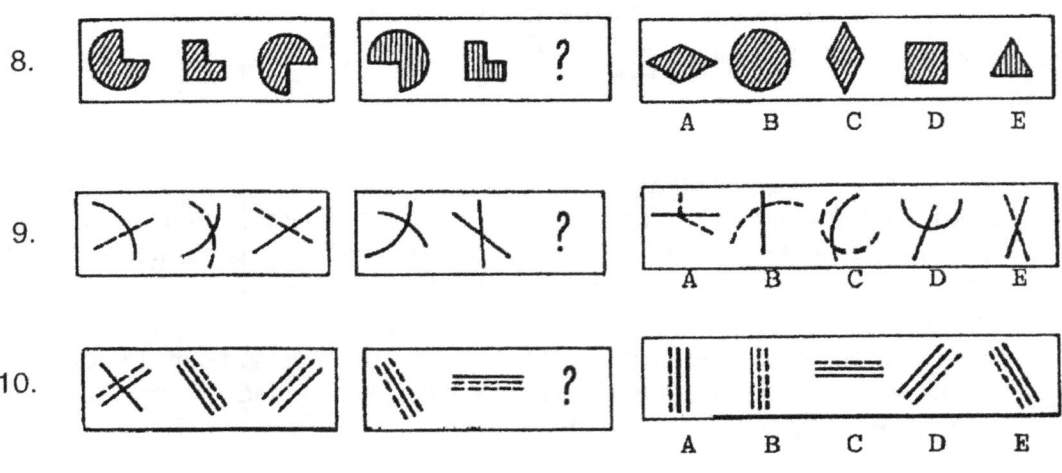

KEY (CORRECT ANSWERS)

1. E
2. D
3. B
4. A
5. D

6. D
7. A
8. E
9. D
10. B

TEST 2

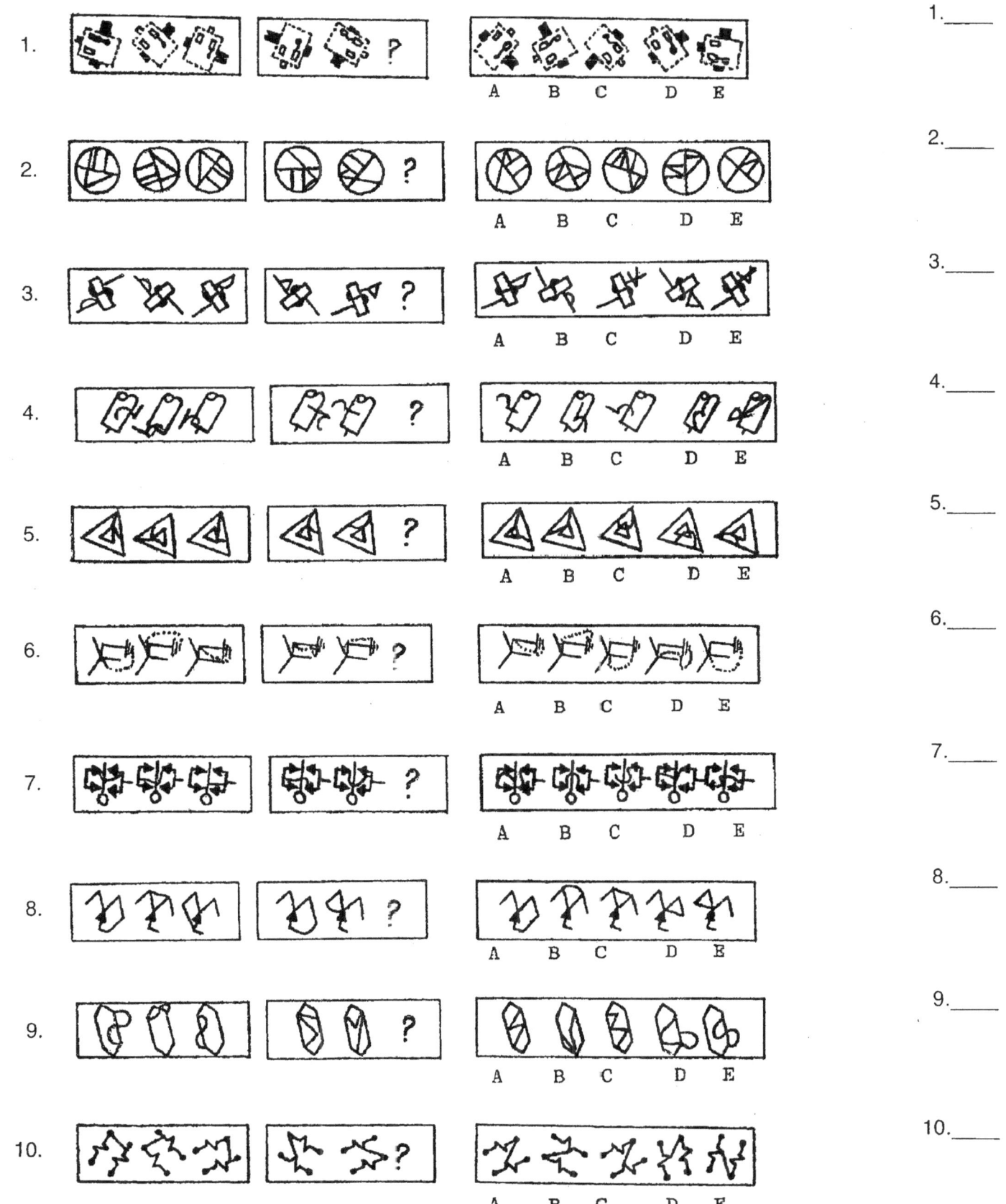

KEY (CORRECT ANSWERS)

1. C
2. A
3. D
4. A
5. E

6. C
7. E
8. B
9. B
10. D

TEST 3

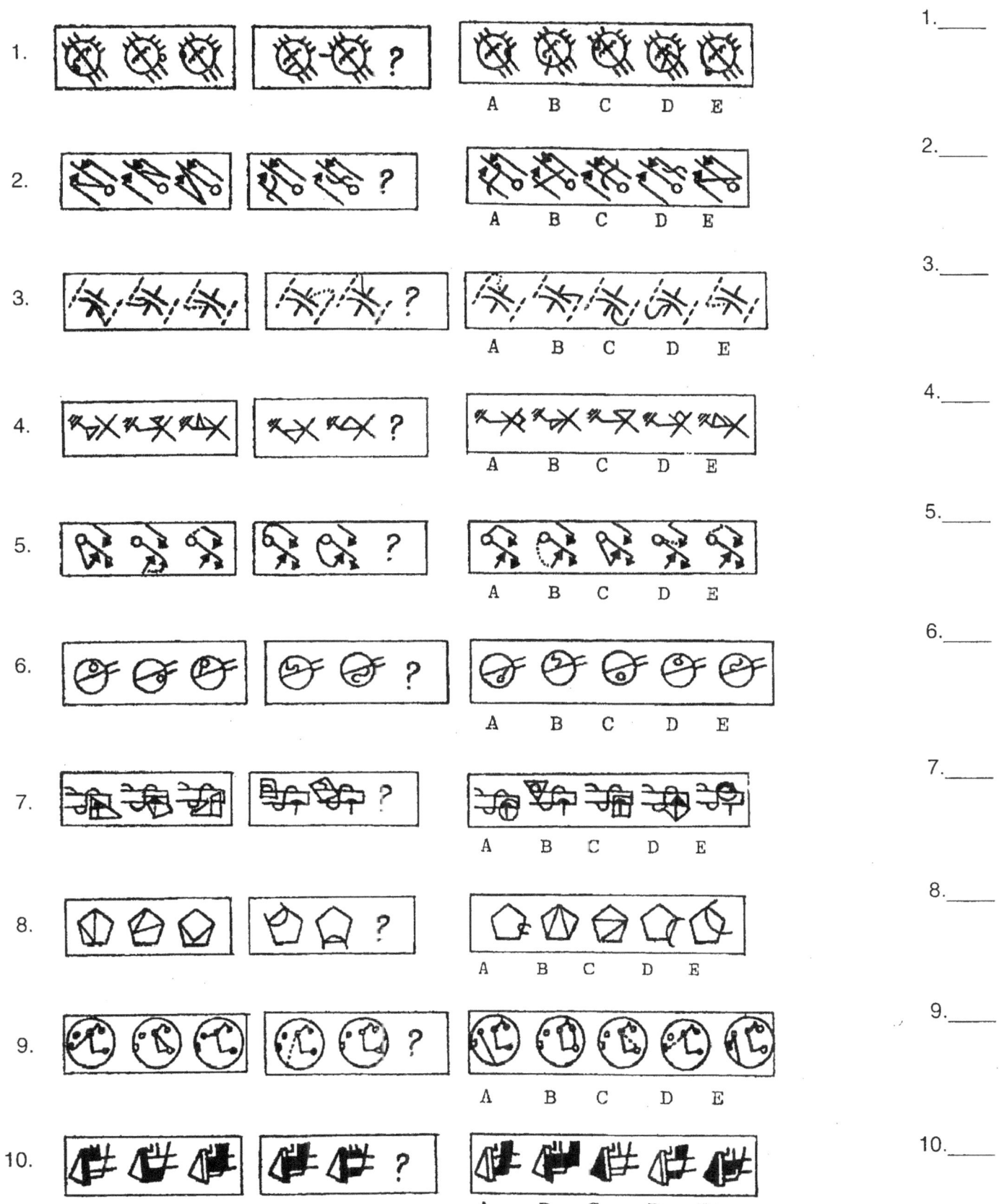

KEY (CORRECT ANSWERS)

1. B
2. D
3. A
4. C
5. B

6. E
7. B
8. D
9. A
10. B

ABSTRACT REASONING
SPATIAL RELATIONS/THREE DIMENSIONS

COMMENTARY

Since intelligence exists in many forms or phases and the theory of differential aptitudes is now firmly established in testing, other manifestations and measurements of intelligence than verbal or purely arithmetical must be identified and measured.

The spatial relations test, including that phase designated as spatial perception, involves and measures the ability to solve problems, drawn up in the form of outlines or pictures, which are concerned with the shapes of objects or the interrelationship of their parts. While, concededly, little is known about the nature and scope of this aptitude, it appears that this ability is required in science, mathematics, engineering, and drawing courses and curricula. Accordingly, tests of spatial perception involving the reconstruction of three-dimensional patterns, are presented in this section.

It is to be noted that the relationships expressed in spatial tests are geometric, definitive, and exact. Keeping these basic characteristics in mind, the applicant is to proceed to solve the spatial perception problems in his own way. There is no set method of solving these problems. The examinee may find that there are different methods for different types of spatial problems. Therefore, the BEST way to prepare for this type of test is to take and study the work-practice problems in three-dimensional patterns provided in this section.

SPATIAL RELATIONS/THREE DIMENSIONS

The tests of spatial relations that follow consist of items which involve the visualization of three dimensions.

Each of the items of these tests consists of a line of figures a question figure in stretchout or open form on the left and five lettered figures on the right, one of which will most closely represent the stretchout or open figure when the latter is folded together.

The candidate is then required to select the figure which will most closely represent the stretchout or open figure when the latter is folded together.

SAMPLE QUESTIONS AND EXPLANATIONS

DIRECTIONS: The items in this part constitute a test of spatial relations involving three dimensions. Each item consists of a line of figures. The first figure is the question figure which appears in stretchout or open form. This is followed by five lettered figures which appear in three-dimensional form. When the stretchout or open figure is folded together, which of the five figures will it most closely represent?

Rules to be followed:
1. The stretchout figure may be folded along the lines or rolled where necessary.
2. The edges of the stretchout figure must meet exactly, with no overlapping or empty spaces between them.

1.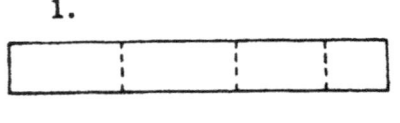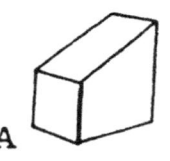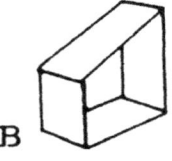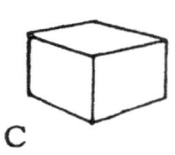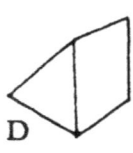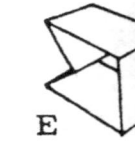
   A   B   C   D   E

The correct answer is B. This is a simple fold of a four-sided figure.

2.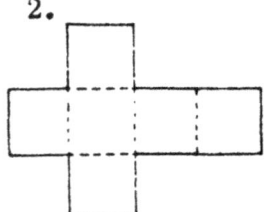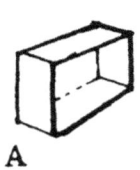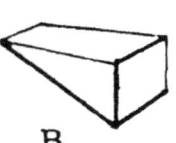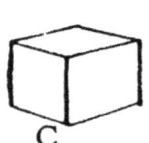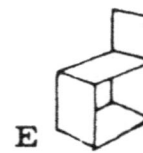
   A   B   C   D   E

The correct answer is C. This represents the product of a continuous fold from any point to form a cube (six-sided solid).

3 (#1)

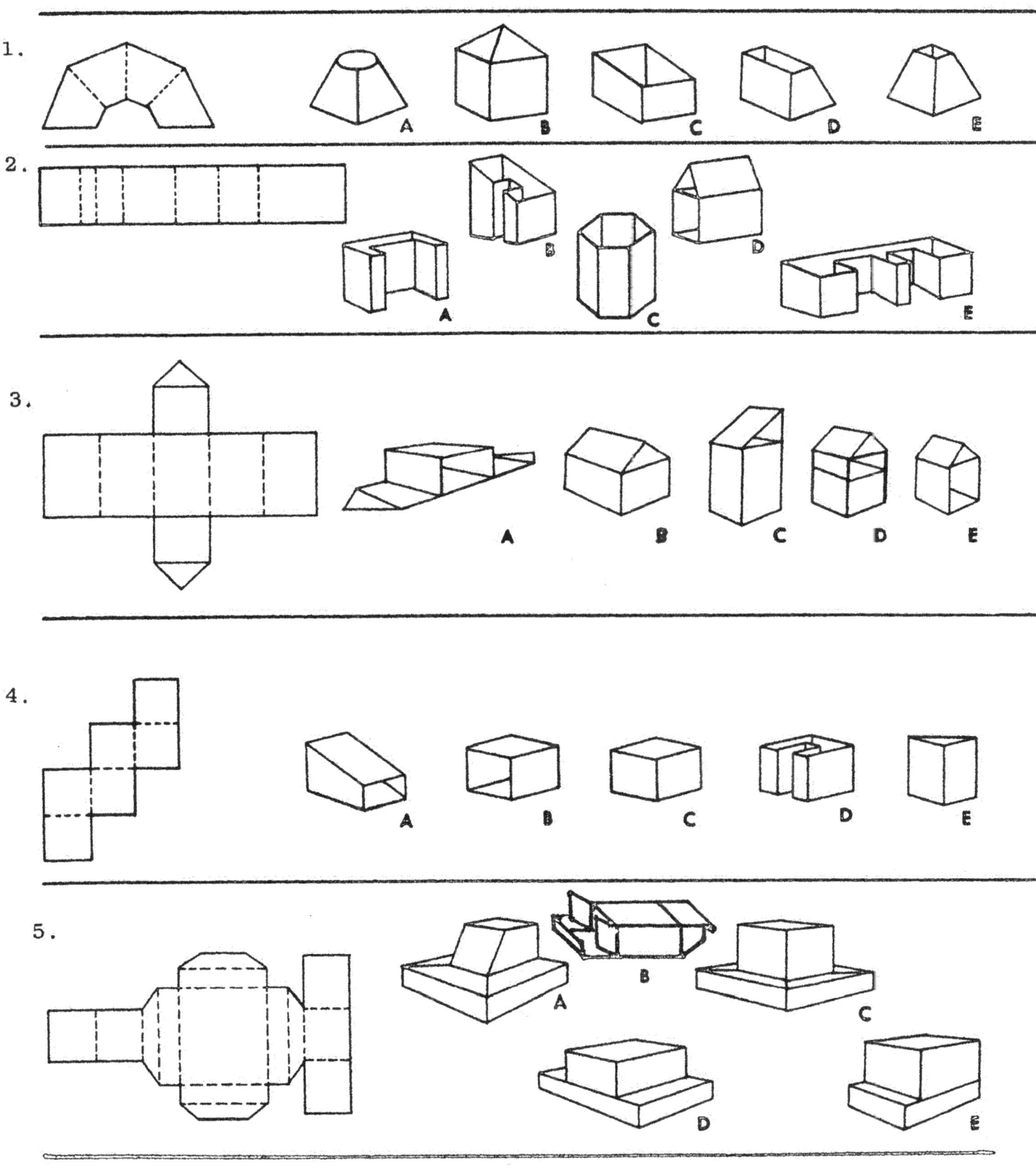

KEY (CORRECT ANSWERS)
EXPLANATION OF ANSWERS

		EXPLANATION
1.	E	Straight edges form square-top hollow pyramid
2.	A	Count panels for key
3.	B	Solid "house" shape
4.	C	Solid cube shape
5.	C	Fold all sides toward center

TEST 2

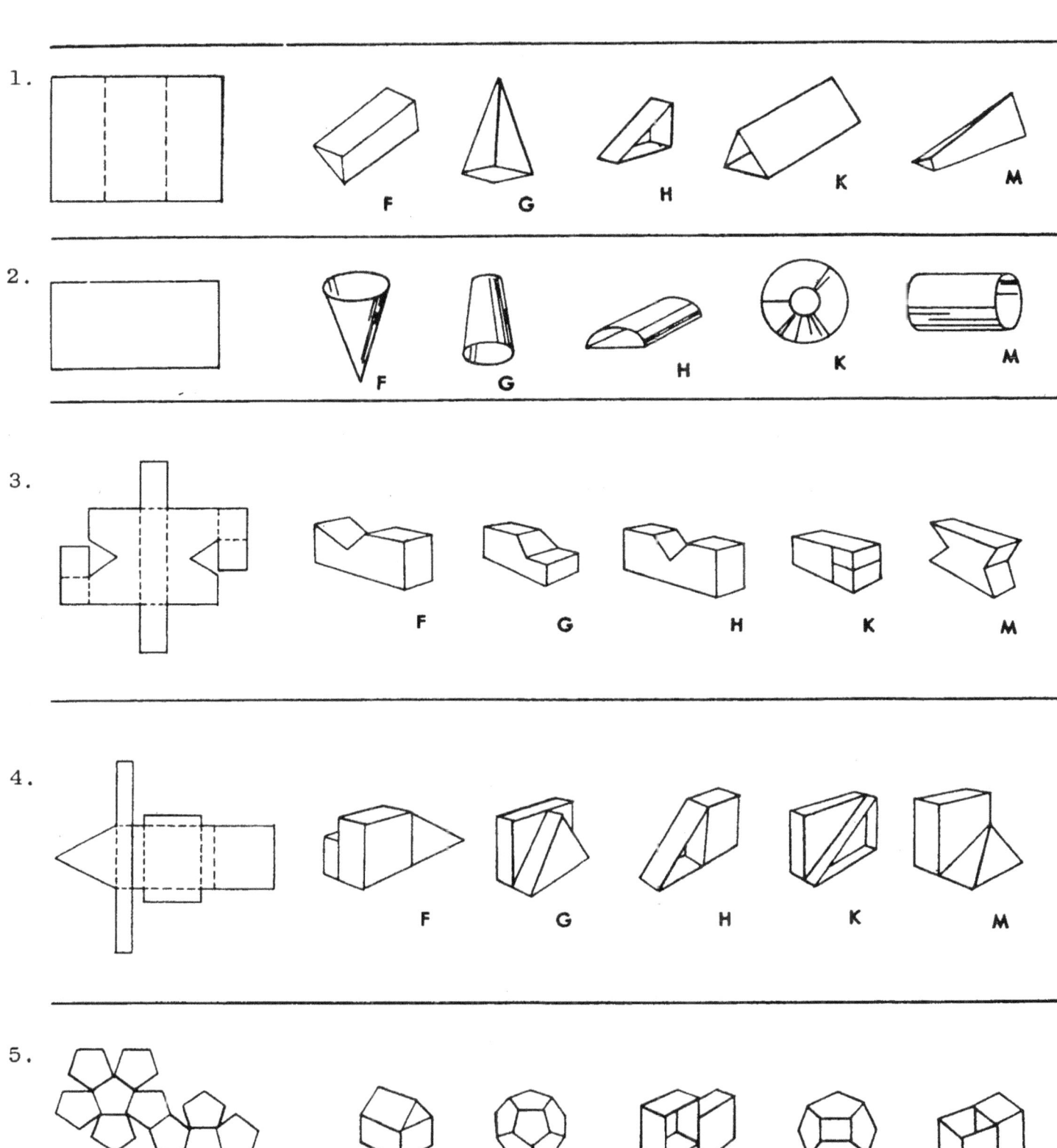

KEY (CORRECT ANSWERS)
EXPLANATION OF ANSWERS

1. K   Simple three-panel fold
2. M   Roll left to right
3. H   Fold all sides toward the center
4. G   Fold all sides toward the center
5. G   A continuous fold from any point to form a dodecahedron (based on a single pentagon form)

TEST 3

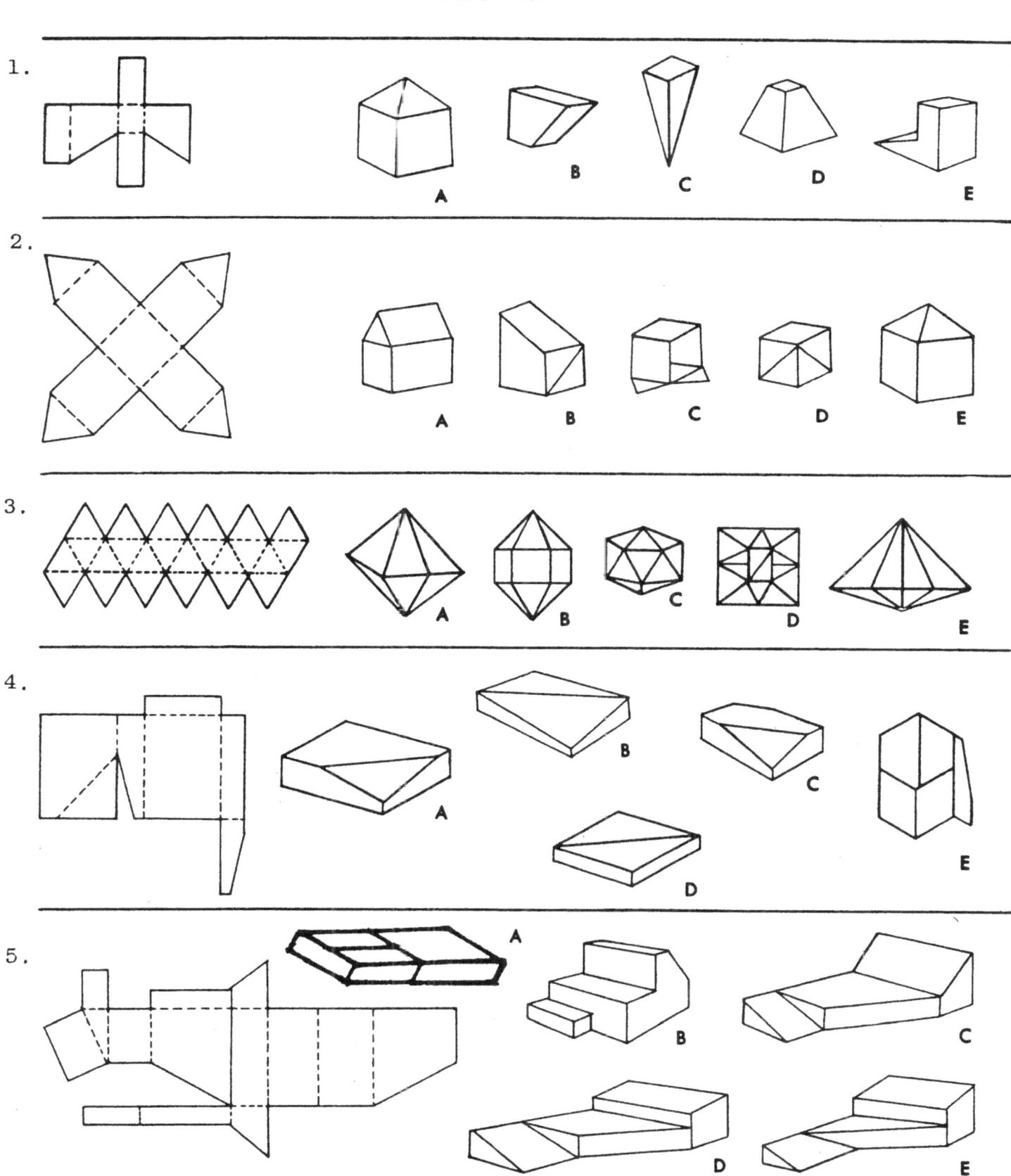

KEY (CORRECT ANSWERS)
EXPLANATION OF ANSWERS

1. B   Fold toward the center
2. E   Cube with pyramid on top
3. C   Continuous fold to form an icositetrahedron (24 planes); based on equilateral triangles
4. A   Size of triangular fold is the key
5. C   Fold all sides toward the center

TEST 4

1.   F   G   H   K   M

2.   F   G   H   K   M

3.   F   G   H   K   M

4.   F   G   H   K   M

5.   F   G   H   K   M

KEY (CORRECT ANSWERS)
EXPLANATION OF ANSWERS

1. H   Fold from left to right
2. F   Pyramid with base
3. M   Continuous fold to form an octahedron, based on two pyramids, bottom to bottom
4. K   Hexagon (solid)
5. G   Count panels and start fold from the center, working both sides together

ELECTRO-MECHANICAL NOTES AND RESOURCES

TABLE OF CONTENTS

		Page
I.	BASIC ELECTRICITY	1
	Ohm's Law	2
	Kirchoff's Voltage Law	3
	Kirchoff's Current Law	3
	Inductors	3
	Capacitors	4
	AC Cycles	4
	Magnetism	5
	Relays	6
	Switches	6
	Diodes	6
	Transistors	7
	Soldering	8
II.	COMPUTERS	8
	Numbering Systems	9
	Flip Flops	10
	Logic Gates	12
III.	OSCILLOSCOPES	12
	Meters	13
IV.	SCIENTIFIC NOTATION	14
V.	GEARS	14
	Pulleys	16
	Lubricants	18

ELECTRO-MECHANICAL NOTES AND RESOURCES
I. BASIC ELECTRICITY

Resistance is measured in ohms, and its symbol is Ω. Resistance is additive in series circuits. This means that with two resistors in series as shown below, if one resistor is 100Ω's and the other 200Ω's, then the total resistance is 300Ω's.

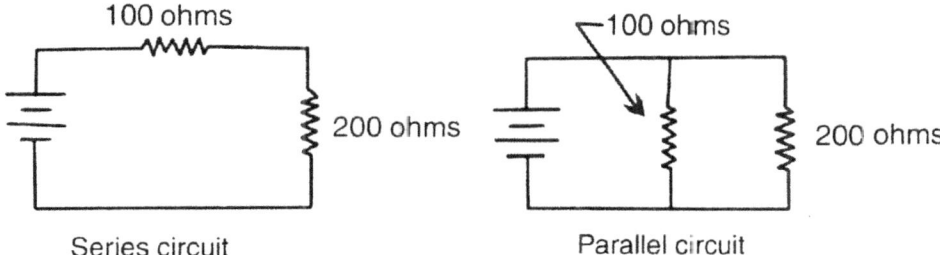

Series circuit   Parallel circuit

Resistance in parallel is summed differently. In the figure shown above in the parallel circuit, if the 100 ohm resistor is considered to be R, and the 200 ohm resistor is R, the formula is:

$$\frac{1}{R_t} = \frac{1}{R_1} + \frac{1}{R_2}.$$

Derivation is as follows:

$$\frac{1}{R_1} = (\frac{1}{R_1} \times \frac{R_2}{R_2}) + (\frac{1}{R_2} \times \frac{R_1}{R_1}) = \frac{R_1}{R_1 R_2} + \frac{R_1}{R_1 R_2} = \frac{R_1 + R_2}{R_1 R_2}$$

So, now we have:

$$\frac{1}{R_t} = \frac{R_1 + R_2}{R_1 R_2}. \quad \text{Inversing,} \quad \frac{R_t}{1} = \frac{R_1 R_2}{R_1 + R_2} = R_t$$

This derivation is for two resistors in parallel; for more resistors in parallel, the same derivation technique would be followed.

Given that all the resistors in a parallel circuit are of the same resistive value, the following is a short calculation of the total circuit resistance.

Take the resistive value of one of the resistors and divide it by the number of resistors in the parallel circuit. Assuming that 5 resistors are in parallel and each one is 500 ohms, to calculate the total circuit resistance, divide 500 by 5 and the result is 100 ohms.

An interesting aspect of resistance is that the inverse (1/R) is conduction, the ease with which electrons can flow through a given material, and is expressed in units of *mhos* with a symbol that is the same as the resistance symbol inverted.

The color codes for resistors are as follows:

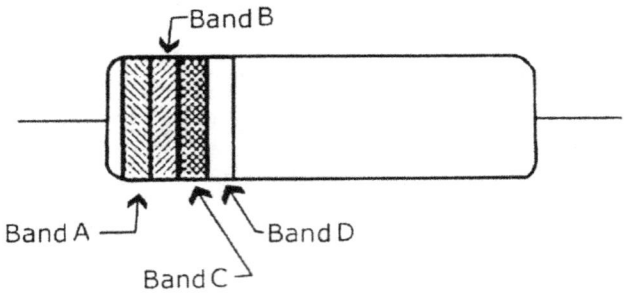

Band A is the first digit of the value of the resistor.
Band B is the second digit of the value of the resistor.
Band C is the decimal multiplier.
Band D is the tolerance of the value of the resistor.

The colors and their values are:

COLOR	VALUE	COLOR	VALUE	TOLERANCE COLORS
BLACK	0	GREEN	5	
BROWN	1	BLUE	6	GOLD 5%
RED	2	VIOLET	7	SILVER 10%
ORANGE	3	GRAY	8	NO COLOR 20%
YELLOW	4	WHITE	9	

So, a resistor colored as:
    1st band   violet
    2nd band   green
    3rd band   blue
    4th band   silver
is computed as:

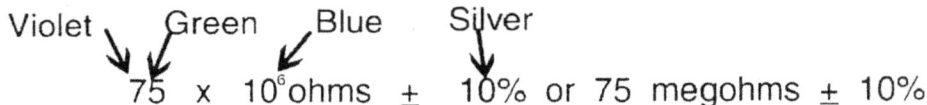

An easy way of remembering the sequence of the color codes above is to remember the following sentence and use the first letters of each word: *Bad Boys Race Our Young Girls Behind Victory Garden Walls.*

Ohms' Law

Ohm's law is the law that establishes the mathematical relationship of current, voltage, and resistance in a circuit. The formula is: $E = IR$, where E = the circuit or component voltage, I = the circuit or component current, and R = the circuit or component resistance.

In the circuit shown below, we know $E = 10$ volts and $I = 5$ ohms. Deriving the formula, we get $I = E/R$. So, $I = 10/5 = 2$ amps.

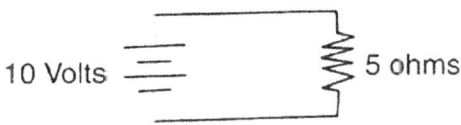

The power consumed by a component is equal to E x I. So, P = EI, and this calculated value is expressed in units of watts.

Kirchoff's Voltage Law

Kirchoff's voltage law states in technical terms that in a simple series circuit, as shown below, the algebraic sum of the voltages around the circuit is zero. Basically, this means that the supply voltage, Vsupply, is equal to VA + VB + VC, which are the voltage drops across the respective resistors in the circuit below. In the parallel circuit shown below, the voltages in each of the individual branches are equal to each other as well as equal to the total circuit voltage.

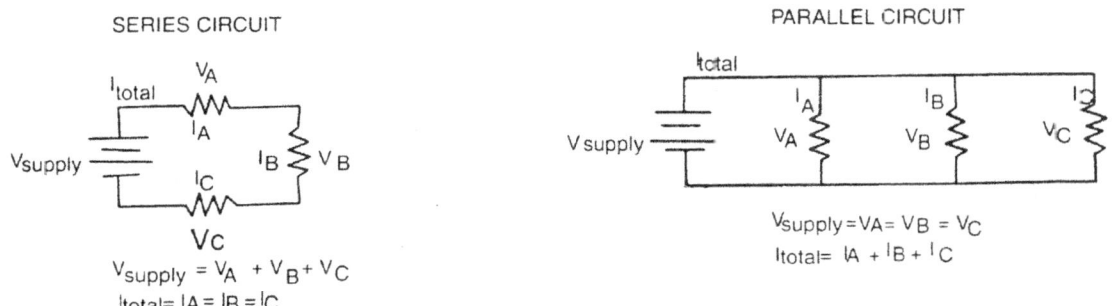

Kirchoff's Current Law

Kirchoff's current law states that at any junction of conductors in a circuit, the algebraic sum of the currents is zero. On a series circuit shown above, current is equal across each individual component as well as equal to the total circuit current. In a parallel circuit, the current across each individual branch when added is equal to the total circuit current, as in the parallel circuit shown above.

Inductors

Inductors are coils that oppose changes in current, which also store energy in a magnetic field. Induction is expressed in units of henries, and represented by an h. Inductance in series and parallel circuits is summed in the same manner as resistance. Inductors tend to block AC signals and pass DC voltages. An inductor's ability to oppose AC current is called inductive reactance. Inductive reactance is expressed in ohms just like resistance, but is represented by the symbol ZL, where Z means impedance and L added specifies inductive reactance or impedance. The impedance symbol Ω should not be confused with the resistive symbol, which is the same. The formula for inductive reactance is: $X_L = 2\pi fL$, where $\pi = 3.14$, f = the frequency of the AC signal to be used, and L = the inductance in henries. The schematic symbol for an inductor is ⏜⏜⏜⏜

Adding two lines on the top of the symbol means that it is an iron core filled inductor. Since they have a magnetic field, they are used in transformers and electromagnetic switches.

Capacitors

Capacitors consist basically of two metal plates in parallel separated by an insulator (dielectric). Capacitors have the ability to store a charge in an electrostatic field between its two plates. This charge is dependent upon two things, the capacitance of the circuit and the difference in the potential of the circuit. The capacitance of a capacitor is measured in farads, and is depicted by the letter C. Capacitance is summed in a manner that is exactly opposite to that of resistors, since it is directly summed when in parallel as shown below.

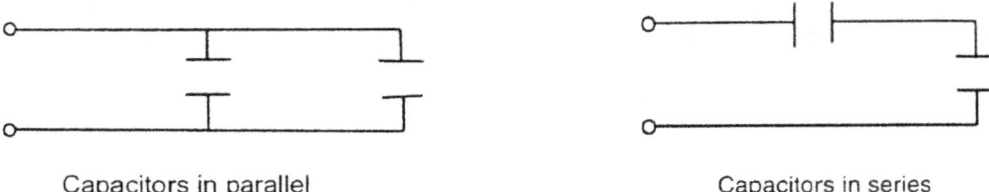

Capacitors in parallel   Capacitors in series

In the parallel circuit shown above, if one of the capacitors is 1 farad and the other is 2 farads, then total circuit capacitance is 3 farads. Capacitance of such a high value is rare and usually limited to industrial use. More realistic values would be in the microfarad range. When capacitors are in series as shown above, they are added, as are resistors in parallel. So, the formula would be: $Ct = \dfrac{C_1 C_2}{C_1 + C_2}$

As with inductors, capacitors are also measured by the opposition that they may give to AC current flow, which is called capacitive reactance. Capacitive reactance, X_c, is expressed also in units of ohms, and its formula is:

$$X_c = \frac{1}{2\pi f C}$$

where f = the frequency in hertz of the AC signal, and C = the capacitance, in farads. Electrolytic capacitors are polarized, which means that they must be placed in circuits with polarity considerations.

AC Cycles

The five main forms of AC signals are sawtooth, sinusoidal, square, rectangular, and trapezoidal waveforms.

Sawtooth waveform   Sinusoldal waveform   Square waveform   Rectangular wavefrom   Trapazoldal waveform

There are also parts of sinewaves that are of interest.

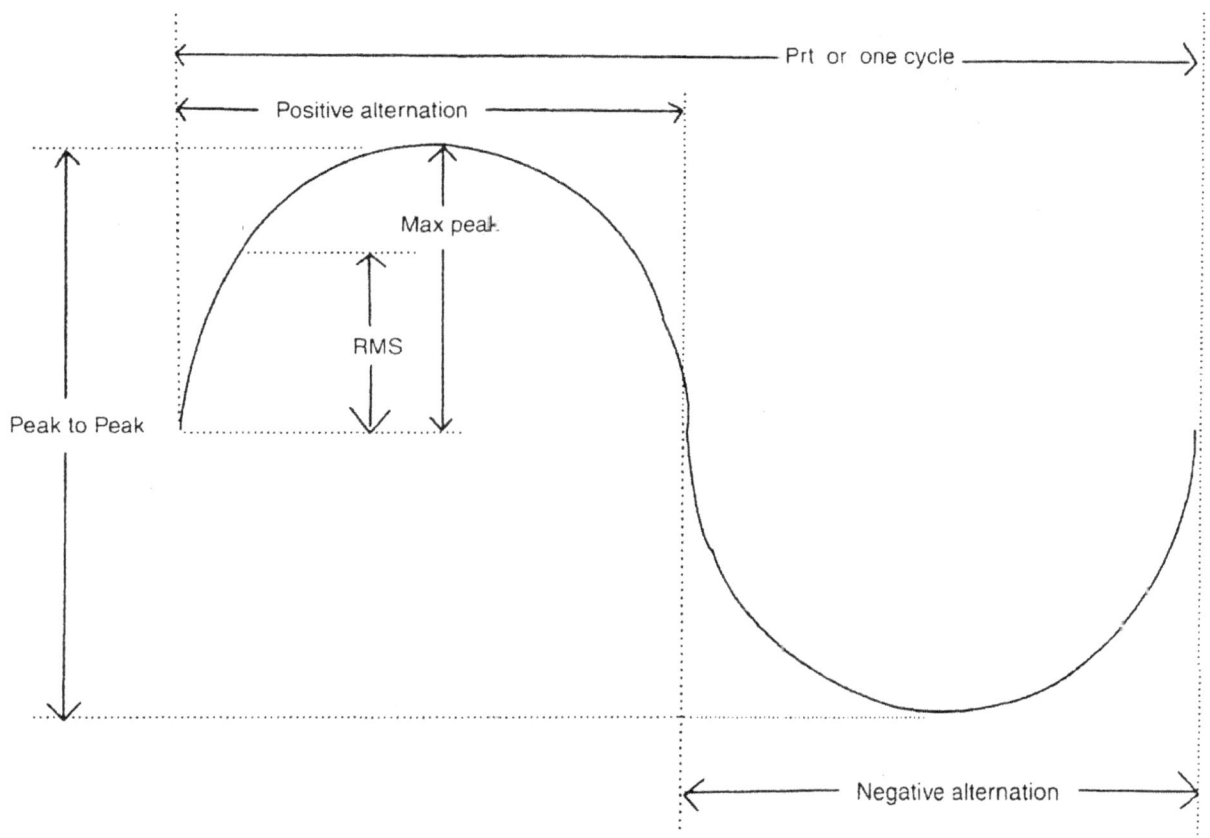

The RMS value (root mean square) is the same as the effective value, which is the value of an AC signal that has the same power or heating effect as a DC voltage. With sinusoidal waveforms, this value is equal to .707 times the AC voltage peak.

The average value is the value of an AC signal of a positive alternation and in a sinusoidal waveform is equal to .637 times the maximum voltage or peak.

Magnetism

The basic properties of magnetism are permeability, reluctance, and retentivity.

Permeability is the property of the ease with which a metal will allow magnetic lines of flux to pass through it.

Reluctance is a property of a metal that opposes lines of flux going through it.

Retentivity is the ability of a magnetized metal to stay magnetized.

Permanent magnets have high retentivity. Steel has high retentivity, low permeability, and high reluctance. Soft iron has low retentivity, high permeability, and low reluctance.

When a wire has current passing through it, the wire will have an electromagnetic field around it. The left hand rule can be used to determine the direction of the electromagnetic lines. To do this, place your left hand with fingers wrapped around the wire and your thumb pointed in the direction of current flow. The direction in which your fingers are pointing is the direction of the electromagnetic lines of flux.

Relays

The three types of relays are power relays, control relays, and sensing relays. Power relays control high voltages going to circuits such as motors. Control relays are used to energize and de-energize other relays and associated circuitry. Sensing relays are used to detect such items as over or under, current or voltages. When sensed by the sensing relay, power sources will be disconnected.

Switches

The various types of switches are identified by the number of poles, throws, and positions that they have. The number of *poles* that a switch has indicates the number of terminals through which voltages may enter the switch. The number of *throws* refers to the number of circuits that could be completed or disconnected by each blade or contacter. The number of *positions* indicates the number of different places that the toggle of the switch can be placed in.
The four kinds of switches are shown below.

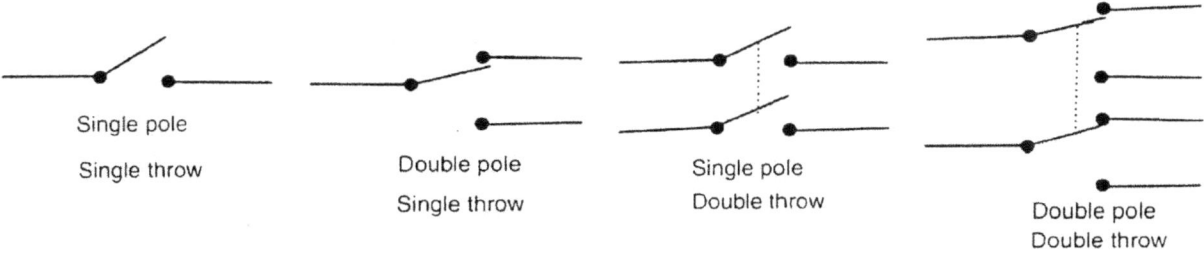

Single pole
Single throw

Double pole
Single throw

Single pole
Double throw

Double pole
Double throw

Diodes

As its name implies, a simple rectifier diode is used for signal rectification. The schematic symbol is shown below. Zener diodes are designed for specific reverse breakdown voltages; and since they keep the voltage across the diode constant, they are used for voltage regulation. Tunnel diodes will give negative resistance for specific ranges of forward bias voltages. Because of this phenomenon, tunnel diodes are used as amplifiers or oscillators. Silicon controlled rectifiers (SCR) are triggered diodes. These are used to control AC voltages on one particular half cycle. Diacs work on both sides of the cycles of an AC signal. Triacs are gated diacs. Basically, SCRs, diacs, and triacs are used to pick out desired portions of AC signals.

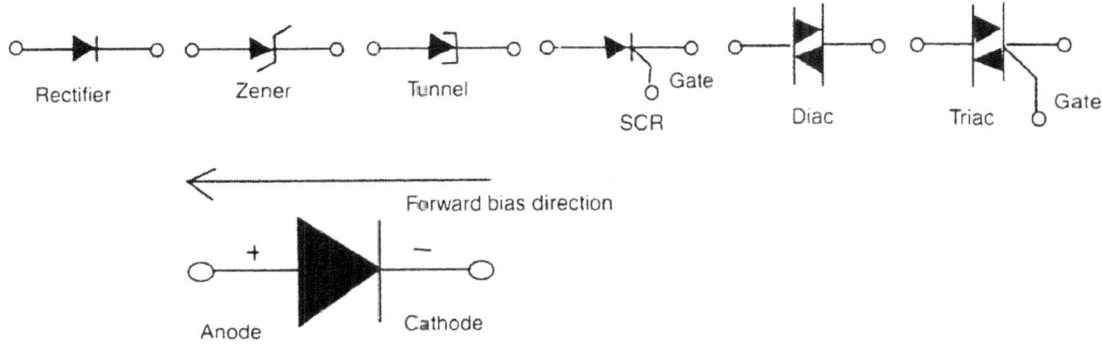

Transistors

Transistors are solid state devices that can act as amplifiers or switches. They are classified as bipolar and field-effect transistors. The bipolar transistor allows current flow in either direction. The two types of bipolar transistors are PNP and NPN transistors, which are shown below.

When used strictly as a switch, the PNP transistor requires a negative input signal on the base to turn it on or conduct. Conversely, the NPN transistor requires a positive signal on the base to turn it on.

Bipolar transistors are not only used as switches and have several configurations. The different transistor configurations and their respective traits are shown below:

BEC
VPI
ABG
LMH
HML
IOI

The <u>first</u> line is the type of configuration, i.e., common base, emitter, or collector. The particular transistor's configuration traits are shown vertically below the transistor. Line <u>two</u> shows electrical gains (voltage, power, or current). Line <u>three</u> shows the type of gain (alpha, beta, or gamma). Line <u>four</u> shows the input impedance of the configuration (low, medium, or high). Line <u>five</u> shows the output impedance (high, medium, or low).

Line _six_ shows the output signal phase relationship with the input (in-phase or out-of-phase).

There are two types of field effect transistors (FET) - JFETs and MOSFETs. <u>JFETs</u> stand for junction field transistors and control large voltages with very small inputs and, therefore, can be used as amplifiers. <u>MOSFETs</u> stands for metal-oxide-semiconductor field effect transistors and have a higher input impedance and can use even smaller signals. They are also smaller and are configured by the thousands to form chips.

Soldering

Electrical connections are joined by soldering. Soldering requires a high heat source and an alloy that melts at a relatively low temperature when compared to other metals. The basic soldering technique is to first heat the joint to be soldered with a soldering device and then place the solder directly onto the joint with the soldering device still in contact. Allow the solder to melt and flow onto the joint surface covering the joint area. Once this occurs, remove solder and device, allowing to cool without any movement of the joint area. After the solder hardens, inspect the solder joint. The joint should look smooth, bright, and shiny, with the surface area of the joint smoothly covered. If the solder has the appearance of being partially balled up instead of a smooth semi-flat flow, it is called a *cold solder* joint. A possible cause of a cold solder joint might be wrongly applying the solder to the solder device and then dropping onto the area to be soldered. If the solder joint is not shiny but dull and gray instead, then the connection was probably moved prior to the solder hardening completely.

Solder is an alloy usually made up of various ratios and combinations of tin and lead. Some that are resin filled are also called flux. Soldering fluxes are used to de-oxide surfaces that are being soldered. One type of flux is acid-core resin, which is very corrosive to electrical connections and should be avoided.

Soldering devices come in various sizes, depending on the job required to be done. One of the most delicate of soldering jobs, soldering components with very small connections onto printed circuit boards, is usually done by pencil irons. These miniature irons are ideal for providing low heat to small areas. Soldering jobs that require more heat use items such as solder guns. These produce high heat and heat up very quickly.

The types of solder tips most commonly used in electrical work are made of copper or copper alloys, since copper has high heat conductivity and good tinning quality. The tinning of a soldering tip increases heat transfer/conductivity to the area to be soldered and also reduces scaling of the solder tip. Tinning consists of getting a good layer of solder on the working surface of the copper tip. Cleaning tips that become dirty or discolored requires dipping the tip in water while hot, and quickly removing it or wiping with a damp sponge or towel.

II. COMPUTERS

The 5 major components of a computer are input, storage, control unit, arithmetic and "logic unit, and output. The <u>input</u> device allows information such as data and commands or instructions to be fed into the computer system. The most common type of input device is the keyboard. Other input devices are magnetic and optical readers. Storage devices are used to store memory, such as instructions or data until they are needed. Memory is stored in bits, which is the most basic element of binary numbers, a 1 or 0. Bytes are groups of eight bits. A nibble is half of a byte. The control unit coordinates the operations of the entire computer. It interprets programs and issues instructions to accomplish the program. The output device communicates the progress or results of a program used in the computer to the operator/user. The devices range from monitor screens to high speed printers.

Numbering Systems

Computers and associated circuitry use several numbering systems that have different bases. We are all familiar with base 10 numbering system. This is the system we use in everyday life. In this system, each decimal/digit place represents a value of 10, whether it is the first digit to the left of the decimal point, which is a 10 to the 0 power or one's. The second digit to the left represents the number of 10's and the third represents the number of 100's.

The other base sytems work in the same fashion with their own respective bases. The other base systems used are base 2 (binary), base 8 (octal), and base 16 (hexadecimal). It is easy to convert from one system to another.

	5th digit	4th digit	3rd digit	2nd digit	1st digit
Base 10	10^4	10^3	10^2	10^1	10^0
Base 2	2^4	2^3	2^2	2^1	2^0
Base 8	8^4	8^3	8^2	8^1	8^0
Base 16	16^4	16^3	16^2	16^1	16^0

The largest number in base 10 is a 9, for base 2 it is 1, for base 8 it is 7, for base 16 it is 15. The numbers for base 16 greater than 9 are expressed by letters, i.e., 10 = A, 11 = B, 12 = C, 13 = D, 14 = E, and 15 = F.

The following is a conversion of the base 16 number to the other bases. The number will be $2B7_{16}$

```
        7
   2  B*    +    Base 16     So 2B7₁₆ = 695₁₀
  x16  +   688
   32  32  695              *B = 11
       43
        x
       16
       688
```

So $2B7_{16} = 695_{10}$

*B = 11

The procedure for calculating is to start with the most significant digit and multiply it by the value base used. In this case, the most significant digit is a 2 and the base value is 16. Next, take the result of the multiplication and add this to the next lower digit and then multiply by the digit place value. This was (32+11) x 16 = 688. This procedure continues until the least significant digit is reached. At this point, just add the accumulated value so far with the last digit.

This same process is used for converting any other number of a different base to base 10 number, using the respective base values.

To convert a base 10 number to its base 16 (or any base), the process is as follows: First, the base 10 number is divided by the base number of the base system it is to be converted to. To reconvert 695 base 10 back to base 16, 695/16 = 43 with a remainder of 7. The remainder (7) is the least significant digit of the new base number. Next, 43/16 = 2 with a remainder of 11. 11 is the next digit because we are going to base 16, 11 = B. Since it is less than the base number (16), 2 becomes the most significant digit. So, the converted number is 2B7 base 16.

To convert the base 10 number to base 8, 695/8 = 86 with a remainder of 7, which will be the least significant digit. Now, 86/8 = 10 with a remainder of 6, which is the next digit. Finally, 10/8 = 1 with a remainder of 2, which is the next digit. 1 is left as the most significant digit. So, 695 base 10 = 1267 base 8.

We can reverse this to see if it is correct. Multiply the most significant digit 1 by 8. 1x8=8. Add this to the next digit and multiply by 8, (8+2) x 8 = 80. Add the result to the next digit and multiply by 8, (80+6) x 8 = 688. Now, add the result to the last (least significant) digit, 688 + 7 = 695. So, 695 base 10 does = 1267 base 8.

Performing base 2 calculations is just as simple. Take 21 base 10 and convert to base 2. 21/2 = 10 with a remainder of 1, which is the least significant digit. 10/2 = 5 with a remainder of 0, which will be the next digit. 5/2= 2 with a remainder of 1, the next digit. 2/2 = 1 with a remainder of 0, the next digit. The remaining number will be the next most significant digit. So, 23 base 10 = 10101 base 2.

Reverse this to check: 1x2=2. (2+0) x 2 = 4. (4+1) x 2 = 10. (10+0) x 2 = 20. (20+1) = 21. So, 23 base 10 does equal 10101 base 2.

Flip Flops

Flip flops have one of two stable states. They change states by receiving input pulses. The reset-set flip flop (RS FF) is one of the most basic forms of flip flops made by interconnecting two NAND gates.

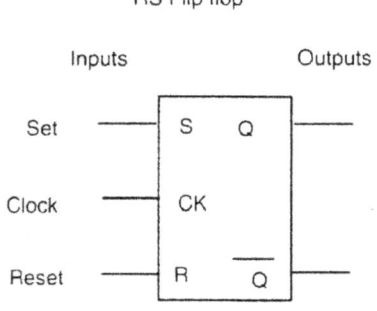

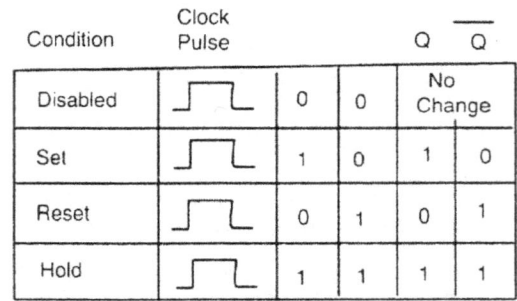

Condition	Clock Pulse	S	R	Q	Q̄
Disabled	⎍	0	0	No Change	
Set	⎍	1	0	1	0
Reset	⎍	0	1	0	1
Hold	⎍	1	1	1	1

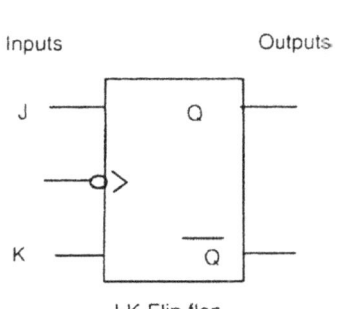

Condition	Clock Pulse			Q	$\overline{Q}$
Hold	⎍	0	0	NO Change	
Set	⎍	1	0	1	0
Reset	⎍	0	1	0	1
Toggle	⎍	1	1	Change to Opposite state	

J-K Flip flop

A flip flop with a clock input is called a synchronous device; without a clock input it is called an asynchronous device.

The most common type of flip flop is the J-K flop flip (shown on the previous page). The J + K inputs are data inputs. The arrowhead > at the clock input means that the flip flop is edge triggered. The bubble 0 means that the flip flop is negative edge triggered. Flip flops can be put together to make counters such as:

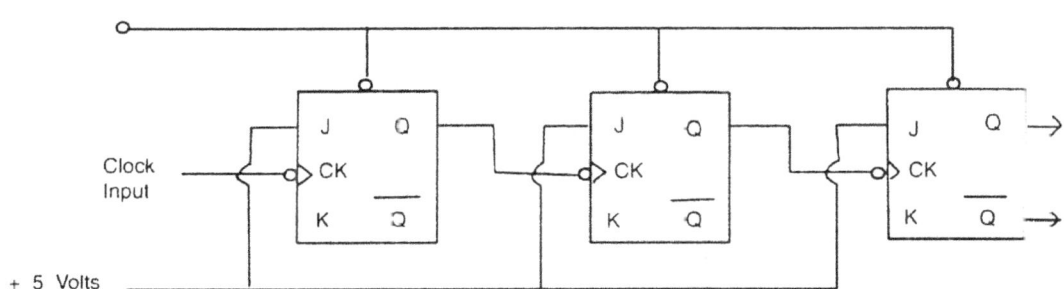

Shift registers also use flip flops in which data is loaded serially (one bit at a time). Once the FF's are loaded with data, they can be shifted left or right (depending upon how they are wired), by clock pulses. Shifting the data to the left or right will either divide by 2 or multiply by 2, depending on which FF has the least significant digit.

The following represent adders which perform arithmetic operations:

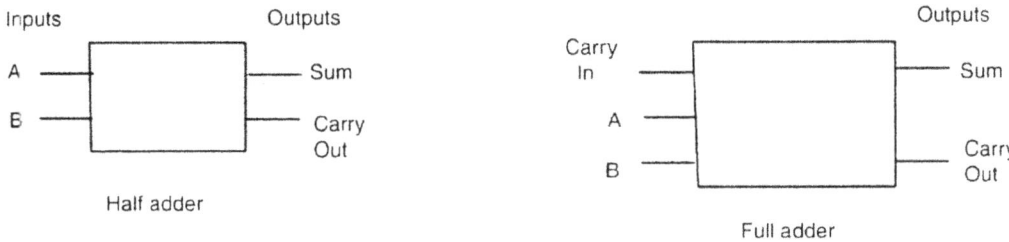

Half adders add binary numbers like the full adder, but do not consider previous carry inputs.

The significance of flip flops is that they can be grouped together to form units of memory, such as RAMs, ROMs, PROMs, and EPROMs. RAM (random access memory) is volatile memory, meaning that when power is turned off, the stored memory is lost. RAM is considered a read-write memory, meaning that you can read data from or write data into the memory. ROM (read-only memory) is non-volatile, meaning that when power is turned off, memory is not lost. ROMs are permanently programmed by the manufacturer and is often called firmware. PROMs (programmable read-only memory) are special ROMs designed to allow the user to program the ROM. EPROMs (erasable programmable read-only memory) are also special ROMs that allow the user to program memories and erase the programs.

Logic Gates

Logic gates use binary inputs. In positive logic, a 1 is a high input and a 0 is a low input. In negative logic, a 1 is a low input and a 0 is a high input.

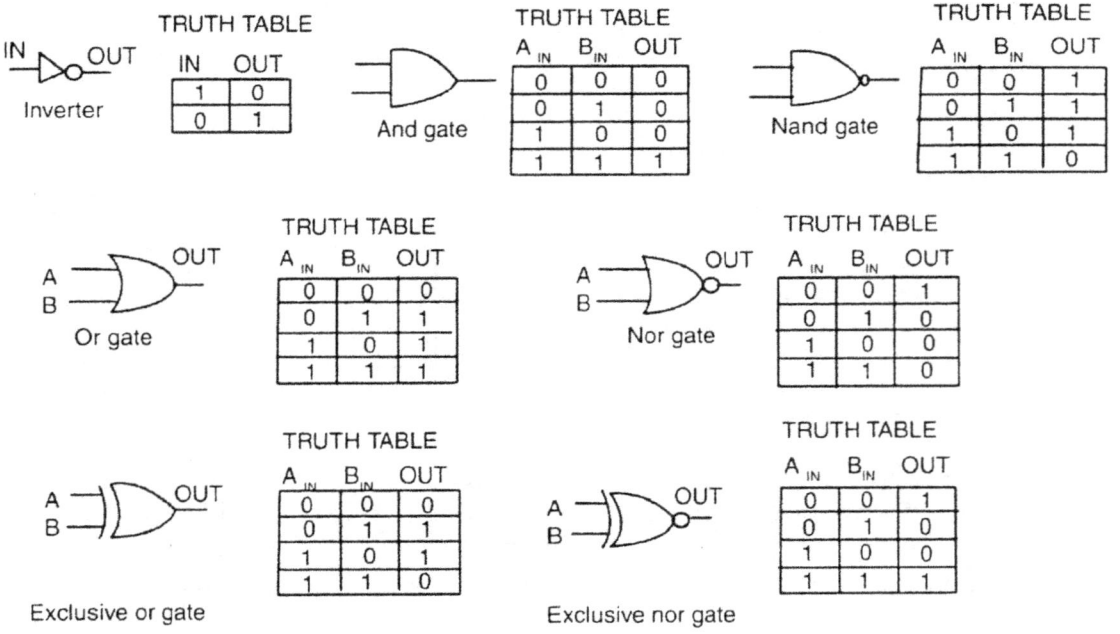

III. OSCILLOSCOPES

Oscilloscopes are used to display instantaneous voltage waveforms in graphic form. The display screen is set up and divided vertically and horizontally in 1 cm divisions. There are 8 vertical divisions in which waveform amplitude is displayed and 10 horizontal divisions in which the time of the wavelength is displayed.

The VOLTS/DIV knob allows the user to select the waveform voltage amplitude in each vertical division to be displayed. The SEC/DIV knob allows the user to select the sweep speed of the waveform in each horizontal division to be displayed.

Proper use of the oscilloscope requires the ability to analyze displayed waveforms by observing the number of divisions a cycle of a given waveform covers both vertically and horizontally.

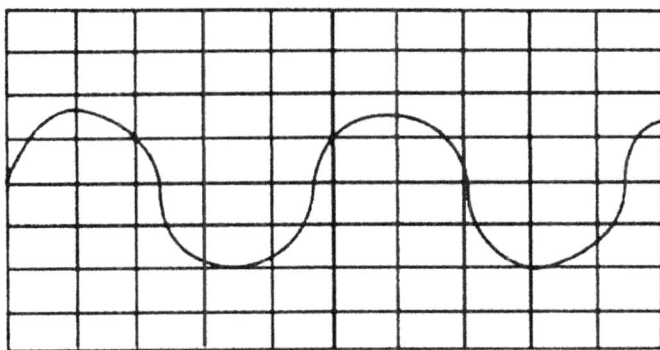

In the waveform shown above, the VOLT/DIV knob is set on 5 volts/div and the SEC/DIV knob is set to 1 msec/div.

Count the number of divisions covered vertically by the waveform, which is 3 1/2 divisions. To get the actual peak-to-peak amplitude of the sinewave, perform the following calculation: 3 1/2 divisions x 5 volts/division = 17.5 volts peak to peak.

Now count the number of divisions covered horizontally by one complete cycle of the waveform, which in this case is 4 1/2 divisions. To find the PRT (pulse repetition time), perform the following calculation: 4 1/2 divisions x .001 sec/division = .0045 seconds. .0045 seconds x msec/.001 sec = 4.5 msec for the PRT.

To find the frequency, simply invert the PRT: Frequency = 1/PRT = 1/.0045 sec = 222.22 cycles/sec or hertz.

The same process could be reversed to find the settings to use on an oscilloscope when you know the amplitude and frequency of a given waveform/signal that you would like to view on the oscilloscope.

Meters

The following are the basics of measuring meters: Always measure current *in series* with the circuit to be measured and always measure voltage in parallel with the circuit.

When performing resistance measurements, always ensure that the component or circuit has no voltage on it and consider whether a specific component may need to be isolated from the rest of the circuit so that the resistance measurement does not follow an alternate path. This can be accomplished by removing one of the *electrical* legs of the component from the circuit. When unsure of the amount of voltage on a circuit to be measured, start with the highest meter setting or range.

When using analog or needle deflection type meters, ensure that you have the proper polarity of leads when checking for DC voltages. One of the most popular analog type multimeters used is the Simpson 260. For copyright reasons, a copy of the meter cannot be given but here are some tips that will work using any analog multimeter. When performing DC measurements, look at the range setting that you have the meter set up for, and find the same corresponding scale on the meter face for proper readings. When performing resistance measurements, read the resistance value on the resistance scale where the needle is deflected to and then multiply this by the resistance range setting. An example of this is with the needle setting on a value of 8 on the resistance scale and the range knob on *RX1000,* then the value of resistance is 8000 ohms.

IV. SCIENTIFIC NOTATION

Scientific notation is a way of expressing large numbers. For example, 100,000,000 ohms could be written as 100×10^6 ohms or 100 megohms. Other prefixes like meg are listed below.

FACTOR	PREFIX	SYMBOL	FACTOR	PREFIX	SYMBOL
10^{12}	tera	T	10^{-2}	centi	c
10^9	giga	G	10^{-3}	milli	m
10^6	mega	M	10^{-6}	micro	μ
10^3	kilo	K	10^{-9}	nano	n
10^2	hecto	h	10^{-12}	pico	p
10^1	deka	da	10^{-15}	femto	f
10^{-1}	deci	d	10^{-18}	atto	a

V. GEARS

Gears are wheels with teeth that are used to transmit mechanical motion from one point to another. The usual configuration is that of two gears meshed together. In this configuration, the larger gear is simply called a *gear* and the smaller gear is called a *pinion*. If the pinion drives the gear, the system is called a speed reducer. If the gear drives the pinion, then the system is called a speed increaser.

When gears are used in increasing or decreasing speeds, they are configured in gear ratios. This allows specific speed changes. For example, for a gear to turn 100 revolutions per minute, if the shaft of the driving motor turns at 1000 revolutions per minute, to achieve the desired speed, it is necessary to use a reducer configuration. This is accomplished by changing the gear ratios. Since gears are made with a certain number of teeth per inch, reducing the number of teeth per inch on the gear attached to the motor shaft to one-tenth of that of the other gear that is being driven would reduce the speed of the driving shaft from 1000 revolutions per minute to 100 revolutions per minute on the driven shaft.

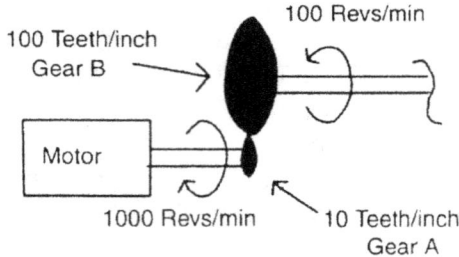

The basic formula for calculating the relationship between the gears and their respective speeds is: Revs/min(gear A) x Teeth/inch (gear A) = Revs/min(gear B) x Teeth/inch(gear B).

When two gears mesh, they turn in opposite directions. Adding a third gear called an idler gear and placing it in-between the two gears will allow them to turn in the same direction. There are four basic types of gear configurations, and they are spur, worm, helical/herringbone, and bevel gears.

<u>Spur gears</u> are the most common type, having straight teeth. They are used to transmit power between two parallel shafts.

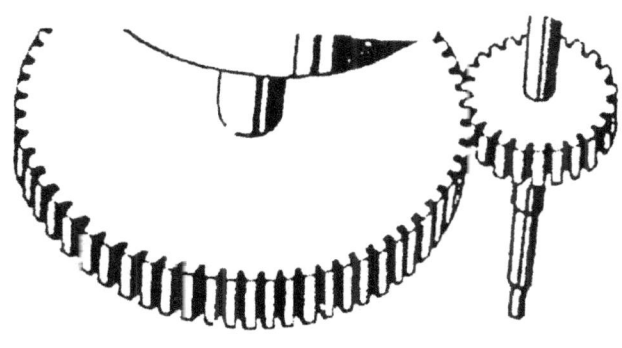

TYPICAL SPUR GEAR

<u>Worm gears</u> having helical teeth are used to transmit power between two shafts whose axis intersect, but not in the same plane. This is probably the most common method of speed reduction, especially in conveyers because the speed of a very fast rotating motor can be greatly reduced.

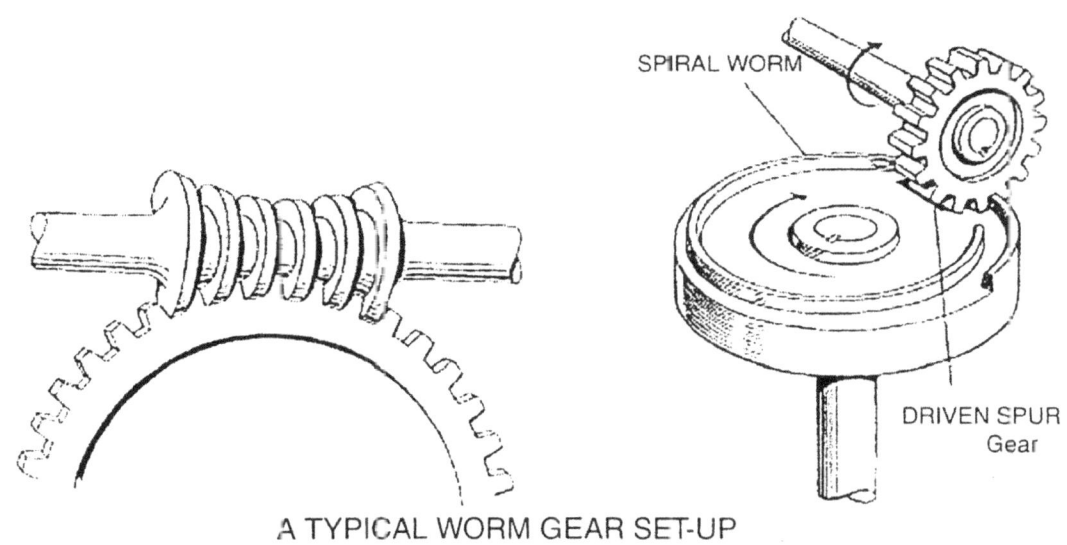

A TYPICAL WORM GEAR SET-UP

<u>Helical/herringbone gears</u> have spiral teeth which allows them to transmit power between two shafts at any angle.

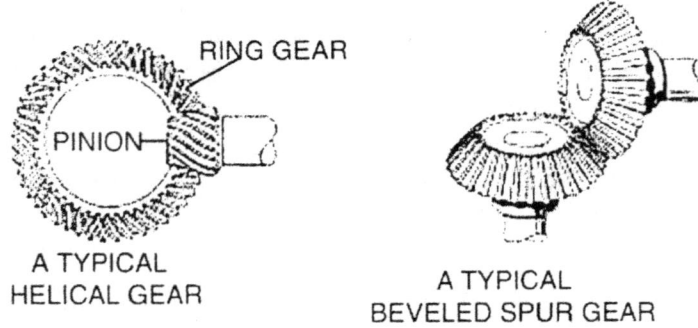

A TYPICAL HELICAL GEAR

A TYPICAL BEVELED SPUR GEAR

<u>Bevel gears</u> are shaped like sections of cones and used to transmit power between shafts whose axis intersect.

Pulleys

Pulleys are wheels used to transmit power such as pulleys used to transmit power from a motor to drive the roller of a conveyer belt. The main feature of a pulley is its ability to change speeds or revolutions per minute. When a pulley drives another pulley with a smaller diameter, the rpms of the second pulley will be greater. This results in a speed increase similar to that in gear systems.

A formula for calculating the circumference around a pulley is: $C = 2\pi r$, where r is the radius of the pulley, and $\pi = 3.14$. Through a series of derivations, the relationship of respective rpms between two connected pulleys is as follows.

Arpms = Brpms x rB/rA where:
        Arpms = revolutions per minute of pulley A
        Brpms = revolutions per minute of pulley B
        rB = radius of pulley B
        rA = radius of pulley A

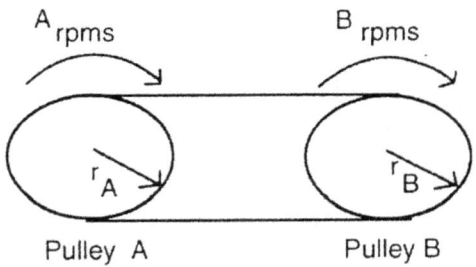

Pulley A   Pulley B

Another use of pulleys is compounding. Compound bows used for archery take advantage of the physics involved in compounding to allow archers to draw bows at high weight pulls with relative ease. For example, to pull up a 100 lb. weight, instead of having to pull with a force of 100 lbs., pulleys can be used to lessen the force required.

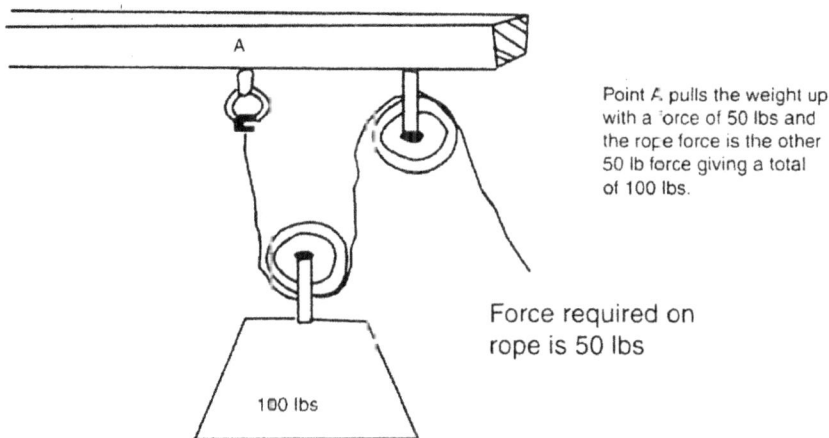

Point A pulls the weight up with a force of 50 lbs and the rope force is the other 50 lb force giving a total of 100 lbs.

Force required on rope is 50 lbs

A pawl is a device used to allow a wheel to turn in one direction and lock the wheel from turning in the other direction. Pawls are commonly found in winching or come-along set-ups.

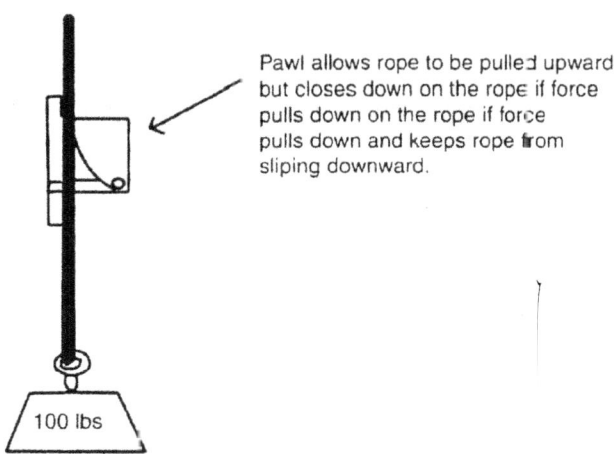

Pawl allows rope to be pulled upward, but closes down on the rope if force pulls down on the rope if force pulls down and keeps rope from sliping downward.

Special coupling is required in power transmissions in order to get mechanical power from one point to another. There are four general types of coupling. The first type is rigid coupling and is rarely used because the shafts must be exactly parallel and, therefore, do not allow for misalignment. The second is flexible coupling which allows for some misalignment although excessive misalignment increases wear. The third type is chain coupling which has been mostly replaced by flexible coupling which requires the most maintenance of all couplings. The last is fluid coupling which uses steel shot as a flow charge. This allows the motor to pick up loads gradually.

Chains should be mounted horizontally or not more than 60 degrees off the horizontal plane. They do allow for the most misalignment. Hook-shaped sprocket teeth show excessive wear. Misalignment may be identified by inspecting for wear on the sides of teeth on the inner surface of roller link plates. The chain sag should not be greater than 2% of the distances from the sprockets, which is 1/4 inch per foot.

A cam is a device connected to a rotating shaft used to convert rotary motion into reciprocal motion.

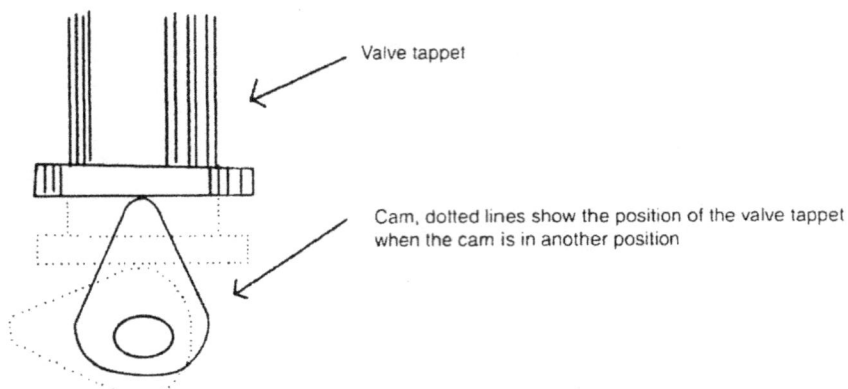

Valve tappet

Cam, dotted lines show the position of the valve tappet when the cam is in another position

Lubricants

Lubrication materials occur in many mediums. Three that will be discussed here are oils, greases, and solids.

Multigrade oils are the most versatile of the oil types. They have additives that allow them to be used in a wide range of temperatures. For example, in an oil labeled 10 w/30, 10 is the SAE viscosity number at 0 degrees Fahrenheit, and the SAE viscosity number at 210 degrees Fahrenheit is 30.

Greases are used in the lubrication of ball or idler bearing systems. Generally speaking, greases are oils that have had thickening agents or *soaps* added. The different kinds of greases are graded from 000, which is a *semi-fluid,* to 6 which is described as being very stiff or thick.

Another type of lubricant is solids. The most common type of solid lubricant is graphite. Another type is molybdenumdisulphide. Solid lubricants are extremely useful as anti-seize compounds to protect rubbing surfaces under high pressures and temperatures from metal pick-up.

ELECTRIC MOTOR AND GENERATOR REPAIR

CONTENTS

	Page
I. TROUBLESHOOTING DATA FOR GENERATORS AND MOTORS	1
<u>Section I. DC Generators</u>	1
1. Failure to Build up Voltage	1
2. Output Voltage too Low	1
3. Output Voltage too High	1
4. Armature Overheats	1
5. Field Coils Overheat	2
6. Sparking at Brushes	2
<u>Section II. DC Motors</u>	2
7. Failure to Start	2
8. Stops After Running a Short Time	2
9. Attempts to Start, but Overload Relays Trip Out	2
10. Runs too Slow	3
11. Runs too Fast Under Load	3
12. Sparking at Brushes	3
13. Overheating	3
<u>Section III. AC Generators</u>	3
14. Noisy Operation	3
15. Overheating	3
16. No Output Voltage	3
17. Output Voltage Unsteady	4
18. Output Voltage too High	4
19. Frequency Incorrect or Fluctuating	4
20. Voltage Hunting	4
21. Stator Overheats in Spots	4
22. Field Overheating	4
23. Alternator Produces Shock When Touched	4
<u>Section IV. AC Induction Motors</u>	4
24. Failure to Start	4
25. Noisy Operation	4
26. Overheating	5
<u>Section V. AC Wound Rotor Motors</u>	5
27. Runs Slow with External Resistance Cutout	5
<u>Section VI. AC Synchronous Motors</u>	5
28. Failure to Start	5
29. Runs Slow	5
30. Failure to Pull into Step	5
31. No Field Excitation	5
32. Pulls Out of Step, or Trips Breakers	6
33. Hunting	6
34. Stator Overheats in Spots	6
35. Field Overheats	6
36. Overheating	6
<u>Section VII. AC Repulsion Induction Motors</u>	6
37. Failure to Start	6
38. Runs Slow	7
39. Overheating	7
40. Noisy Operation	7
41. Motor Produces Shock when Touched	7

continued ....

ELECTRIC MOTOR AND GENERATOR REPAIR (cont'd)

CONTENTS

	Page
Section VIII. AC Split-Phase, Capacitor-Start, and Transformer-Capacitor Motors	7
42. Failure to Start	7
43. Overheating	7
44. Noisy Operation	8
II. TROUBLESHOOTING DATA FOR DC AND AC CONTROLLERS	9
Section I. DC Controllers	9
45. Failure to Close	9
46. Failure to Open	9
47. Sluggish Operation	9
48. Erratic Operation (Unwanted openings and closures, and failure of overload protection)	9
49. Overheating of Coils	10
50. Contacts Welded Together	10
51. Overheating of Contacts	10
52. Excessive Arcing of Contacts	10
53. Pitting or Corroding of Contacts	11
Section II. AC Controllers	11
54. Failure to Close	11
55. Failure to Open	11
56. Sluggish Operation	11
57. Erratic Operation (Unwanted openings and closures, and failure of overload protection)	12
58. Overheating of Coils	12
59. Contacts Welded Together	12
60. Overheating or Contacts	12
61. Arcing at Contacts	13
62. Pitting or Corroding of Contacts	13
63. Noisy Operation (Hum or Chatter)	13
64. Vibration After Repairs	13

ELECTRIC MOTOR AND GENERATOR REPAIR

I. TROUBLESHOOTING DATA FOR GENERATORS AND MOTORS

Section I. DC GENERATORS

1. Failure to Build up Voltage

Probable cause	Remedy
Voltmeter not operating	Check output voltage with separate voltmeter. Replace voltmeter.
Open field resistor	Repair or replace resistor.
Open field circuit	Check coils for open and loose connections. Replace the defective coil or coils. Tighten or solder loose connections.
Absence of residual magnetism in a self-excited generator.	Flash the field.
Dirty commutator	Clean or dress commutator.
High mica	Undercut mica.
Brushes not making proper contact	Free, if binding in holders. Replace and reseat if worn.
Newly seated brushes not contacting sufficient area on the commutator.	Run in by reducing load and use a brush-seating stone.
Armature shorted internally, or to ground	Remove, test, and repair or replace.
Grounded or shorted field coil	Test, and repair or replace.
Shorted filtering capacitor	Replace.
Open filter choke	Replace.
Open ammeter shunt	Replace ammeter and shunt.
Broken brush shunts or pigtails	Replace brushes.

2. Output Voltage too Low

Probable cause	Remedy
Prime mover speed too low	Check speed with tachometer. Adjust governor on prime mover.
Brushes not seated properly	Run in with partial load, use brush-seating stone.
Commutator is dirty or film is too heavy	Clean, or if film is too heavy, replace brushes with a complete set of proper grade.
Field resistor not properly adjusted	Adjust field strength. Tighten all connections. Make shim adjustment.
Reversed field coil or armature connection	Check and connect properly.

3. Output Voltage Too High

Probable cause	Remedy
Prime mover speed too high	Check speed with tachometer. Adjust governor on prime mover.
Faulty voltage regulator	Adjust or replace.

4. Armature Overheats

Probable cause	Remedy
Overloaded	Check meter readings against nameplate ratings. Reduce load.
Excessive brush pressure	Adjust pressure or replace tension springs.
Couplings not alined	Aline units properly.

Probable cause	Remedy
End bells improperly positioned	Assemble correctly
Bent shaft	Straighten or replace
Armature coil shorted	Repair or replace armature
Armature rubbing or striking poles	Check for bent shaft, loose or worn bearings. Straighten and realine shaft. Replace bearings, tighten pole pieces, or replace armature.
Clogged air passages (poor ventilation)	Clean equipment
Repeated changes in load of great magnitude. (Improper design for the application).	Generator should be used with a steady load application.
Unequal brush tension	Equalize brush tension
Broken shunts or pigtails	Replace brushes
Open in field rheostat	Repair or replace rheostat

5. Field Coils Overheat

Probable cause	Remedy
Shorted or grounded coils	Repair or replace
Clogged air passages (poor ventilation)	Clean equipment. Remove obstructions.
Overload (compound generator)	Check meter reading against nameplate rating. Reduce load.

6. Sparking at Brushes

Probable cause	Remedy
Overload	Check meter readings against nameplate ratings. Reduce load.
Brushes off neutral plane	Adjust brush rigging.
Dirty brushes and commutator	Clean brushes and commutator.
High mica	Undercut mica.
Rough or eccentric commutator	Resurface commutator.
Open circuit in the armature	Repair or replace armature.
Grounded, open- or short-circuited field winding	Repair or replace defective coil or coils.
Insufficient brush pressure	Adjust or replace tension springs.
Brushes sticking in the holders	Clean holders. Sand brushes.

Section II. DC MOTORS

7. Failure to Start

Probable cause	Remedy
Open circuit in the control	Check for open. Replace open resistor or fuse.
Low supply voltage	Check with voltmeter and apply proper voltage.
Frozen bearing	Replace bearing and recondition shaft.
Overload	Reduce load or use larger motor.
Excessive friction	Check for air gap, bent shaft, loose or worn bearings, misalined end bells. Straighten shaft, replace bearings, tighten pole pieces, aline end bells.

8. Stops After Running a Short Time

Probable cause	Remedy
Failure of supply voltage	Apply proper voltage, replace fuses, or reset overload relay.
Overload	Check meter readings against nameplate ratings. Reduce load.
Ambient temperature too high	Ventilate space to reduce ambient temperature.
Overload relays set too low for application	Adjust relays for the application.

9. Attempts to Start, But Overload Relays Trip Out

Probable cause	Remedy
Motor field weak or non-existent	Check field circuit. Repair or replace defective field coils. Tighten all connections.
Overload	Check meter readings against nameplate ratings. Replace motor with one suitable to the application.
Relays adjusted too low for the application	Adjust relays for the application.

10. Runs too Slow

Probable cause	Remedy
Line voltage low	Apply proper voltage.
Bushes ahead of neutral plane	Adjust brush rigging.
Overload	Check meter reading against nameplate readings. Reduce load.

11. Runs too Fast under Load

Probable cause	Remedy
Weak field	Check field circuit. Replace open coils or open starter resistors.
Line voltage too high	Reduce line voltage.
Brushes off adjustment with neutral plane	Adjust brush rigging.

12. Sparking at Brushes

Probable cause	Remedy
Same as dc generator (par. 6)	Same as dc generator (par. 6).

13. Overheating

Probable cause	Remedy
Same as dc generator (par. 4 and 5)	Same as dc generator (par. 4 and 5).

Section III. AC GENERATORS

14. Noisy Operation

Probable cause	Remedy
Unbalanced load	Balance load.
Coupling loose or misalined	Reline coupling and tighten.
Improper air gap	Check for bent shaft, loose or worn bearings. Straighten and realine shaft. Replace bearings.
Loose laminations	Tighten bolts. Dip in varnish and bake.

15. Overheating

Probable cause	Remedy
Overloaded	Check meter readings against nameplate ratings. Reduce load.
Unbalanced load	Balance load.
Open load-line fuse	Replace fuse.
Restricted ventilation	Clean, and remove obstructions to ventilation.
Rotor winding short-circuited, open-circuited, or grounded.	Check, and replace defective coil or coils.
Stator winding short-circuited, open-circuited, or grounded.	Check, and replace defective coil or coils.
Bearings	Check for worn, loose, dry, or overlubricated bearings. Replace worn or loose bearings, lubricate dry bearings, relieve overlubrication.

16. No Output Voltage

Probable cause	Remedy
Stator coils open- or short-circuited	Check, and replace defective coil or coils.
Rotor coils open- or short-circuited	Check, and replace defective coil or coils.
Shorted sliprings	Disconnect field coils and check ring-insulation resistance with megger. Repair.
Internal moisture	Check with megger and dry windings.
No dc voltage at the slipring brushes. (No dc exciter voltage.)	Check for defective switch or blown fuse in exciter feeder lines. Repair switch or replace fuses. Check feeder cables for opens or shorts. Repair connections or replace cables. Refer to FAILURE TO BUILD UP VOLTAGE (par. 1).
Voltmeter defective	Check with a voltmeter known to be working properly. Replace.
Ammeter shunt open	Replace ammeter and shunt.

17. Output Voltage Unsteady

Probable cause	Remedy
Poor commutation at sliprings	Clean sliprings and brushes. Reseat brushes.
Loose terminal connections	Clean and tighten all connections and contacts.
Maladjusted voltage regulator and speed governor	Readjust speed governor and voltage regulator.

18. Output Voltage too High

Probable cause	Remedy
Overspeeding	Adjust speed-governing device.
Overexcited	Adjust voltage regulator.
Delta-connected stator open on one leg	Remake connection, repair or replace defective coil or coils.

19. Frequency Incorrect or Fluctuating

Probable cause	Remedy
Speed incorrect or fluctuating	Adjust speed-governing device.
Dc excitation fluctuating	Adjust belt tension of exciter generator.

20. Voltage Hunting

Probable cause	Remedy
External field resistance in total out position	Readjust resistance.
Voltage regulator contacts dirty	Clean and reset contact points.

21. Stator Overheats in Spots

Probable cause	Remedy
Short-circuited phase winding	Check and replace defective coils.
Rotor off center. (Improper air gap.)	Check for bent shaft, loose or worn bearings. Straighten and realine shaft. Replace bearings.
Unbalanced winding circuits	Balance winding circuits.
Loose winding connections	Tighten winding connections.
Wrong phase polarity connections	Correct connections for proper phase polarity.

22. Field Overheating

Probable cause	Remedy
Shorted field coil or coils	Check and replace defective coil or coils.
Dc excitation current too high	Reduce exciter current by adjusting dc voltage regulator.
Clogged air passages (poor ventilation)	Clean equipment. Remove obstructions.

23. Alternator Produces Shock when Touched

Probable cause	Remedy
Reversed stator field coil	Check polarity. Make correction to connections.
Static charges or grounded stator field coil	Check generator frame-ground connection or connections, clean and tighten. Repair or replace stator field coil.

Section IV. AC INDUCTION MOTORS

24. Failure to Start

Probable cause	Remedy
Circuit breaker or fuse open	Check for grounds. Close breaker or replace fuse.
Overload relay open	Wait until motor cools and relay closes.
Low supply voltage	Apply correct voltage.
Stator or rotor windings open or shorted	Check and replace shorted coil or coils.
Winding grounded	Check and replace grounded coil or coils.
Overload	Check meter readings against nameplate ratings. Reduce or install larger motor.

25. Noisy Operation

Probable cause	Remedy
Unbalanced load or coupling misalinement	Balance load and check alinement.
Air gap not uniform	Center rotor by replacing bearing.
Lamination loose	Tighten bolts. Dip in varnish and bake (chapter 4, par. 70). Repeat several times.
Coupling loose	Tighten.

26. Overheating

Probable cause	Remedy
Overloaded	Check meter readings against nameplate ratings. Reduce load.
Electrical unbalance	Balance supply voltage.
Open fuse	Replace line fuse.
Restricted ventilation	Clean. Remove obstructions.
Rotor winding shorted, open, or grounded	Check and replace defective coil or coils.
Stator winding shorted, open, or grounded	Check and replace defective coil or coils.
Bearings	Check for worn, loose, dry, or overlubricated bearings. Replace worn or loose bearings, lubricate dry bearings, relieve overlubrication.

Section V. AC WOUND ROTOR MOTORS

27. Runs Slow with External Resistance Cutout

Probable cause	Remedy
Cables to control box have insufficient current-carrying capacity.	Replace with larger cables.
Open circuits in rotor, cables, or controls	Clean, remake connections, and repair.
Excessive brush sparking	Clean sliprings and reseat brushes.

Section VI. AC SYNCHRONOUS MOTORS

28. Failure to Start

Probable cause	Remedy
Open fuse	Replace fuse.
Faulty starter	Check and repair or replace faulty contacts or contactor coils.
Low supply voltage	Apply correct voltage.
Bearings	Check for bent shaft or worn, loose, dry, or overlubricated bearings. Replace and realine bent shaft. Replace worn and loose bearings, lubricate dry bearings, relieve overlubrication.
Overloaded	Check meter readings against nameplate ratings. Reduce load or install larger motor.
Stator coil open or shorted	Repair or replace coil or coils.
Field exciter current is being applied	Make sure that field contactors are open, and that field-discharge resistors are connected.

29. Runs Slow

Probable cause	Remedy
Overloaded	Check meter readings against nameplate. Reduce load or install larger motor.
Low supply voltage	Apply correct voltage.
Field excited too soon	Adjust time-delay relay so that exciter current will not be applied until rotor reaches synchronous speed.

30. Failure to Pull into Step

Probable cause	Remedy
No field excitation. Open rotor coils. Exciter inoperative. Faulty field contactor.	Tighten or solder open or loose connections. Repair or replace defective rotor coils. Be sure field contactor is operating properly.
Overloaded	Check meter readings against nameplate ratings. Reduce load or install larger motor.

31. No Field Excitation

Probable cause	Remedy
Grounded or open rotor coil	Repair or replace rotor coil or coils.
Grounded or short sliprings	Check and reinsulate.
No output from exciter	See dc generator (par. 1).

32. Pulls out of Step, or Trips Breakers

Probable cause	Remedy
Low exciter voltage	Readjust voltage regulator on exciter to increase voltage.
Intermittently open or shorted cables	Check, and replace defective cables.
Reversed field coil	Check polarity. Change coil leads.
Low supply voltage	Increase voltage if possible. Raise excitation voltage.

33. Hunting

Probable cause	Remedy
Fluctuating load	Increase or decrease size of flywheel on load or loads. Increase or decrease excitation current.
Uneven commutator	Recondition commutator.

34. Stator Overheats in Spots

Probable cause	Remedy
Open phase coil	Check and repair or replace faulty coil or coils.
Rotor not centered	Check for bent shaft, loose or worn bearings. Straighten and realine shaft. Replace bearings.
Unbalanced circuits	Repair loose connections, or correct wrong internal connections.
Shorted coil	Check and replace faulty coil or coils.

35. Field Overheats

Probable cause	Remedy
Shorted field coil	Check and replace faulty coil or coils.
Excitation current too high	Reduce exciter current by adjusting dc voltage regulator.

36. Overheating

Probable cause	Remedy
Overloaded	Check meter readings against nameplate ratings. Reduce load or install larger motor.
Underexcited rotor	Adjust to rated excitation.
Improper ventilation	Remove obstructions and clean air ducts.
Improper supply voltage	Adjust to rated voltage.
Reverse field coil	Check polarity. Change coil leads.

Section VII. AC REPULSION-INDUCTION MOTORS

37. Failure to Start

Probable cause	Remedy
Open fuse	Replace fuse.
Overloaded	Check meter readings against nameplate ratings. Reduce load or install larger motor.
Low supply voltage. Lead wires insufficient current capacity.	Apply correct voltage. Install larger lead wires.
Stator coil open	Check and replace open coil or coils.
Stator coil shorted	Check and replace shorted coil or coils.
Stator coil grounded	Check and replace defective coil or coils.
Centrifugal mechanism not operating properly	Disassemble, clean, inspect, adjust, repair or replace.
Incorrect brush setting	Locate neutral plane by shifting brushes until there is no rotation when current is applied. Shift brushes in the direction of the desired rotation, 1⅓ bars from neutral on 4-pole motors of ½ hp and smaller, and 1¾ bars on larger 4-pole motors. On 2-pole motors, set ⅓ bar farther than setting given above.
Bearings	Check for bent shaft or worn, loose, dry, or overlubricated bearing. Straighten and realine bent shaft. Replace worn and loose bearings, lubricate dry bearings, relieve overlubrication.

38. Runs Slow

Probable cause	Remedy
Overloaded	Check meter readings against nameplate rating.
Centrifugal mechanism not operating properly	Disassemble and clean.
Bearings binding	Clean and lubricate bearings.

39. Overheating

Probable cause	Remedy
Overloaded	Check meter readings against nameplate ratings. Reduce load or install larger motor.
Incorrect supply voltage	Apply correct voltage.
Centrifugal mechanism not operating properly	Disassemble, clean, inspect. Repair, adjust, or replace.
Bearings	Check for bent shaft, or worn, loose, dry, or overlubricated bearings. Straighten and realine bent shaft. Replace worn or loose bearings, lubricate dry bearings, relieve overlubrication.

40. Noisy Operation

Probable cause	Remedy
Bearings	Check for bent shaft, or worn, loose, dry, or overlubricated bearings. Straighten and realine bent shaft. Replace worn or loose bearings, lubricate dry bearings, relieve overlubrication.
Excessive end play	Adjust end-play takeup screw, or add thrust washers to shaft.
Motor not alined properly with driven machine	Realine.
Loose motor mounting and accessories	Tighten all loose components.

41. Motor Produces Shock when Touched

Probable cause	Remedy
Grounded stator coil	Replace defective coil or coils. Check motor-frame connection or connections to ground. Clean and tighten.
Static charge	Check motor-frame connection or connections to ground. Clean and tighten.

Section VIII. AC SPLIT-PHASE, CAPACITOR-START, AND TRANSFORMER-CAPACITOR MOTORS

42. Failure to Start

Probable cause	Remedy
Open fuse	Replace fuse.
Low supply voltage	Apply correct voltage.
Stator coil open	Replace open coil or coils.
Centrifugal mechanism not operating properly	Disassemble, clean, inspect. Adjust, repair, or replace.
Defective capacitor	Replace capacitor.
Stator coil grounded	Check and replace grounded coil or coils.
Bearings	Check for bent shaft, or worn, loose, dry, or overlubricated bearings. Straighten and realine bent shaft. Replace worn or loose bearings, relieve overlubrication.
Overloaded	Check meter readings against nameplate ratings. Reduce load or install larger motor.

43. Overheating

Probable cause	Remedy
Shorted coil	Replace shorted coil or coils.
Centrifugal mechanism not operating properly	Disassemble, clean, inspect. Adjust, repair, or replace.
Incorrect voltage	Apply correct voltage.
Overloaded	Check meter readings against nameplate ratings. Reduce load or install larger motor.
Bearings	Check for bent shaft, or worn, loose, dry, or overlubricated bearings. Straighten and realine bent shaft, replace worn or loose bearings, lubricate dry bearings, relieve overlubrication.

44. Noisy Operation

Probable cause	Remedy
Worn bearings	Replace. Realine.
Shaft bent	Straighten shaft. Realine or replace rotor.
Excessive end play	Adjust screw of end-play takeup device, or put shim washers on shaft between end bells and rotor.
Loose motor mounts or accessories	Tighten all loose components.

II. TROUBLESHOOTING DATA FOR DC AND AC CONTROLLERS

Section I. DC CONTROLLERS

45. Failure to Close

Probable cause	Remedy
No power	Check power source. Replace faulty fuses.
Low voltage	Check power-supply voltage. Apply correct voltage.
Inadequate lead wires	Install lead wires of proper size.
Loose connections	Tighten all connections.
Open connections and broken wiring	Locate and repair or replace. Remove dirt from controller contacts.
Contacts affected by long idleness or high operating temperature.	Clean and adjust.
Contacts affected by chemical fumes or salty atmosphere.	Replace with oil-immersed contacts.
Inadequate contact pressure	Replace contacts and adjust spring tension.
Open circuit breaker	Check circuit wiring for possible fault.
Defective coil	Replace with new coil.
Overload-relay contact latched open	Operate hand- or electric-reset.

46. Failure to Open

Probable cause	Remedy
Interlock does not open circuit	Check control-circuit wiring for possible fault. Test and repair.
Holding circuit grounded	Test and repair or replace grounded parts.
Misalinement of parts; contacts apparently held together by residual magnetism.	Realine and test for free movement by hand. Magnetic sticking rarely occurs unless caused by excessive mechanical friction or misalinement of moving parts.
Contacts welded together	See paragraph 50, below.

47. Sluggish Operation

Probable cause	Remedy
Spring tension too strong	Adjust for proper spring tension.
Low voltage	Check power-supply voltage. Apply correct voltage.
Operating in wrong position	Remount in correct operating position.
Excessive friction	Realine and test for free movement by hand. Clean pivots.
Rusty parts due to long periods of idleness	Clean and renew rusty parts.
Sticky moving parts	Wipe off all accumulations of oil and dirt. Bearings do not need lubrication.
Misalinement of parts	Check for proper alinement. Realine to reduce friction, and test for free movement by hand.

48. Erratic Operation (Unwanted openings and closures, and failure of overload protection)

Probable cause	Remedy
Short circuits	Test and repair or replace defective parts.
Grounds	Test and repair or replace defective parts.

Probable cause	*Remedy*
Sneak currents	These are usually caused by intermittent grounds or short circuits in the machines or wiring circuit. Test and replace faulty parts or wiring.
Loose connections	Tighten all connections. Eliminate any vibrations or rapid temperature changes that may occur in close proximity to the controller.

49. Overheating of Coils

Probable cause	*Remedy*
Shorted coil	Replace coil.
High ambient temperature or poor ventilation	Relocate controller, use forced ventilation, or replace with suitable type controller.
High voltage	Check for shorted control resistor. Check power-supply voltage. Apply correct voltage.
High current	Check current rating of controller. Check for high voltage, above. If necessary, replace with suitable type controller.
Loose connections	Tighten all connections. Check for undue vibrations in vicinity.
Excessive collection of dirt and grime	Clean but do not reoil parts. If covers do not fit tightly, realine and adjust fasteners.
High humidity, extremely dirty atmosphere, excessive condensation, and rapid temperature changes.	Use oil-immersed controller or dusttight enclosures.

50. Contacts Welded Together

Probable cause	*Remedy*
Improper application	Check load conditions and replace with a suitable type controller.
Excessive temperature	Smooth off contact surface to remove concentrated hot spots.
Excessive binding of contact tip upon closing	Adjust spring pressure.
Contacts close without enough spring pressure	Replace worn contacts. Adjust or replace weak springs. Check armature overtravel.
Sluggish operation	See paragraph 47, above.
Rapid, momentary, touching of contacts without enough pressure.	Smooth contacts. Adjust weak springs. Where controller has "JOG" or "INCH" control button, operate this less rapidly.

51. Overheating of Contacts

Probable cause	*Remedy*
Inadequate spring pressure	Replace worn contacts. Adjust or replace weak springs.
Contacts overloaded	Check load data with controller rating. Replace with correct size contactor.
Dirty contacts	Clean and smooth contacts.
High humidity, extremely dirty atmosphere, excessive condensation, and rapid temperature changes.	See paragraph 49, above.
High ambient temperature or poor ventilation	See paragraph 49, above.
Chronic arcing	Adjust or replace arc chutes. If arcing persists, replace with a more suitable controller.
Rough contact surface	Clean and smooth contacts. Check alinement.
Continuous vibration when contacts are closed	Change or improve mounting of controller.
Oxidation of contacts	Keep clean, reduce excessive temperature, or use oil-immersed contacts.

52. Excessive Arcing of Contacts

Probable cause	*Remedy*
Arc not confined to proper path	Adjust or renew arc chutes. If arcing persists, replace with more suitable controller.
Inadequate spring pressure	Replace worn contacts. Adjust or replace weak springs.
Slow in opening	Remove excessive friction. Adjust spring tension. Renew weak springs. See paragraph 47, above.
Faulty blowout coil or connection	Check and replace coil. Tighten connection.
Excessive inductance in load circuit	Adjust load or replace with proper size controller.
Faulty capacitor	Replace with new capacitor.

53. Pitting or Corroding of Contacts

Probable cause	*Remedy*
Too little surface contact	Clean contacts and adjust springs.
Service too severe	Check load conditions and replace with correct size controller.
Corrosive atmosphere	Use airtight enclosure. In extreme cases, use oil-immersed contacts.
Continuous vibration when contacts are closed	Change, or improve, mounting of controller.
Oxidation of contacts	Keep clean, reduce excessive temperature, or use oil-immersed contacts.

Section II. AC CONTROLLERS

54. Failure to Close

Probable cause	*Remedy*
No power	Check power source. Replace faulty fuses.
Low voltage	Check power-supply voltage. Apply correct voltage. Check for low power factor.
Inadequate lead wires	Install lead wires of proper size.
Loose connections	Tighten all connections.
Open connections and broken wiring	Locate opens and repair or replace wiring. Remove dirt from controller contacts.
Contacts affected by long idleness or high operating temperature.	Clean and adjust.
Contacts affected by chemical fumes or salty atmosphere.	Replace with oil-immersed contacts.
Inadequate contact pressure	Replace contacts and adjust spring tension.
Open circuit breaker	Check circuit wiring for possible fault.
Defective coil	Replace with new coil.
Overload-relay contact latched open	Operate hand- or electric-reset.

55. Failure to Open

Probable cause	*Remedy*
Interlock does not open circuit	Check control-circuit wiring for possible fault. Test and repair.
Holding circuit grounded	Test and repair or replace grounded parts.
Misalinement of parts; contacts apparently held together by residual magnetism.	Realine and test for free movement by hand. Magnetic sticking rarely occurs unless caused by excessive mechanical friction or misalinement of moving parts. Wipe off pole faces to remove accumulation of oil.
Contacts welded together	See paragraph 59, below.

56. Sluggish Operation

Probable cause	*Remedy*
Spring tension too strong	Adjust for proper spring tension.
Low voltage	Check power-supply voltage. Apply correct voltage.
Operating in wrong position	Remount in correct operating position.
Excessive friction	Realine and test for free movement by hand. Clean pivots.
Rusty parts due to long periods of idleness	Clean or renew rusty parts.
Sticky moving parts	Wipe off all accumulations of oil and dirt. Bearings do not need lubrication.
Misalinement of parts	Check for proper alinement. Realine to reduce friction and test for free movement by hand.

57. Erratic Operation (Unwanted openings and closures and failure of overload protection)

Probable cause	*Remedy*
Short circuits	Test and repair or replace defective parts.
Grounds	Test and repair or replace defective parts.
Sneak currents	These are usually caused by intermittent grounds or short circuits in the machines or wiring circuit. Test and replace faulty parts or wiring.
Loose connections	Tighten all connections. Eliminate any vibrations or rapid temperature changes that may occur in close proximity to the controller.

58. Overheating of Coils

Probable cause	*Remedy*
Shorted coil	Replace coil.
High ambient temperature or poor ventilation	Relocate controller, use forced ventilation, or replace with suitable type controller.
High voltage	Check for shorted control resistor. Check power-supply voltage. Apply correct voltage.
High current	Check current rating of controller. Make check for high voltage, above. If necessary, replace with suitable type controller.
Loose connections	Tighten all connections. Check for undue vibrations in vicinity.
Excessive collection of dirt and grime	Clean but do not reoil parts. If covers do not fit tightly, realine and adjust fasteners.
High humidity, extremely dirty atmosphere, excessive condensation, and rapid temperature changes.	Use oil-immersed controller or dusttight enclosures.
Operating on wrong frequency	Replace with coil of proper frequency rating.
DC instead of ac coil	Replace with ac coil.
Too frequent operation	Adjust to apply larger control.
Open armature gap	Adjust spring tension. Eliminate excessive friction or remove any blocking in gap.

59. Contacts Welded Together

Probable cause	*Remedy*
Improper application	Check load conditions and replace with a more suitable type controller.
Excessive temperature	Smooth off contact surface to remove concentrated hot spots.
Excessive binding of contact tip upon closing	Adjust spring pressure.
Contacts close without enough spring pressure	Replace worn contacts. Adjust or replace weak springs. Check armature overtravel.
Sluggish operation	See paragraph 56, above.
Rapid, momentary, touching of contacts without enough pressure.	Smooth contacts. Adjust weak springs. Where controller has "JOG" or "INCH" control button, operate this less rapidly.

60. Overheating or Contacts

Probable cause	*Remedy*
Inadequate spring pressure	Replace worn contacts. Adjust or replace weak springs.
Contacts overloaded	Check load data with controller rating. Replace with correct size contactor.
Dirty contacts	Clean and smooth contacts.
High humidity, extremely dirty atmosphere, excessive condensation, and rapid temperature changes.	See paragraph 58, above.
High ambient temperature or poor ventilation	See paragraph 58, above.
Chronic arcing	Adjust or replace arc chutes. If arcing persists, replace with a more suitable controller.

Probable causes	*Remedy*
Rough contact surfaces	Clean and smooth contacts. Check alinement.
Continuous vibration when contacts are closed	Change or improve mounting of controller.
Oxidation of contacts	Keep clean, reduce excessive temperature, or use oil-immersed contacts.

61. Arcing at Contacts

Probable cause	*Remedy*
Arc not confined to proper path	Adjust or renew arc chutes. If arcing persists, replace with more suitable controller.
Inadequate spring pressure	Replace worn contacts. Adjust or replace weak springs.
Slow in opening	Remove excessive friction. Adjust spring tension. Renew weak springs. See paragraph 56, above.
Faulty blowout coil or connection	Check and replace coil. Tighten connection.
Excessive inductance in load circuit	Adjust load or replace with more suitable controller.

62. Pitting or Corroding of Contacts

Probable cause	*Remedy*
Too little surface contact	Clean contacts and adjust springs.
Service too severe	Check load conditions and replace with more suitable controller.
Corrosive atmosphere	Use airtight enclosure. In extreme cases, use oil-immersed contacts.
Continuous vibration when contacts are closed	Change or improve mounting of controller.
Oxidation of contacts	Keep clean, reduce excessive temperature, or use oil-immersed contacts.

63. Noisy Operation (Hum or Chatter)

Probable cause	*Remedy*
Poor fit at pole face	Realine and adjust pole faces.
Broken or defective shading coil	Replace coil.
Loose coil	Check coil. If correct size, shim coil until tight.
Worn parts	Replace with new parts.

64. Vibration After Repairs

Probable cause	*Remedy*
Misalinement of parts	Realine parts and test for free movement by hand.
Loose mounting	Tighten mounting bolts.
Incorrect coil	Replace with proper coil.
Too much play in moving parts	Shim parts for proper tightness and clearance.

ANSWER SHEET

TEST NO. _____ PART _____ TITLE OF POSITION _____
(AS GIVEN IN EXAMINATION ANNOUNCEMENT - INCLUDE OPTION, IF ANY)

PLACE OF EXAMINATION _____ DATE _____
(CITY OR TOWN)   (STATE)

RATING

USE THE SPECIAL PENCIL. MAKE GLOSSY BLACK MARKS.

Make only ONE mark for each answer. Additional and stray marks may be counted as mistakes. In making corrections, erase errors COMPLETELY.

www.ingramcontent.com/pod-product-compliance
Lightning Source LLC
Chambersburg PA
CBHW081759300426
44116CB00014B/2172